JOSEPHINE BUTLER

JOSEPHINE BUTLER
About 1869

[Frontispiece

JOSEPHINE BUTLER

Flame of Fire

by

E. MOBERLY BELL

"There is no Evil in the world so great that God cannot raise up to meet it a corresponding beauty and glory that will blaze it out of countenance." (J. B., Edinburgh 1871.)

CONSTABLE AND CO LTD
LONDON W. C. 2

LONDON
PUBLISHED BY
Constable and Company Ltd
10–12 ORANGE STREET W.C.2

First Published 1962

THIS book is based on comprehensive correspondence collected from every branch of the International Abolitionist Federation as well as from many of Josephine Butler's personal friends, and lent to me by the Josephine Butler Society. The correspondence had been dipped into but never before fully used or put into any sort of order.

May 1962.   E. M. B.

PRINTED AND BOUND IN ENGLAND BY
HAZELL WATSON AND VINEY LTD
AYLESBURY AND SLOUGH

THE BUTLER FAMILY

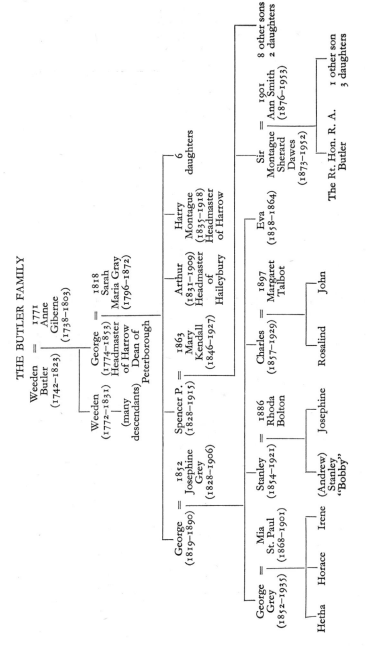

THE GREYS OF NORTHUMBERLAND
GREY OF FALLODON—GREY OF MILFIELD—GREY OF HOWICK

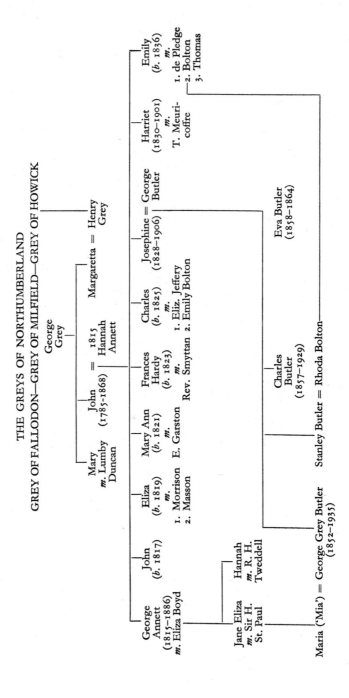

CONTENTS

THE FLAME KINDLED

CONSUMING FIRE

GLOWING EMBERS

ILLUSTRATIONS

AUTHOR'S NOTE AND
ACKNOWLEDGEMENTS

THIS book was written with the encouragement of the
Josephine Butler Society, which felt the need of an
authoritative biography of Josephine Butler that
could be put into the hands of the present generation of its
workers.
I have to thank:—

The Society for giving me access to the great mass of
Josephine Butler's correspondence and other writings housed
at the Fawcett Library, and Miss Douie, the Librarian there
for her ever-ready help.
Josephine Butler House in Liverpool and the Liverpool
University Library for letting me read their collections of
letters.
Chelsea Public Library for housing these letters and making
work on them easy for me.
Miss Ena Steel, and the Rev. G. R. Dunstan of the Church of
England Council for Social Work and many others for reading
my script and giving me much advice and criticism.
Members of the Butler family, Mr Horace and Miss Hetha
Butler and Miss Gwendolen Garston for guidance about
illustrations and family memories.

Finally, I would express my gratitude to Miss Anne Lupton who
read, sorted and catalogued the Fawcett Library letters, bringing
order out of chaos, and without whose collaboration and continuous help I could never have undertaken this book.

May 1962   E. M. B.

PREFACE
by the
Rt. Hon. R. A. BUTLER, C.H., M.P.

W E the descendants of the family into which "Aunt" Josephine married have always been kept well aware of the details of her single-minded and courageous life. I am therefore glad to write this short preface to Miss Moberley Bell's book.

Josephine never wanted a biography written, nor did she have her papers arranged for that purpose. But fortunately one or two studies have been done including my cousin Andrew—S. G. Butler's portrait. I am in some doubt how Josephine would have reacted to a preface written by one recently Home Secretary! I think that she would have been pleased to note how the cause for which she fought is upheld in the present clear and sympathetic life story. Besides, the author brings out two aspects of this remarkable life, first the perpetual struggle against, and triumph over, ill-health, and second the calm handling of a subject which in her days was regarded as usually unmentionable. Perhaps Gladstone's words when he met her in 1872 sum up the best impression the reader can obtain. He says:

"I had a good deal of conversation with Mrs. Butler and was greatly struck and pleased with her. Knowing her feelings about *the* topic I appreciated her perfect abstention. Also I was struck with the force of her mind, and I thought her perfectly and rather remarkably feminine, notwithstanding the said material, which under a strong impulse of conscience she has to handle."

"Rather remarkably feminine" is the memory which her portrait and photographs convey to us nearly a hundred years later. With the increase in prosperity and, alas, the spread of vice, the nature of the problem with which she grappled has changed. Methods now also have to be adapted to meet conditions as they are. But the fundamentals remain, that is the need to enhance and to establish firmly the proper status and dignity of women. This biography is valuable since it puts this issue in a broad setting in which Josephine Butler's life is viewed side by side with those famous Victorian figures engaged primarily with the Education of girls in the practice of medicine and philanthropy such as Elizabeth Garrett Anderson, Miss Beale, Miss Buss and Miss Clough.

Just as the Victorian age was enriched by the life of Josephine Butler, so this biography will help to fortify and inspire us in the bustle of modern times.

August 1962   R. A. BUTLER

THE FLAME KINDLED

CHAPTER ONE

NOT MENTIONED

"I was not disobedient unto the heavenly vision". (Acts XXVI. 19)

WE are just getting far enough away from the Victorian age to be able to see it. Those who made its history are dead, the controversies in which they were involved are no longer live issues. As the dust of conflict settles down we can discern with some clarity the stature of the protagonists and the permanent importance of the battles in which they took part. Few will doubt that the revolution in the position and status of women was one of the most significant issues of the period, or will deny the greatness of those women who effected it. For they were remarkable, by whatever standard they are judged. Florence Nightingale, who not only saved the army in the Crimea but also brought to the care of the sick a new attitude and standards of efficiency which transformed the hospitals and made a profession in which thousands of women have found a vocation; Elizabeth Garrett and Sophia Jex-Blake, those dauntless fighters, who not only made a success of medical practice but also battered at the doors of the Colleges of Medicine and Surgery, forcing a way for countless other women; Octavia Hill who, with a new conception of social relations and responsibilities, might almost be said to have invented the professional social worker and brought to birth a profession now universally acknowledged; and the women who made all these things possible by the provision of education for girls, Miss Beale and Miss Buss, Miss Davies and Miss

Clough—all these are gratefully remembered. Their names are household words.

It is strange that the greatest of them all, Josephine Butler, is relatively unknown today. The mention of her name rouses no more in the average educated man or woman than a vague uneasy searching of memory for something once heard but forgotten. Yet of all the women engaged in fighting for the woman's cause she alone saw the whole question as one. She alone perceived that the various things for which women were asking could be comprised in the simple demand that a woman should be regarded as an individual with needs and rights like any other human being—the right to work, to be regarded as equal with men in the eyes of the law, to share with men the responsibility of making the conditions in which both must live. The fact that her immense gifts and energy were spent in freeing the country from a system which sanctioned and encouraged vice is almost accidental. She would have achieved immensely valuable results in other fields had not the demands of this particular work been too great to leave room for anything else. None of the other women saw the whole situation with so penetrating an intelligence. Mrs. Fawcett kept herself clear of Josephine's movement for fear of compromising the suffragists; the women doctors stood by the British Medical Association, keeping in step with the men; but Josephine, once she had seen her principle clearly, could not be deflected by anyone's opinion. She saw and constantly reiterated the necessity for building a society in which men and women should play an equal part. The woman's question was all one; if women had the vote, these laws would never have been passed; if women were given education they would be able to hold their own, proving themselves as efficient as men; if women were trained for industry and allowed to take their place there, they would not be driven by sheer starvation into prostitution.

It is difficult to determine why Josephine Butler has been almost forgotten by the ordinary citizen today. It was natural enough that this should be so in Victorian times. Sex was then a subject "unbecoming to a gentlewoman"; she could not be altogether ignorant of the fact, but the less said about it the better and in public no "nice" woman would mention or hear of it. Josephine insisted on bringing it out into the open. She, "a woman who called herself a lady", made speeches in public about things of which she ought to have been ignorant. No wonder she was not mentioned. In fact the kindest thing to do was to forget her existence. In the obituary notice in *The Times* when she died in 1906 her work is discreetly referred to as "the social question", thus carefully obscuring its nature and avoiding offence. But the First World War changed all this. When Mrs. Fawcett's *Life of Josephine Butler*, written in 1928 for the centenary of her birth, was reviewed, the reviewer in *The Times* commending it said it was not a book to conceal from the daughters of the house, but should be put where they could see it and they should be encouraged to discuss it. After another World War, the present generation shows no smallest reluctance to discuss prostitution or any other problem arising from sex.

It is clearly not delicacy that consigns Josephine Butler to oblivion. What then is the cause? She expressed a strong wish that no biography of her should ever be written and she wrote to her sons and intimate friends begging them to destroy any private letters she had written to them, as she could not bear the idea of people digging into her correspondence to find out details of her private life. This reluctance would seem to have arisen from a very real humility, a conviction that she was no more than an instrument—one of many—in the Hand of a Divine Power, and a dread lest a biographer should exalt her at the expense of other equally essential instruments. Actually there is no temptation to violate her privacy. She was not reticent; indeed in a sense her biography is already written—in her Life of her Father, John Grey of Dilston; in her Memoir of her Husband, George Butler; in her Life of Catharine of Siena; in the columns of the *Storm-Bell*, in which she reveals most intimate details of her domestic life and of her spiritual and religious experiences.

It is all there, but these works are out of print and even if they were accessible, their idiom, naturally enough, belongs to her day and not to ours; the rising generation would read them with difficulty and would be unlikely to appreciate the importance of her contribution to the problems of society. Emphatically, she has something to say to the modern world in her own field, and it is hoped that this account of her work and thought, this presentation of a very remarkable personality, may throw some light on the problems that are still with us. If Josephine Butler was right in believing that her work was based on eternal principles, then though the conditions have changed and new methods must be used, the fundamentals remain the same. This is my justification for writing a biography in defiance of her wishes.

CHAPTER TWO

THE GREYS OF DILSTON

"It was a house, the door of which stood wide open to welcome all comers." (J. B. in *John Grey of Dilston*)

JOSEPHINE GREY was born in 1828, the seventh child in a large and prosperous county family.

No one needs to be told that the Greys were and are one of the great families in the Border country. Their roots go deep in Northumbrian soil. In the early days they sent warriors to battlefields and they have served the country both locally and nationally, fighting battles military or political as occasion demanded for the last 600 years. There are three branches of the family: Greys of Howick of Reform Bill fame, Greys of Fallodon and Greys of Milfield. Josephine's father, John Grey, belonged to this last branch of the family and was a man of considerable importance and influence in his day. He was by far the most important person in Josephine's life until her marriage and he played so large a part in her intellectual and spiritual development that no study of her life can be adequate which does not start with him.

John Grey was born in 1785 at Milfield, his father's estate in Glendale close to Flodden Field and in sight of Cheviot. John, the eldest of four, was only eight when his father died, so the upbringing of the family fell on Mary Grey, his very remarkable mother. She was a woman of unusual ability; left a widow with four small children she cheerfully undertook the management of the estate, the crops, herds, labourers and accounts; she took an interest in local affairs, advising the Wooler library as to the choice of books. She managed her home and her children and, believing passionately in the importance of education, she saw to their intellectual as well as their physical needs. In the early stages she taught them herself, reading first to, and then with, them, reciting Pope's translations of Homer to them as she sewed or occupied herself with household jobs and expecting them to be able to reply with passages they had learned. More important than this, she spoke and read to them of the events going on in the contemporary world and awoke in them a real interest in other nations and in mankind generally. Above all, she excited them about the slave trade and the struggle for its abolition, reading them Clarkson's *History of the Trade* and firing them with her own bitter hatred of oppression in any form. Thus she laid the foundations of a solid and humane education.

When she felt the children needed more than she could give, she sent them away to be professionally taught. Even the girls were sent to school in London and this at that date—the end of the 18th century—shows a very remarkable concern for the minds of her daughters. Margaretta, the younger of the two, was quickly responsive. Even before she went to school she astonished her brother, who was kindly playing marbles with her to amuse her, by breaking away and standing up to her full height declaiming against some social evil which she had perceived, while her brother looked on, puzzled at the outburst. She always felt and spoke very bitterly about the limitations imposed on women by their lack of education and opportunity. In school in London she conceived a great desire to see Parliament and, since at that time there was no admission for women, she dressed up as a boy and, with the connivance of some friend, actually visited the Chamber. She married her cousin, Henry Grey, a minister of the Scottish Church, and kept closely in touch with her brother's family. No doubt her influence on Josephine was considerable.

Perhaps the most remarkable feature in Mrs. Grey's character was her determination not to dominate her son. Before he was well in his teens she made a practice of speaking of him always as "my man John", and as soon as he was eighteen she handed over the management of the estate entirely to him and receded into the background. No doubt she kept an anxious eye on him and she was glad, when he went riding to Wooler for the market, to notice that a neighbour, Mr. Culley, a notable scientific farmer, always ordered his horse and John's at an early hour after dinner, and then rode back with John, conversing as they came. It was not long after John had entered on his estate that first his mother and then he himself became very ill. We are told, in the curious idiom of that day, that they caught a severe cold and "it turned to typhus". Whatever the diagnosis, they were both very seriously ill and it was in this bout of illness that Mary Grey, expecting death, turned to the Bible for comfort and found it there. This peace of mind greatly facilitated her recovery, and her children were deeply impressed by it. John, albeit rather shyly, followed his mother's example and studied the Bible assiduously through illness and convalescence. After they had both recovered, as he pondered on his experience, he determined to have family prayers every evening. This resolution he carried out and, for the rest of his life, no day ended without the assembling of his family and household for an act of worship.

In 1815 John Grey married Hannah Annett, a girl of Huguenot descent, whose forebears had settled at Alnwick after the Revocation of the Edict of Nantes. Like her future husband, she had inherited a passionate conviction of the importance of freedom and a hatred of all injustice. They made a striking pair, he dark, largely built and handsome, she slight, graceful and very fair. They were ideally suited to one another and settled down at Milfield, while Mary Grey, eschewing all the reputed characteristics of the mother-in-law, retired to a cottage at Humbledon and, as occasion offered, became the perfect grandmother.

The young couple led a busy, active life; children came regularly at suitable intervals, till they had three sons and seven daughters. John Grey was by no means absorbed in domesticity; he was a man of boundless vitality with a great fount of good-will to all mankind. The period was a difficult one for those connected with the land. The Napoleonic Wars, like all wars, had left an aftermath of depression and anxiety. In times of war there is a very general belief among the less thoughtful that peace, when it comes, will inevitably bring prosperity in its train. In fact, war being destructive, produces not prosperity but poverty and disorganisation and the disappointed optimists feel cheated and discontented. John Grey had studied Arthur Young's writings and with the help of his friend and neighbour Mr. Culley had learned about scientific methods of agriculture. He was convinced that by these methods and by a reasonable economic system prosperity could return to farmers. He proceeded to apply all these principles to his own estate and it flourished. But he could not stop there. He was distressed by the evil conditions under which too many of his poorer neighbours lived and he entered with zest into the struggle to improve them. This drew him into politics. In the fierce fight of the ten years which preceded the passing of the great Reform Bill of 1832, John Grey was the steadfast supporter and chief lieutenant in the North of his kinsman Lord Grey; and the drawing up of petitions and getting signatures for them, which was to play so large a part in his daughter's activities, was in full swing in the home into which she was born.

The repeal of the Corn Laws; the reform of the Poor Law; the education of the masses; all these causes found in John Grey a hearty and energetic supporter. But the cause which above all others called on his energy and devotion was that of the abolition of slavery. He had never been able to forget the stories Clarkson told of the Slave Trade and he could never think of the subject without an inward fury of indignation and shame. He was still a lad when the Trade itself had been abolished, but slavery persisted in British Dominions and this was an evil he could not tolerate. For its abolition he was willing to work tirelessly. When abolition was finally achieved he rejoiced that a very large sum as compensation to the plantation owners was paid with real willingness by the ordinary Englishman; it seemed to him in some slight degree to atone for the shame of the country's long acquiescence in so evil a thing.

Slavery was abolished in 1834; in the preceding year John Grey was appointed Receiver of the Greenwich Hospital Estates in Northumberland. These estates were those forfeited by Lord Derwentwater after the '15 and bestowed on Greenwich Hospital; they covered a large area on both sides of the Tyne. John Grey became agent for all this property, responsible for the tenant farmers and for the care of fields and woodlands. The appointment was a recognition of his services to agriculture in his county. He abundantly justified the choice. In the forty years in which he administered the estates their value and their revenue vastly increased, the farms were kept in good order and the whole countryside profited. The work was very hard; it involved riding all over the estates, getting to know every tenant farmer, advising, encouraging, criticising, caring for every farm and every home as if it was his own. The ignorance of scientific agriculture shown by most of his neighbouring landlords struck him forcibly and he never ceased to hope that the Universities of Oxford and Cambridge at least would institute Schools of Agriculture for undergraduates, many of whom were destined to become great landowners in the future. He was happy in the work and he was universally trusted and respected.

When John Grey was first appointed, the Trustees decided to give him a house on the estate and he and his wife walked over the hills and moors to find the site they liked. They chose one quite close to the ruined castle of Dilston, and there their home was built and in 1835 the family moved in. By this time there were nine children, one having died in infancy. Of these Josephine was the seventh. Dilston—the name is a corruption of Devil's Stone—was a happy home. It stood on a hill and the Devil's Water ran at the bottom of the garden to join the Tyne. The house was spacious and comfortably built; throughout the summer the children ran freely in and out of the doors, which stood wide open, welcoming all-comers. The garden was not formally laid out; it was wild, a matter of heath and coppice with the sound of water continually to be heard. It was a perfect playground for children and they enjoyed it to the full.

Josephine was seven when they moved to Dilston, her sister Hattie less than two years younger and as they came in age between Charlie who was ten and Emmie still a baby, they made a natural pair and shared their lessons, their joys and their sorrows. They were taught to ride as soon as they could sit on a pony's back and rode freely on the moors and in the pleasant country round their home, their dogs following wherever they went. Dogs and horses always played a large part in their lives and are mentioned again and again in their letters. Many years later Josephine was still mourning over the death of her pony Apple Grey, and it almost broke Hattie's heart when one of the dogs was shot on a charge of sheep worrying. Hattie's affections extended to less interesting animals too. She was convinced that all animals, even newts, had souls. At one time she had a collection of newts, snails and other small water beasts in glass jars kept on a little shelf above their bed. When an accident precipitated the jars into the bed, it was Hattie who rescued the animals, with an agony of apprehension about their sufferings, and restored them to fresh water in more jars, while Josephine did her best with the bed. The close friendship which began in the nursery became only closer as years went by and though their lives lay far apart, they turned to one another instinctively at every crisis. They spent any holiday they could get together and their loving intimacy was broken only by Hattie's death in 1901.

Of formal schooling the children had little. Josephine and Hattie went to a school in Newcastle for a couple of years. We hear of a party from the school to Durham to see the Cathedral and Castle, in the course of which one young lady fell into the river and was rescued without her bustle, which was found floating on the stream. Apart from this incident, the school seems to have been fairly dull; Hattie resisted efforts to make her work, but illustrated the history book she was studying with very original and charming pictures on the margins. Josephine, on the contrary, found no difficulty in her lessons, but she does not seem to have been greatly inspired by the experience. Looking back on those early days Mrs. Butler writes: "We had none of the educational advantages of the girls of today." This may be a just reflection on what was offered to her at the school she attended, but it is a serious under-estimate of her whole mental training; and it is a judgment from which anyone may dissent who has seen children crowded into just-adequate class rooms, driven relentlessly from one subject to another in a valiant effort to cover a vast syllabus. Such an observer may well feel that the advantage is not entirely on the side of the "girls of today". This is no criticism of the modern policy in education. Few children in the forties of the last century had the advantages of the Grey family. The lot of the vast majority of the girls of today has of course immensely improved, but it remains true that parents are the great factor in all liberal education, and here the Grey children were very fortunate. For it was their parents who really opened their minds and taught them to think and to work, not in that insufferably self-conscious and dogmatic manner exhibited in Victorian works of fiction for children, such as *Harry and Lucy*, but by encouraging them to take an interest in the things their parents were doing and thinking about. Mrs. Grey contributed whatever was formal in the business. She collected the children in the mornings and made them read to her from some serious book. At the end of the reading she questioned them about what had been read, to ensure that they had understood. She further taught them to draw and to paint in water colours, and if neither of them attained professional standards, they at least learned to derive great pleasure from sketching and from making accurate drawings of plants and architectural features. More than all, they learned to look at the world with a seeing eye, a faculty which appears continually in Josephine's letters and writings. For the rest Mrs. Grey gave them tasks and insisted that these must always be done perfectly. This insistence on excellence she regarded as the foundation of their moral training.

The stimulating part of their education came from their father. They rode with him as he went about his business over the estates; as they rode he talked about their neighbours, about agricultural problems, about the news of the great world and whatever else seemed to him interesting or important. No doubt his talk was often above the heads of the younger of them, but as they grew older they understood more and they caught from him the conviction of the importance of every individual, the dignity of every man as man and the hatred of any sort of injustice or oppression. When they were at home he read to them a great deal especially out of the Bible and the sonorous words of the Hebrew Prophets became part of their consciousness long before they could understand the great themes of prophesy. He would tell them too of the fights in which he had engaged, more especially that for the abolition of slavery, and he could never speak of this without strong emotion. Josephine was perhaps, of all his daughters, the closest to him in mind and temperament. She herself felt she had inherited from him her hatred of injustice. His indefatigable energy, his acutely sensitive reaction to anything evil, his instinctive sympathy for every sufferer and his fundamental friendliness to all mankind were all reproduced in her. Josephine resembled him in another way. In spite of his immense activities, he yet managed to read more than many a man of sedentary and studious life. When he was quite an old man, he was invited to address an agricultural association at a social evening on any subject he chose. The subject, surprisingly, was Poetry, and he spoke for an hour and a half, illustrating his remarks by copious extracts quoted from memory from Homer, Virgil, Shakespeare and Milton. Considering that all his life he was actively riding over his great estates, farming, doing accounts, making speeches and working at one thing and another, it is difficult to conceive when he found time to read so much and with so great thoroughness that in old age he could still recite long passages from memory. We find the same extraordinary power in his daughter. Writing, organising, addressing meetings, travelling to an almost incredible extent, she yet managed to find time to read and digest, so that she could quote from or refer to a large variety of rather obscure books in various languages and show a surprising familiarity with mediaeval history and constitutional law.

Among other stimulating features of life at Dilston was the constant influx of visitors. These came to consult John Grey about agricultural questions. They came from all over Europe; from Finland, Russia, France and Italy and they were always welcomed cordially and stayed a week or a few days or even a few months as suited their convenience. There were others who came too; men from America, who were fighting the battle for the abolition of slavery there, who knew of Grey's part in the British fight and came to him seeking the sympathy they could not fail to find. It was thus absolutely impossible for the children to grow up with an insular outlook; since their father regarded the whole world as his parish. Moreover the eldest of the Grey sisters married a business man who worked in China, whence she wrote letters eagerly read aloud in the family circle; her daughter married an Italian; Hattie married a Swiss who worked in Italy. It is not surprising that as soon as Josephine tackled any social or political problem, she considered it internationally rather than as a purely domestic concern.

The art of conversation has languished in modern society; in the Dilston home it played a large part and when Grey came home from his out-of-door activities he and his guests would sit in the comfortable, homely room and the talk flowed freely. The young people listened. The talk was not all technical and concerned with agriculture, much of it was about the conditions of contemporary life abroad. More especially the American visitors spoke of the horrors of slavery in their country, in their indignation sparing no harrowing detail. Josephine was a sensitive child and possessed of a visual imagination; as she listened she saw the scenes the visitors described; the things that men and women were suffering at that very moment became terrifyingly vivid to her and she passed from pity to wrath and from wrath to despair. She had been brought up in the belief that the world was ruled by a God of love and justice. Could this be so? And if not, was there any sanity or safety in this world which had seemed so secure? It was indeed the problem with which Job and many another has wrestled; but she was only a child, feeling with all the intensity of a child and without any maturity to steady her. With the natural reticence of an adolescent, she found it impossible to speak of her misery to her parents or even to her beloved Hattie; in the woodlands round her home she found solitude and in solitude she struggled with her pain. It was a long and dreary time; she says it was nearly a year before the Lord spoke to her through the darkness. She emerged with the conviction, on which the whole work of her life was based, that the Lord is not indifferent to the sufferings of his creatures, but that caring infinitely for each individual He is crucified afresh in every act of cruelty and injustice practised by man on man. At that moment she dedicated herself to the service of the Master, whom for the rest of her life she served with utter trust and confidence. She was destined again to have periods of desolation, that experience which the mystics call "the dark night of the soul"; but she never again doubted the existence and the love of God.

So she was able once more to join in and enjoy the family life and social pleasures. The girls were keen followers of the hunt. Josephine and Hattie were in the habit of going over to Milfield to stay with their brother George, who was M.F.H., to hunt with him in the Christmas holidays; and when they passed from childhood to girlhood they attended all the local social functions. The Hunt Ball at Alnwick was definitely an occasion. All the great families from the neighbourhood attended. Josephine tells how her father and Lord Grey and the other Liberals would gather in the middle of the ballroom discussing their political hopes and plans until the Duke of Northumberland and his party appeared, when the Liberals would sink into the background and presently the ball would open. But in the ballroom, politics were as nothing to the Grey sisters. They danced, thinking and caring nothing for the views of their partners, and they were greatly in demand, for in their book-muslin dresses "with garlands of natural flowers on their heads and round their waists" they were much sought after. Tall, slight and very graceful, they all had that charm and those good looks that come from youth, intelligence and freshness. Josephine had something more; her finely moulded features, the form of her bones, her steady eyes combined with a sensitive mouth gave her real beauty, the kind that does not pass away with youth but survives in the grace of that "autumnal face" so greatly admired by John Donne. Painters and sculptors throughout her life begged her to sit for them and all the portraits, from the youthful one by Richmond to the painting in old age by Watts, bear witness to the beauty of her sensitive face.

Josephine was exceedingly musical and the serious study of that art filled much of her time in these last happy years of her girlhood. There is no one now alive who can speak with any authority of her attainment as a pianist, though those who heard her play all affirmed that she reached a standard quite beyond that of the ordinary amateur. Certainly she derived enormous pleasure from hearing, as well as from playing, music, and often when she was abroad and strained and tired, she thought longingly of her beloved piano and hungered to refresh herself by playing thereon.

In 1851 the Grey sisters went to London to see the Great Exhibition in Hyde Park. They stayed part of the time with their cousin Charles Grey, who was equerry to Prince Albert, and though none of them ever learned even to tolerate London as a place to live in, they enjoyed themselves immensely. As usual, they were a success; their genuine interest in everyone they met, and their pleasure in all that was offered to them, made them delightful guests. In addition to social engagements Josephine took the opportunity of having piano lessons from Sterndale Bennett and her cup was full when her cousin Charles Grey bought a Broadwood Grand at the Exhibition and gave it to her as a wedding present. For by this time Josephine's heart had been captured and she was engaged to George Butler.

CHAPTER THREE

OXFORD 1852—1857

"They know no better, poor fellows". (George Butler to Josephine Butler)

JOSEPHINE met George Butler in 1850, when he held a post as lecturer at Durham University. He was a man of quite remarkable ability and power, who could have made a name for himself and won distinction in either of the professions he followed, but he chose rather to give himself with unstinted devotion to the support of his wife in her arduous struggle. It is not too much to say that without his strength of purpose and serenity of temperament, she could have achieved little. If, as a result, he is remembered, if at all, not in his own right but merely as her husband, he would be content to have it so, for no man ever lived with less personal ambition or self-importance.

George Butler came of a scholastic family. His grandfather, Weeden Butler, was head of a 'School for the Sons of Gentlemen' in Chelsea. When George was born his father was Head Master of Harrow and all his three brothers attained positions of eminence in the same profession. George was the eldest son and by the time he entered Harrow School his father had retired to a country living in Northampton. At Harrow he distinguished himself chiefly on the playing field, where a good eye made him excel in all ball games; indeed, long before he was old enough to go to school he won fame, or perhaps one should say notoriety, for his excellent marksmanship, the target being the chimneys of neighbouring houses. From Harrow, following the Butler tradition, he went up to Cambridge, where new friends and new sports—Harrow had offered no boating opportunities—proved so much more attractive than the lecture room that his performance in examinations at the end of his first year convinced his father and his tutors that he had better pursue his studies elsewhere. This was a shock to the young man; his father took the matter seriously and sent him to a coach for some weeks in the summer; and in the autumn, fortified by good resolutions, he went up to Exeter College, Oxford.

George Butler had now finished with frivolity and he proceeded to cover himself with academic honours. He won a college scholarship, a Latin scholarship, a Fellowship and then took a First in his Finals. In the process he found a delight in intellectual work, which he had not before experienced; he read deeply rather than widely, but he impressed all who worked with him by his great ability, the depth of his understanding and the soundness of his judgments. From the University George Butler carried away far more than academic distinction. There he made friends who remained intimate with him till death separated them; he belonged to a society called the Cosmopolites, designed to extend the interests of its members beyond the limits common to Oxford undergraduates, and he was delighted when Jowett invited him to join a very select discussion group, consisting of no more than twelve members. Among these were Coleridge, afterwards Lord Chief Justice, Matthew Arnold, Max Muller, Froude and Arthur Stanley.

George Butler was a man of magnificent physique. There was no game at which he did not excel; he rode, he shot and he fished when he had the opportunity and he was a great lover of mountains and wild country. When he came down, he determined to make his livelihood by taking pupils and he spent the first Long Vacation after his Schools conducting a reading party on a tour to the Lake Country. Here they all climbed indefatigably and were entertained by Wordsworth, Hartley Coleridge and the Arnold family. This expedition was followed by others to Ireland, to

27

Coblenz and the Rhine and to various parts of the Alps. The fishing, the mountain climbing and the long tramps over miles of cross-country tracks delighted and never exhausted him; he acquired also the pleasures of sketching and for art he developed a considerable talent.

When George Butler met Josephine Grey he had just been offered the post of Examiner to the University of Oxford and this made it possible for him to embark on matrimony. He went to stay at Dilston, where he was accepted wholeheartedly by all the Grey family. His politics were Liberal and his hatred of injustice and appreciation of individual values were as strong as those of his host, while he shared the older man's enthusiasm for hunting, fishing and shooting. Many years later Josephine was to recall how, "Standing at the front door of my father's house and looking down on the Tyne valley, I could see him pacing the stubble with his dogs in the plain below, and could hear through the clear, frosty September air the plaintive voice of the keeper who was with him 'Mr. Butler, sir! Wait a bit sir!' The keeper was a stout walker, yet he had difficulty in keeping up with my husband's pace through a whole day's walking."

While Josephine was enjoying the pleasures of the Great Exhibition in London, George was living in an attic at the top of Durham Castle, turning out his drawers, sorting and destroying letters, and writing to her about all his hopes and aspirations. In a letter a short time before they were married he wrote: "I wish I could give you some of my stamina. I think I should be all the better if I were less robust, more sympathising with others, more considerate of weak or delicate persons. If I can help you by my strength of physique, depend upon it I will do so. In other matters I think you are more capable of giving me aid than of borrowing it." George Butler and Josephine Grey were married in January 1852 in Corbridge Parish Church; she went from her father's house to her husband's in perfect confidence that the security of love which she had known in her childhood would again be hers in married life. Nor was she mistaken, for in all the difficult years that were to follow, in all the distresses that came to her, she was to find support in her husband's abundant faith and security in his serenity—so reassuring to her mercurial temperament.

They went to Oxford, to a house which they had taken in the High. To every bride the entry into her new home is a joyous adventure. She looks forward to the pleasure of entertaining friends, her own family and with less assurance, perhaps, her husband's. Josephine, in this as in everything to do with her marriage, was singularly blessed, for the Butlers had welcomed her into their family as cordially as the Greys had accepted George. For her father-in-law Josephine conceived a deep affection and respect. "I love him best, next to George, of this family," she wrote to her sister. "I often sit looking at him for a long time together, that I may never forget his face. We have nice long talks together. . . . He is going blind and cannot tell who you are unless you go near him, and then his bright look of recognition and pleasure, and his 'God bless you, dear' are so beautiful." He was too old and frail to visit them in Oxford and Hattie was the first visitor there. Others came too, and the Butlers were seldom without guests.

John Grey provided his daughter with a chestnut thoroughbred for the first two years of her married life and on this horse she rode with her husband in the summer evenings through Bagley Woods, exploring the hills which lie about Oxford. Josephine's grand piano was the source of great joy. When she was alone she practised. In the evenings guests arrived and they had musical parties—sometimes duets with Max Muller, sometimes quartets in which Mr. Blagrove played the violin, and "old Mr. Donkin" the violoncello. Many men came, "and listened in rapt silence". It was a stimulating life, full of new pleasures. It was delightful to be able to entertain. Hattie came for the first Christmas, and later on Emmie, with one of George's young sisters, also in her teens. Picnics were planned for them, one on a barge, another to Witchwood Forest on horseback and in carriages, which Josephine described in a letter to her parents; "Emmy rode on a spirited horse with other riders of the party;

but changes were made occasionally, and at one time she constituted herself 'whip' in a light dogcart with a high-stepping horse, and with Mr. Jowett at her side. We did not fancy these two could have many subjects in common to furnish conversation; and after our return, we asked her how they got on. 'Oh very well,' she replied. 'I asked him questions, and if he was long in replying I drove the dogcart over some bumps on the roadside, and this joggled the answers out of him.' It was touching to see how calmly Mr. Jowett confided himself to the guidance of a wild young girl of fifteen, but she drove well." An even more delightful visitor was Josephine's father. He sat listening "with grave attention" to "conversations in which he took little part, not being professedly a literary man". He enquired the meaning of the Professorship of Rural Economy there, and the lessons taught. He was told that the Professor gave lectures from year to year on the Georgics of Virgil. His answer was gentle: "*Very good*; but I think your young men will scarcely learn from Virgil how to keep pace with the progress of the present day." Josephine appreciated afresh the solid force of her father's wisdom.

During their first two years at Oxford George Butler was coming to an important decision. When he had come down from the University in 1843, his father had confidently expected him to take Holy Orders and wrote to his son to that effect. George sincerely loved and respected his father, but he could find in himself no vocation for the Ministry. He was interested primarily in study and he felt that the treatment accorded by some of the senior clergy to Darwin and Huxley might make it difficult to combine loyalty to one's superiors with loyalty to truth. However, as he worked first at Durham and afterwards at Oxford, among young men, he became increasingly involved in their problems. He easily won the confidence of his pupils and he found himself, not by his own choice, exerting influence over them; he began to feel the need of some pastoral authority. Being older, he was now confident that he could preserve his own independence of mind. He determined therefore to seek ordination, and in 1854 he was ordained by the Bishop of Oxford at Christchurch Cathedral and the Vicar of St. Giles gladly accepted his help in the parish.

Josephine wrote to her mother about the service: "George and I are so accustomed to do everything together, that I thought I should feel like Edith when she crept secretly to the church and looked on while her own Harold was married to another. But I did not feel so. I quite identified myself with my Harold; and when the Bishop's hands rested on his shining curls I felt as if I was being ordained too."

It was at about this time that the Butlers met Mr. Gladstone and conceived for him a very sincere admiration, which they never entirely lost in spite of the exasperation often induced by his inability to come to a decision and stand by it.

George's influence in the University was growing, and he was able to persuade the Vice-Chancellor that there was a need for a hall of residence for students who wished to read without becoming members of any college. This idea, now generally accepted, was a new one to Oxford. A house was found near St. Giles, a pleasant house with a garden and behind the garden some tall trees where the nightingales sang in the spring. Here the Butlers established themselves and with larger rooms and more space than had been available in the little house in the High they were able not only to house the young men who came to live with them, but also to entertain more freely. To Josephine, brought up as she had been, it seemed natural to welcome to her house as many as it would hold. The drawing-room was constantly full and the talk was always good and stimulating. The young men who lived there brought in their friends; Arthur Butler was an undergraduate at this time and he delighted in joining in the talk at his brother's house. George had so many new ideas. It is difficult now, when the whole conception of University life has changed, to realise the atmosphere of the University in the middle of last century. It still retained the mediaeval conception of learning. The classics, philosophy and theology were the studies recognised as important; the only science admitted was that of mathematics. In the 1850's there was no single laboratory. There were, however, some advanced thinkers who believed that a study of the natural sciences might not be without value. Dr. (Sir Henry) Acland was notable among these, and as a preliminary, he obtained permission from the Vice-Chancellor to build a museum in the Parks. George was keenly interested in the project, which was resisted by some of the more conservative, who obscurely felt a danger to orthodoxy in the venture. But the project prospered and when the museum was being built all were invited to contribute ideas: Josephine describes how she sat in the Fellows' Garden of St. John's and made drawings of Solomon's seal for the capital of one of the slender pillars in the central hall.

One of George's peculiar ideas was that there was a value in the study of geography. He was encouraged and helped in this by de Bunsen, the Prussian Minister in London—a debt which he acknowledged many years later in a letter to de Bunsen's son: "Your father not only gave me some very useful hints, but wrote down memoranda for me which I have now. One of the most noteworthy features of his character was his readiness to assist young men who were embarking on a course of scientific and literary study." Official opinion in Oxford was very different. It was generally conceded that this "infantile subject" had its place in the curriculum of a little boys' school. When George persuaded the Vice-Chancellor to allow him to give lectures on the subject and to advertise them and notify the colleges about them, the principal reaction was derision; but it was good-tempered derision, for George was both liked and respected, and many senior members of the University attended the lectures. Josephine describes how she helped her husband prepare for the lectures, drawing great outline maps of Europe with the Mediterranean and the north coast of Africa, to put on the board: "It happened that several fellows and tutors of colleges called at that moment. I continued my work while they chatted with him on the curiosity of his introduction in Oxford of so elementary a study. The conversation then turned on letters we had just received from Arthur Stanley and Theodore Walrond, who were visiting Egypt. 'Where is Cairo?' someone asked, turning to the map spread on the table. I put the question to an accomplished college tutor. His eye wandered hopelessly over the chart; he could not even place his hand on Egypt! I was fain to pretend that I needed to study my performance more closely, and bent down my head in order to conceal the irreverent laughter which overcame me." The ignorance of these learned men gave great amusement to the whole family. Hattie, being told by Josephine that Palgrave, of *Golden Treasury* fame, had not even *heard* of Damascus, replied: "There is an ancient book which has been translated into English, and can be had at most bookshops, called 'The Bible,' where I believe he could find mention made of the place." George and Josephine, however, reflecting that many of the young men in the University would be entering the diplomatic service and might well find themselves sent to a country of which they had barely heard and of whose resources and alliances they were totally ignorant, did not feel so wholeheartedly amused.

Among the guests at their house was Aurelio Saffi, who had worked with Mazzini in the cause of Italy, and who was at that time an exile in Oxford. The Butlers sought him out and made him welcome in their home. They were themselves at the moment studying Italian, and the cause of Italian freedom could not fail to appeal to them. They asked him to lecture on the Italian cause in their drawing-room and collected a considerable audience to hear him. Dante Gabriel Rossetti, who at that time was working on his book *Dante and his Circle*, found it worth while to consult George Butler about his translations of some of Dante's Sonnets, and a friendship sprang up between him and the Butlers based on a common interest, not only in Italy but also in Art. Butler indeed, was the first person to introduce into Oxford the serious study of Art. In the winter of 1854, with the approval of the Vice-Chancellor and the Curators, he gave a course of lectures on the Principles of Art in the Taylor Institute. Josephine helped him in preparing for these lectures, which involved, among other things, a thorough investigation of Turner's paintings. There was other work in which his wife could help him. Butler was invited by the publishers to make a collation of some of the mediaeval black-letter manuscripts of Chaucer's poems in the Bodleian Library, and in the Life of her husband she describes the pleasure of "many quiet hours in that venerable edifice, sitting side by side in one of the silent recesses, puzzling out the old English black letter, which was sometimes partly defaced, and transcribing it in modern characters".

The Oxford of that date was very different from the Oxford of today; it was far more masculine. Not only were there no women members of the University, but there were no married Fellows, since a Fellow who married sacrificed his Fellowship. Oxford—the home of lost causes—still clung with conviction to a belief in the inherent superiority of the male, doubting indeed whether any woman had even the apparatus for thought. It remained a city not only of "dreaming spires," but also of scholars and professors who lived in a world of dreams, such as Tennyson portrayed in his refined and bowdlerised version of the Round Table of Mallory, a world in which woman was certainly exalted, honoured, prized as a spiritual being, but in which as a human being she had no rights or interests worth considering. That a woman had any relation to real life, that she had any function beyond that of ornamenting the home, producing the next generation, and ministering to the comfort of some man, was an idea too manifestly absurd to be entertained. With confidence the *Saturday Review* wrote: "Women are fatally deficient in the power of close consecutive thought. Men have too much experience of the sex's charming ways ever to trust them with Government or politics." Josephine found conversation based on these assumptions very hard to endure; it was so different from what she had been accustomed to at Dilston. It happened that Mrs. Gaskell's *Ruth* had just been published. Those who are sufficiently old-fashioned to read Mrs. Gaskell will remember that it is the story of a girl who has been seduced by a man of fashion and left to struggle with the child she has borne. The character of Ruth is drawn with great delicacy and calls for the reader's sympathy rather than condemnation. When someone mentioned this book in the Butler's drawing-room a stream of denunciation burst forth. It was agreed that to show any sympathy for a "woman of that sort" was subversive of morality and that this book should have been written by a woman made it so much worse. One of the company indeed declared that he would on no account "allow" his mother to read such a book. When the guests had gone and Josephine turned indignantly to her husband, he replied gently, "They know no better, poor fellows," and this was balm to her soul; to be able to pity them was comforting.

It was not always so simple. What they said could be dismissed as ignorance, what they did could hurt intolerably. With her instinct for making contact with the unhappy, Josephine came to know a girl who had been deserted by her seducer, and who was in severe financial straits, as well as almost in despair as she contemplated her immediate future. She told Josephine the name of the man involved and he was one well thought of in the University—a man of wealth and good standing, who had returned to his pleasant easy life among friends and associates without the faintest sense of responsibility to his child, shortly to be born. To Josephine this seemed quite intolerable. She reflected on all the prominent members of the University whom she knew and she went to see the one who seemed to her, from all she had heard him say, the wisest and most sincerely Christian. Hoping that he might bring the father to a sense of his financial responsibilities, at least, she told the story. Her wise Christian was shocked indeed, but not so much at the plight of the unhappy girl or the behaviour of a senior member of the University, but at the impropriety of mentioning the case at all. It would do infinite harm, he said, ever to speak of such a thing; silence was the only course which could rightly be pursued. Josephine was crushed in spirit. She was to learn by bitter experience that society as a whole would infinitely rather suffer this evil than allow its complacency to be disturbed by mentioning it. In her record of the incident she wrote, "I resolved to talk little to men, much to God."

Sometimes a way to help was made plain. There was a young mother in Newgate prison, condemned for the murder of her illegitimate child. This time Josephine consulted no one but

George, who suggested writing to the chaplain of the prison about her, with the result that when the girl had completed her sentence she came to Oxford into the Butler household and served them with devotion for many years. This action was not likely to commend itself to Oxford opinion, but George Butler, as always, was entirely indifferent to this. This girl was only the first of many unhappy women he welcomed into his own home.

There was another subject about which Josephine found herself at odds with Oxford current opinion. Religious orthodoxy was no longer in fashion. Tennyson had written "There lives more faith in honest doubt, believe me, than in half the creeds"; and honest doubt had become the fashion. To Josephine orthodoxy meant nothing, but she suspected that "honest doubt" might be an easy refuge for those who lacked the will to consider seriously the grounds of belief. But this was their own affair. What she resented was the attitude expressed also by Tennyson when he wrote:

> "Leave thou thy sister when she prays
> Her early Heaven, her happy views;
> Nor thou with shadow'd hint confuse
> A life that leads melodious days."

It was this attitude of superiority—regarding religion as a hobby for any delicately nurtured woman—which emerged in a conversation recorded by Josephine about a painting by Raphael. She had said that she had found the face of the praying saint "insipid". The "distinguished college tutor" to whom she spoke dismissed this criticism as invalid on the ground that more than made clear that his idea of prayer was "a kind of sentimental dreamy devoutness of feeling", no doubt suitable for the female. More directly was she shocked by another man, who, when she made some remark "from the Christian point of view", replied "with a smile of pity, almost of contempt," "But you surely don't imagine that we regard as of any authority the ground upon which you base your belief?" Josephine made no answer to this, but she was not prepared to leave the matter there.

She was determined to discuss religion seriously, and having a deep respect for Jowett's sincerity, she entered into a correspondence with him. "I think there prevails among clever men who do not know intimately the hearts of many women, an idea that women generally accept Christianity without a thought or a difficulty; that they are in a measure instinctively pious, and that religion is rather an indulgence of the feelings with them, than anything else. . . . For myself I can say that to be guided by feeling would be simply dangerous; that I am obliged to give feeling a subordinate place, and to be guided by a stern sense of *right*. . . . I believe there are few honest women knowing anything of religion, who would not confess the same. . . ." She proceeds to say that while she deeply respects those who base their faith on an intellectual study of philosophy in the search for truth, yet she believes that for those who, like herself, have neither time nor ability for such an intellectual exercise, there is a more direct way. This way she describes: "I began to address myself immediately to God Himself . . . I spoke to Him in solitude, as to a person who could answer. . . . Do not imagine that . . . I worked myself into any excitement, there was much pain . . . and dogged determination required. . . . I will say nothing of what followed except this —that whereas I doubted before whether there was a God who communicates *directly* with a spirit which seeks Him, *now I do not doubt it*. . . . To a man who doubts whether God can and does enlighten and instruct the mind of man in this direct manner, in spiritual things, I would only answer 'Try this manner of seeking God; persevere in it for years, and you will be answered.' I cannot help feeling that there is a great poverty in the minds and teaching of those, even wise and honoured teachers, who, however painful a search they may be pursuing, never speak to God directly and in solitude. Since my childhood it has seemed to me a poor and mean thing to choose to converse with all the servants of a great King, and to hear what we can of Him only from them, *if* it is granted to us to enter into the presence of the King Himself and speak with Him." This expresses Josephine's attitude throughout her life. She never regarded herself as a member of any particular sect or branch of the Church. She could worship

God in any society and she consciously sought His guidance in every decision that she took.

By 1857, George Butler began to be anxious about his wife's health. The climate of Oxford, never very salubrious, was far worse then than now. The surrounding marshes were undrained and through the autumn a thick, unwholesome fog shrouded the city. Josephine's lungs had never been very robust, and she now caught one cold after another and suffered perpetually from a low fever. No remedy afforded more than very temporary relief and in the spring of 1857, after a wretched winter, she was persuaded to consult a London specialist. He took a serious view of her condition, spoke of the threat of consumption and finally declared that it was impossible that she should ever be well in Oxford.

CHAPTER FOUR

CHELTENHAM 1857—1865

"Audacious dissenters against society".   (J. B.)

THE doctor's verdict was a blow to the Butlers, but there was no possibility of appeal against it. Things looked very difficult, more especially as John Grey, to whom Josephine would naturally have turned with confidence, was in no position to help. He had been heavily involved in the failure of a bank in Newcastle—one of those failures so frequent in the 1850's. George had no income except what he earned; he had lately been made an examiner in the new Public Service Examinations and examined for the Royal Artillery, the Royal Engineers and the East India Company, but there were now three little sons to support, as well as a wife, and for this, without his Oxford work, his income was quite inadequate. The doctor had forbidden Josephine even to go back to Oxford to settle up the family affairs there, and George sent her to his sister, who lived in Clifton, while he returned to Oxford to do this rather depressing business. His project of making a home for unattached students had been dear to both their hearts; they had planned their house and furnished it lovingly; to give it up was a real sorrow, and the settling of the young men and disposing of their own household goods was no light task, but it had to be done, and George was helped by the kindness and hospitality of all their Oxford friends, who much regretted their going. These arrangements completed, he joined his wife in Clifton.

Fortunately George Butler's literary reputation afforded him one way of escape from his present difficulties. He was invited to write for the *Edinburgh Review* and other periodicals. He accepted gladly and there was consolation in the work. He and his wife worked together and, as they tackled translations of Dante in French, German and English, discussing eagerly the adequacy of each language to the task in hand, they forgot their anxieties in the joys of scholarship. In the summer of 1857 George was offered a temporary chaplaincy at Blackheath and they moved there for a few months. There they renewed their friendship with Froude and made the acquaintance of Charles Kingsley, for whom Josephine conceived a great admiration. In the autumn George was offered the post of Vice-Principal of Cheltenham College and accepted it with gratitude, for it gave him the prospect of a permanent post with a steady regular income. He had never been a schoolmaster before, but it was work for which he was admirably suited, for he combined sound scholarship and an enthusiasm for knowledge, very infectious to his pupils, with a real care for the individual boy.

They found a large house in Cheltenham, where they took pupils, and then followed perhaps the happiest years of their married life. The change from the climate of Oxford to that of Cheltenham was beneficial to Josephine's health, as was the change in the intellectual atmosphere to her spirits. Conversation in Cheltenham was perhaps not as stimulating as in Oxford, but a very real belief existed there in the possibility of educating girls. Cheltenham Ladies' College had been founded in 1853; and in 1858, just as the Butlers came to the town, Miss Beale was appointed Principal, and under her leadership the College became of outstanding importance.

George Butler was very successful in his profession. He remained an innovator, insisting that geography and science were worthy of serious study, and expressing what was then an original view about the importance of physical education. The Duke of Wellington may or may not have said that the Battle of Waterloo was won on the playing fields of Eton—certainly the playing fields of public schools were growing increasingly important. But George Butler's conception of the place of athletics in education had little to do with the winning of matches, or battles. He believed that the hardness and self-control necessary to give success in athletics was of immense moral value in the training of young men. The fact that, himself an athlete, he so greatly enjoyed the exercises he recommended, eliminated the danger of any self-conscious priggishness in pursuit of these ends. He developed this theme many years later in a paper "Gymnastics and Athletic Games in relation to Morals" which he read (in French) at Geneva in 1877. Half a century later Edward Lyttelton tried to teach the same doctrines at Eton, but perhaps at Eton he had a tougher proposition.

In their first year at Cheltenham Josephine gave birth to a daughter, and this completed their contentment. George found the company of Cheltenham congenial. He was soon invited to join a society called "Friends in Council", which included members of the College Staff and other Cheltenham residents, among whom was Macready, the actor, then retired. Members in turn read papers on subjects of their own choice and George's choice fell on modern Italian literature, in which he was perfectly at home. The subject was topical, for Italy was at the moment very much in the public eye. The Italian struggle had entered on a new phase with the arrival of Garibaldi, and since the Meuricoffres were living in Naples when Garibaldi landed there in 1860, they were very much in the centre of things. Harriet was helping to nurse the wounded and had much to tell of her contacts with Garibaldi himself. She told him that her brother-in-law had offered a prize in the College for the best essay on the Unification of Italy, and he thereupon sent a letter of congratulation, signed with his own hand, to be given to the prizewinner.

On this question of the Risorgimento there were no two opinions in Cheltenham or, for that matter, throughout the country. The Butlers, hearing directly from Harriet in her long and interesting letters, might be better informed about the progress of events there, but their point of view was identical with that of their colleagues and friends.

In the other upheaval which agitated the world in the last years of the 50's and early '60's, the situation was quite different. When the war in America between the North and the South broke out, English public opinion was markedly on the side of the South. In an essentially conservative place like Cheltenham, this sympathy was even more pronounced. The men of the South, it was said, were gentlemen, landowners, cultured people, almost like the British aristocracy. Those of the North, on the other hand, were hardheaded business men, sharp, money-making—the word nowadays, unknown then, is Tycoon. *Uncle Tom's Cabin*, published in 1852, roused indignation. It was alleged to give an unfair picture of the situation in the South where, the public was assured, the slaves liked being enslaved. To the Butlers all this was intolerable; Josephine heard the trumpet cry summoning her to an army in which she had been enlisted in her babyhood. She could not regard the issue as remote, or the two sides as representing merely two points of view on a question of policy; to her the contest was between liberty and slavery and hence between right and wrong.

Nor could the Butlers get any comfort from their revered leader W. E. Gladstone on this subject. Josephine describes the dismay with which they heard him speak:

". . . with his accustomed fiery eloquence wholly in favour of the spirit and aims of the combatants of the Southern States, speaking of their struggle as one on behalf of liberty and independence, and wishing them success. Not one word to indicate that the question which, like burning lava in the heart of a volcano, was causing that terrible upheaval in America, had found any place in that great man's mind, or had even 'cast its shadow before' in his thoughts. It appeared as though he had not even taken in the fact of the existence of those four millions of slaves, the uneasy clanking of whose chains had long foreboded the approach of the avenging hand of the Deliverer. The obscured perception of the question was that of a great part, if not of the majority, of the Press of that day, and of most persons of the 'privileged' classes; but that *he*, a trusted leader of so many, should be suffering from such an imperfection of mental vision, was to us an astonishment and sorrow. As we left that crowded hall, my companion and I, we looked at each other in silent amazement, and for a long time we found no words."

The Butlers withdrew slightly from the life of the community; this was difficult for them; they had been kindly received and had made many pleasant associations.

"Feeling ran very high; public opinion among the upper and educated classes, led by *The Times*, was almost universally in favour of the Southern party. Anyone with a contrary opinion . . . was regarded as a person of unsound judgment, if not of low and vulgar prejudices . . . We were impelled to give up visiting, finding ourselves out of sympathy with the persons we met daily, among whom we were scarcely welcome and by whom we were looked at askance, as audacious dissenters from the verdict of that august authority, Society. . . . This was one of several occasions in our united life in which we found ourselves in a minority, members of a group at first so insignificant that it scarcely found a voice or a hearing anywhere, but whose position was afterwards fully justified by events. It was a good training in swimming against the tide, or at least in standing firm and letting the tide go by, and in maintaining, while doing so, a charitable attitude towards those who conscientiously differed, and towards the thousands who float contentedly down the stream of the fashionable opinion of the day. In this case, the feeling of isolation on a subject of such tragic interest was often painful; but the discipline was useful; for it was our lot again more emphatically in the future to have to accept and endure this position, for conscience sake."

The Butlers had left Cheltenham before the assassination of Lincoln changed the whole current of public opinion, a reaction entirely illogical (some would say typically British) since the fact of his murder could not affect the rightness of his policy, one way or another. But before this happened a personal tragedy had overtaken them, which raised a wave of sympathy and obliterated all differences of politics.

Their only daughter, Eva, was now a little girl of five. One evening the Butlers had gone out, leaving the four children playing happily. When the children heard their parents returning, they rushed out to meet them and the little Eva somehow tripped and fell, precipitating herself over the banisters into the hall below. She was still alive when her father picked her up, but she died in his arms without recovering consciousness. To any mother such a blow must be shattering; to lose a child at perhaps its most appealing stage, before there has been time for disappointments and misunderstandings is desolation enough; to lose her with such suddenness seemed almost intolerable. Both parents were upheld by their faith and by the need of each for the help of the other. Fortunately, they both had much to do.

While Josephine was wrestling with this sorrow, her second son, Stanley, provided a diversion. He became very ill of diphtheria and for some time hung between life and death. His mother nursed him devotedly and no doubt this new anxiety did help her at the moment to get over the immediate shock of her loss. When the child was better, it was clear that a change of scene and of occupation was imperatively necessary, even more for her than for him. One of the advantages of being a Grey was that there were certainly friends and probably relations in whatever part of the world they might wish to visit. Edith Leupold, the daughter of Josephine's eldest sister, was married and settled in Genoa, an easily accessible spot with the right kind of climate. Thither Stanley and his mother were sent. The kind niece also invited Harriet to bring her two little boys, rightly judging that no one could do more than Hattie to help Josephine recover from the strain she had undergone. The weather was good, the sun shone, the garden was lovely and the two sisters sat and talked while the little boys played together. Stanley recovered his strength and spirits. Josephine became less strained, more like herself. Josephine very much wanted to see Hattie's home in Naples and they determined to go there together. When the time came for starting, the railways, owing to floods, were out of action and they decided to travel on the mail-boat. The sea was calm and the sky blue when they set out, but this kindly weather was deceptive. They had hardly left the shelter of the shore when a storm arose and the little mail-boat was battered. Josephine all her life was a desperately bad sailor, but this time, after the strain of the preceding weeks, she was quite unable to endure the tossing, and succumbed with distressing completeness. The doctor was called. She remained rigid and unconscious and the doctor saw no hope unless she could be put ashore—a thing which seemed out of the question. The captain and his officers were moved by pity for the miserable little party—Josephine so beautiful and apparently dying; Harriet so deeply distressed, and the three little boys forlorn, frightened and wretched. The officers took the little boys away and played with them, and just when Hattie had reached the point of composing a letter to George telling him news of his wife's death, the captain sighted the mail-boat going the other way, hailed her and trans-shipped the whole party to her. So, in a very short time they were landed in Leghorn and the situation was saved. Josephine crept back to life and as soon as possible George came out to take her home.

Back at home, Josephine tried to take up her life again, but it was very difficult. The house was so full of memories and the spring seemed to have gone out of her. George was glad when in the following winter, 1865, he was offered the Principalship of Liverpool College. Professionally this was promotion and showed satisfactory recognition of his success as a schoolmaster, but he was glad mainly because he believed a change of scene would help his wife to make a fresh start.

Josephine's health was still a serious anxiety. It is a puzzling subject. She distrusted the medical profession and would always have preferred not to consult a doctor. She had discovered for herself that sleeping with all her windows open was a help to her lungs—a practice in which she was well ahead of contemporary opinion. When she did consult doctors the diagnoses, as reported by her, are very remarkable. For instance, on one occasion when she was away from home and unwell, hearing from George that all their servants fell ill of diphtheria in one day in Liverpool, she commented: "I daresay some evil influence" (might it have been drains?) "has had to do with my own sufferings and the feverish attacks the children had." There is, however, no doubt that she battled against great physical weakness with enormous courage.

Again and again she had a serious breakdown—her lungs, her heart, her head, her eyesight gave her acute pain. One is tempted to think her life was one long struggle against ill health. Yet, when one considers the amount of work she accomplished, the long journeys undertaken all over Europe without the money to buy what luxuries could then be procured; the intellectual effort involved in her letters, her books, her speeches, written and delivered not only in English but also in French and Italian; her successful management of home and family—one sees there was no time for ill health. Her own explanation was given in a letter to Mr. Wilson in June 1873:

"I broke a blood vessel in my lungs when I was eighteen, and everybody gave me up and said I would die, but I didn't . . . and I belong to a family remarkable for *vitality* . . . None died in their beds—I don't mean they were *hanged*."

No doubt she was right; her family was fundamentally very tough. When she first went to live in Liverpool some of her friends gave her a horse, hoping that riding, so congenial to her, would give her exercise without over fatigue. In writing in 1868 to one of these friends, who had suggested also that she should see a doctor, she says:

"Please never mention to me consulting doctors. I have consulted nine doctors now on this very matter of my heart. Among them two well-known English ones, a good Parisian doctor and a good Italian doctor. *All* said the same thing (you must know I was *much* worse in this way when I went abroad three years ago) and the best doctors were hunted up. They all said rest and quiet were the only things. They all said I would *never* be strong; and they all said the medical art could do positively nothing for me, that general advice might help me, and they all gave me general advice. Not one attempted any *medicine* except slight palliatives and soothing things with which I am now surrounded and know how to use. Every doctor has told me that God is my only physician (which I know) and that all my ailments were so complicated with the spiritual and intellectual being that it would be an impertinence in them to think they could manage me. The Frenchman said just the same. He looked up to Heaven sentimentally and said it would not be a case for an earthly cure. Of course

I have followed out most eagerly every suggestion in the way of tonics, etc.

"But for Miss Garrett (afterwards Dr. Garrett Anderson) I must say of her that I gained more from her than from any other doctor, for she not only repeated exactly what all the others had said, but entered much more into my mental state and way of life than they could do, *because* I was able to *tell* her so much more than I ever could or would tell to any *man*. She too said she could never promise me I should be well."

Many years later she remarked about M. Humbert, whom she visited in his old age, "the complete putting off of his harness had nearly killed him. . . . It is like myself. When my hands are empty I begin to feel so old and ill." This indeed is probably the crux of the matter. An ailing body was governed by an indomitable mind and no doubt, the more exhausted she grew, the more she drove herself on. It is no uncommon thing to find in her letters: "I am too tired and in pain to write today," followed by some ten or twelve pages of careful and reasoned argument. She lived to be nearly eighty largely because she was never willing to accept the idea that there was nothing more she could do.

CHAPTER FIVE

LIVERPOOL 1866—1869

"So take courage, ladies. You must fight your own battles still".
(George Butler at Sheffield)

THE Butlers established themselves in Liverpool in January 1866. Josephine describes the impression made upon her by her new surroundings:

"Liverpool is one of the largest sea ports in the world. No greater contrast could have been found than it presented to the academic, intellectual character of Oxford, or the quiet educational and social conditions at Cheltenham. Its immense population, with an intermingling of foreign elements, its twelve miles of docks lined with warehouses, its magnificent shipping, its cargoes and foreign sailors from every part of the world and from every nation of the earth, its varieties in the way of creeds and places of worship, its great wealth and its abject poverty, the perpetual movement, the coming and going, and the clash of interests in its midst—all these combined to make Liverpool a city of large and international character . . ."

Liverpool College reflected the character of this cosmopolitan seaport; as the city made a contrast to Oxford, so the College made a contrast to the public schools from which most Oxford undergraduates came. Liverpool College was a day school; its pupils were not living in academic seclusion, accepting the conventions of Society and of the Established Church, studying the Classics and expecting to inherit estates and find their life work in important administrative posts. "Among its eight to nine hundred pupils there were Greeks, Armenians, Jews, Negroes, Americans, French, Germans and Spaniards, as well as Welsh,

HARRIET MEURICOFFRE
Josephine Butler's favourite sister

GEORGE BUTLER
Principal of Liverpool College

Irish, Scotch and English"; they would become traders, merchants, clerks. There were some, of course, who would hope to go to the university and enter some profession, but these were in the minority.

To educate all these boys adequately presented serious difficulties, for whereas in the public schools there was an agreed syllabus to which all boys had to conform, at Liverpool it was necessary to devise a curriculum to conform to the boys. Butler with his passionate belief in the importance and unique value of every individual, was exactly the man to tackle this problem. His own interests were so wide that it was a congenial business. In the Upper School there was already a sound standard of classical scholarship and this was not only maintained but improved during his headship, so that year by year more university scholarships were won from the College. A surprising innovation he introduced for more intelligent boys was a class in Hebrew. George Butler had himself, when he was at Oxford, attended Pusey's lectures in Hebrew, and finding immense pleasure from the study, he pursued it with enthusiasm. There was a considerable minority of Jewish boys in the College, and to some of them the course in Hebrew was of special interest, but it was not confined to them, for George's enthusiasm was infectious, and many boys who had the good fortune to be at the College at that time must have owed to him their first conception of the pleasure of pursuing learning for its own sake.

But the Principal's impact was chiefly felt on the modern studies in the school. Liverpool College already had a laboratory, and the Natural Sciences were seriously studied. To these, Geography and Modern History were added with such conspicuous success that boys from the College—among others young George Butler—won a large proportion of the medals awarded by the Royal Geographical Society for physical and political geography. He attributed these successes partly to the widening of the curriculum in the lower part of the school, and the easing of the strain on the younger children. For he discovered that the little boys in the junior department were being increasingly pressed, to the despair of the conscientious and the increased ingenuity of the shirkers. This, he found, was partly due to pressure from ambitious parents, who believed they were not getting their money's worth out of the fees they paid unless their children came home with a mass of homework and appeared to be doing better than the neighbour's child. George Butler perceived that it was his task to educate parents as well as children and to this he addressed himself with real pleasure. He was very generally liked and he quickly became recognised as a remarkable headmaster. Very shortly after his appointment to Liverpool he could have had any post in the profession for which he cared to apply.

For George Butler, therefore, from the beginning Liverpool was full of interest. For Josephine it was different. She had had no experience of life in a great commercial city. Oxford, before the advent of motor cars, was really a country town, and Cheltenham, too, was on the edge of beautiful country. In both she could feel herself a member of a friendly community. Liverpool was quite different. Sefton Park was a suburb; one did not chat casually with those one met in its streets. There was no corporate life. The men went to their work in city or docks and their wives and daughters remained at home carefully preserving their gentility. There was no easily accessible country. A small garden could be enjoyed, but there was little else of natural beauty to refresh the mind. The Principal's house was not in the College building; Josephine had nothing to do with the school, and when her husband and the boys went off in the morning to their work and she knew she would not see them again until the evening, she was very much alone. She found her new way of life well-nigh insupportable. She had not expected this. She had thought that with her books, her beloved piano and her paint box, she could easily fill the hours when she was alone. But it did not do. These pleasures had no power to distract her from her fundamental sorrow, the aching consciousness of loss could not be forgotten.

Josephine was not one to allow herself to indulge in the subtle pleasures of self-pity. Realising that there must be many in this great city more miserable than she, she determined to find them and to see if her experience of sorrow could enable her to help them. There is no difficulty in finding unhappiness in any part of the world, but perhaps it is more easily found in a great seaport than in most places. Certainly, a hundred years ago, when the *laissez faire* doctrine was very generally accepted and the more vulnerable were left to the chance mercies of benevolent societies, it was easier to find wretched men and women than to avoid them.

In Liverpool itself there was a great deal of charitable work going on. There was a tradition of benevolence among the great families of the city, but the situation had become too difficult. The increasing gap between the classes, the extreme poverty of the masses, the constant immigration of the poorest type of Irish unskilled labour presented a problem which filled the wealthy with an uneasy sense of guilt which they did not know how to relieve. There were a great many charitable societies, but all were administered *de haut en bas* and this was utterly foreign to Josephine's nature. William Rathbone, who had organised and financed a system of District Nurses, endeavoured to clear up the chaos of charitable effort by business methods and conceived the idea of centralising all charitable funds and administering them by a joint committee. This again was a method entirely impossible to Josephine. She turned to her cousin Charles Birrell to help her find what she sought.

Charles Birrell—father of Augustine, responsible in 1905 for the education measure known as the "Birreligious Bill"—was prominent among the Free Church ministers in the city. He was at the moment trying to arrange for religious services in the workhouse, and it was probably he who directed her attention to the Brownlow Hill Workhouse. This was an immense building, grim and forbidding, rather like a prison. It housed those miserable derelicts who had given up the struggle against a ruthless industrial society. The pauper was not exactly a criminal; the State recognised that he could not be allowed to die of starvation in an obvious sort of way; provision was made to keep him alive at the public expense, but it was considered very important that this help should be given in so unpleasant a manner that no one would be tempted to choose it, if it were possible to avoid it. In this workhouse Josephine had no difficulty in finding misery. She went to the oakum sheds. These were immense vaults at the bottom of the workhouse, with stone floors, damp and dreary, where women congregated to engage in oakum picking. There were about two hundred girls and young women in the sheds; some were quite young, still almost children; others were mature, hardened in the ways of the world. They had nothing in common beyond their humanity and the experience of failure. Some were picking oakum as a sentence, having been convicted of brawling or fighting on the quays; others came voluntarily to earn the subsistence given at the workhouse in return for a stint of oakum picking. Among them were hearty young women, employable, had there been any employment open to them. They came to the sheds when trade was bad in the sale of sand or of street refuse, which was otherwise their means of livelihood. Others again were the children of irresponsible parents, who, having brought them into the world, left them to manage as well as they could. These drifted in and out of the workhouse infirmary, many of them were consumptive—a miserable company of derelicts, of whom nothing could be expected and for whom less was done.

Into this company came Mrs. Butler. It is difficult to imagine what they made of her; tall, slight, graceful, beautifully dressed and with a face that held the attention with its sadness and a rare beauty, which even the least perceptive could not miss. They could not imagine what had brought her to that dismal place, but when she spoke, a strange new sense of security embraced them. All who ever heard her speak bear witness to this magical quality of Mrs. Butler's voice. It had some extraordinary influence, so that "her first accents seemed to enfold the unhappy and degraded with an infinite tenderness, and to an incomparable degree she possessed the mysterious power of persuading, touching and convincing". She began to pick oakum and they saw that her hands were wholly incompetent for the task of untwisting the tarry ropes; they were too soft and quite useless. The girls laughed at her and the laughter brought a feeling of friendship with it. She had not come to improve them; why, then, had she come? She talked to them as one talks to friends, about the problems of life, about their concerns and her own, she told them about her little daughter. Sometimes she recited to them and when she noticed that they listened with appreciation to the cadences of the Authorised Version, she suggested that they should all learn a few verses in order to have something themselves to recite. One day after this a tall dark girl stood up and recited the whole of Chapter XIV of St. John's Gospel. The others listened spellbound and at the end, as she said the words "Peace I leave with you, My Peace I give unto you; let not your hearts be troubled, neither let them be afraid," it seemed perfectly easy for Josephine to suggest that they should all pray together. They fell on their knees on the damp stone floor, while she poured forth her heart in intercession for them all. After that her relations with these unhappy women became closer and more intimate. Increasingly they looked to her for help.

So one battle was won. Josephine had learned how to live with a sorrow she neither could nor wished to forget. Time no longer hung heavy on her hands. These girls whom she met in the oakum sheds, in the Infirmary, on the quays or in the streets as she walked through the poorest parts of the city were but samples of Liverpool's refuse; she wanted to know what was being done for the mass they represented. This was very little; there was a Catholic Refuge of the Good Shepherd; a Protestant Penitentiary and two smaller refuges; but for those who had not "fallen," or who had indeed failed but were not habituated to vice, there seemed to be nothing. For these, Josephine felt an overpowering sense of pity. There was one girl in particular, who became very significant to her. She was a prostitute; her story was a common enough one. She had been seduced and abandoned by a man of fashion; she had then become a prostitute because there seemed nothing else to do; she was sure that her parents were too respectable to receive her if she returned home. She had become infected and had been among those who miserably drifted in and out of the workhouse infirmary. There was something about her youth and gentleness that touched Josephine to the core. She brought her back to her own home for the few months that remained of her life. It was perhaps a bold step to take; Sefton Park was like a village in this at least, that everyone knew about everyone else's business. That a schoolmaster should take into his house "that type of woman" was likely to be regarded as "odd," to say the least of it. Josephine's confidence in her husband was fully justified. When he heard the carriage drive up, he went to the front door and, with the elaborate and formal courtesy which belonged to that era, he greeted the guest, and offering his arm, led her upstairs to the guest room. Mary was the first of such guests to be received into the house; she was by no means the last, but she counted for much in the years of work that were to follow. Josephine had not misjudged her character; she was an intelligent and sweet-natured girl, who had succumbed because life was too hard for her. She listened gladly to the teaching George Butler gave her and the whole family became much attached to her. She taught them much, too; there were things that no one who had lived in sheltered conditions could possibly know. Above all, perhaps, she convinced all who came in contact with her of the fact of which Josephine was already aware—that there is no such thing as a "class" or "type" of prostitute. The Butlers wrote to her parents, they came to see her and there was a happy reunion with mutual forgiveness. Mary stayed in the Butler's house till she died. Again and again in after years, when she was discouraged in her work, Josephine went back in her mind to the days when Mary lay dying in her house, and to the things she had learned from her.

It quickly became known among the miserable and the outcasts of Liverpool that kindness could be found at the Butler's house and a constant stream of unhappy women came to the door. Their plight was heart-rending; power to deal with them utterly inadequate. Josephine's reaction was characteristic; obviously the resources at her disposal were infinitesimal. She did not lament the sum of human misery—such a phrase for her indeed had no meaning, since misery is an individual thing and can be dealt with only individually. She did not think up an organisation, for organisations she always distrusted. She simply set to work to do what one person could do with the resources available. She had a dry cellar and two large attics. Into these she invited as many as could be accommodated. Some were consumptive; at one point she remarks that she had five dying women in the house; some were suffering only from exposure and undernourishment; she took them in and did what she could. One day she asked the doctor, who had come to see one of her own children, to look at one of her sick prostitutes. He did so and then offered his services and medicines free to any of Mrs. Butler's protégées. This, Josephine remarks in a letter, was the first "hint" the Lord gave her. The second happened when the doctor at the Infirmary asked to see her. He was "a shabby little Dutchman" and he spoke to her of the work she was doing for these women; exhorted her to extend it and offered his services also free. These "hints" coincided with a state of affairs in the Butlers' establishment which made it necessary to review the situation. There is a point at which the walls of a house can expand no further even if the heart is still welcoming. The attic and cellar were crowded to a degree which would horrify a modern sanitary inspector, and still the women came. The Butlers took counsel together; they determined that some house must be taken in which at least the dying could be given some degree of comfort. As her own hands were very full, Josephine wrote to her sister Fanny, recently widowed, and suggested she should come to help her. Fanny responded with alacrity and threw herself wholeheartedly into the work. A house was secured, not very far from the Butlers'. An appeal was made for money to pay the rent and to furnish it—characteristically Josephine insisted that this appeal should be addressed to "wealthy and fashionable young men!" The response was good, though she lamented that she feared it came only from "the good and pure".

The Home of Rest was a source of happiness to Josephine and all her family. It was very small, but it was a peaceful place. She saw a good deal of the patients, spending what time she could spare with them and she had the satisfaction of real friendship with some of them, and of bringing the sense of security to some who were very young and pitifully ignorant. "Tell them," said one dying child, "that when I get to Heaven I will be very busy. I will ask for a place to be got ready for Mr. and Mrs. Butler and their children. I will see to it!" Tending the sick and the dying was only a part of Josephine's work. There were also all the others—the young, who were not dying and who ought to have before them a prospect of an ordinary, useful life, which, by the conditions imposed on them by society, was denied them. What they needed was work, but they had no skills and no prospect of acquiring any. They must be trained, and while the training was in process they must be housed and fed, and then they must be employed. Obviously a hostel was a first necessity. Josephine approached the Committee of the Workhouse and, fired by her eloquence, it approved the venture and even promised fifty beds and an income of £200 a year for its maintenance. This was far better than Josephine had ventured to hope and, having heard that there was a scheme of this sort being operated in Manchester, she went thither eager to profit by the experience of others. It was a useful visit. She came home full of ideas, only to find that in the interval, "The Committee gentlemen seem to have squabbled among themselves and now withdraw their offer. They say that if I will start a lodge they will subscribe when they see it beginning to be successful." She wondered a little ruefully where the money could be found to make this demonstration, and while she was considering this, she took a room and invited those who desired to work to come to the room and do sewing, for which she offered to pay 6d. a day. To supply the material she begged her friends for anything they had in the way of old clothes which could be unpicked and remade, old bits of curtain or anything else that the wit of woman could work upon. The response was immense; girls flocked to the workroom eager to earn the 6d. with which they would be rewarded and they sewed with such zeal that Josephine and her sister were hard put to it to keep them supplied with material, in spite of the generous gifts of friends. There were other ways of helping. Josephine was in touch with people trying to do this sort of social work all over the country. There were rescue homes such as that started by Mrs. Gladstone in London. As vacancies in these institutions occurred, Josephine was often able to find a girl willing and eager to start a new life in a new place. These girls had to be fitted out with a suitable wardrobe and supplied adequately with the essentials, and then Fanny would escort them to their new home. Josephine was even better satisfied when some of the Irish girls could be enabled to rejoin their families, whether at home in Ireland or in America and she took great pleasure in seeing that these were equipped well enough to give them prestige with their own people.

Meanwhile plans for the hostel were maturing; there were many well-to-do and public-spirited citizens in Liverpool who deplored the poverty of the submerged part of the population with sufficient sincerity to be ready to help to relieve it. From them the Butlers received enough money to enable them to rent a large solid house with adequate space to accommodate the hostel and workshop of their dreams; it was soon opened, George Butler conducting the dedication service. The fact that this was attended by many friends and neighbours showed that the first instinctive hostility was dying down. It now became possible to devise some more satisfactory occupation than adapting cast-off clothing for some doubtfully useful purpose. Among other ventures, a small envelope factory was started; this required neatness and accuracy, but no other intellectual gifts, and it was work that appealed to many of the girls. It was not perhaps remunerative, but it did demand enough skill to take it out of the category of "unskilled labour", and the ensuing sense of superiority was good for girls who had never before experienced such a feeling. Many of the letters and papers belonging to the various branches of the Ladies National Association for the Abolition of the C.D. Acts are preserved in rather small envelopes made of rather thin paper. They come from all parts of Europe and are all marked with a little embossed rose—a sort of trade mark. Are these, one wonders, the envelopes made in Liverpool in Josephine's first factory for the employment of girls?

It was compassion which led Josephine to establish the Industrial Home, but she never allowed her emotions to direct her actions unless they were supported by her reason. The Industrial Home was actually her first practical contribution to a problem which had for years exercised her mind. Indeed from her childhood she had been aware of the problem, since it was a constant theme of her aunt Margaretta Grey, who was always protesting against "the wasting of energy, the crippling of talent under the false ideas of station, propriety and refinement, that seems to shut up a large portion of the women of our generation from proper spheres of occupation. . . ." The provision of work for women had long been a crying need, not only for the unhappy girls in the streets of Liverpool or other industrial centres, but for women in every class of society. The fashionable young lady, who sold herself for security or rank to a man who had nothing but position to offer her, seemed to Josephine little less unhappy than the girl who sold herself in the streets to any man who would take her. Nor was the girl of the new middle class much more fortunate. Since idleness was supposed to be a sign of gentility, the housewifely cares which had filled her mother's days had to be abandoned, and she was reduced to playing the piano and painting in water colours in a desultory sort of way; buying clothes and seeking opportunities for wearing them; even working for bazaars, a new device for easing the conscience of those who felt obscurely that there was something not quite right in the condition of the masses. All the time her main preoccupation was to catch the eye and please the fancy of some eligible young man. Since matrimony was the only career open to women, and there was a large excess of women over men, the competition for husbands was severe, and, naturally enough, a corresponding rise in the value set on himself by every marriageable man. In these conditions the constant reiteration by men and by the well-established ladies that "the woman's place is the home" was stupid as well as exasperating.

Working men frankly admitted that they feared their own wages would fall if women entered the market; the more educated were more subtle, holding up women, as Josephine writes, "as superior beings for worship (a thing every sensible woman rejects with scorn because God alone is to be worshipped) while in practice they are most shallow and cruel in their treatment of women". It was against this state of mind, which had tried Josephine in her Oxford days, that she protested with all the energy she possessed. She entered into an embittered controversy with Frederic Harrison: "I have this morning the most *horrible* letter from F. Harrison . . . he says *no* occupations ought to be opened to women . . . they ought *never* to work nor have the means of working." She sent him a pamphlet she had written about governesses and their salaries, begging him to observe the facts in it: "I do not hope to influence you, we stand on entirely different ground. I see now that you reject the ethics of Christianity altogether. Please reconsider about marriage. Two and a half million women working for bread. They would marry, but there are many more women than men in the country. According to your theory you have $2\frac{1}{2}$ million women for whom there is starvation or prostitution." The correspondence with Frederic Harrison helped to clarify her mind about the whole battle of rights for women. She saw that there was really only one right in question—the right of a woman to be an individual and a citizen like any other citizen, under the law. She must be allowed to work and if she was to work effectively it followed that she must be educated; she must, like any other citizen, have a right to share in determining the conditions in which she was to live and this involved the right to vote; she must, like any other citizen, be allowed to possess the money she herself earned.

The scorn and derision with which these claims were greeted was sufficiently galling and it is no wonder that many of the women involved in the struggle became embittered, coming to look upon all men as their natural enemies and regarding themselves as soldiers in a sex war. Josephine saw this tendency with apprehension. She herself, so secure in the understanding, as well as in the affection, of her husband, was in an easier position. She could trust him utterly to sympathise with and support her. His unshakeable faith in the ultimate victory of righteousness helped her to a sense of proportion and a steadiness of mind which kept her balanced even at the worst moments.

At this time it was the educational aspect of the woman's question which Josephine took up. In 1866 Miss Anne Jemima Clough came to Liverpool from Cambridge, hoping to enlist support for the higher education of women. It was natural that she should come to Liverpool College to find out the views of the leading schoolmaster in the town. In the face of the indifference, if not the open hostility, of many men, it was wonderful for her to be received in a house where no one needed to be converted, where host and hostess alike put their wisdom and experience at her disposal. Out of this visit came the foundation of the North of England Council for the Higher Education of Women, of which Mrs. Butler was made President and Miss Clough Secretary. It was at one of the meetings of this Council in the College, and before a large audience of people interested in education, including Sir Joshua Fitch, that Josephine made her first public speech.

A new ally now appeared. James Stuart was a quite young Cambridge graduate, who, having enjoyed to the full all the advantages of a University, felt acutely the distance between himself and the less fortunate class of the community, and longed to convey to them some of the pleasures of the pursuit of knowledge. He conceived the idea of a peripatetic university, which should open to working classes and the under-privileged (including women) the treasures of learning. It was while he was pondering on this project that he received an invitation from the North of England Council to lecture to women in four large towns— Manchester, Liverpool, Leeds and Sheffield. He was delighted with the idea, and it was agreed that, as a preliminary, addresses should be given on the project in each of the four towns by someone well known in educational circles. George Butler undertook this task. There is a record of his lecture in Sheffield in which he considered the early attempts to secure education for women made by the Ursulines in 1537, relating that when Françoise de Saintange proposed the foundation of a school for girls in Dijon four doctors learned in the law were called in to assure her father and the general public that instructing women was not the work of the devil. Her experiment was justified by its success, and George Butler concluded: "So take courage, ladies, struggling now at this day for the right to cultivate to their full extent the faculties and gifts which God has bestowed upon you. You must fight your own battles still. At all times reforms in the social position of women have been brought about by efforts of their own, for their own sex, supplemented by men, but always coming in the first instance from themselves."

James Stuart delivered his lectures. The subject chosen was astronomy. It is a curious commentary on public opinion of that day that, though the audience was exclusively of women, it was found necessary to invite a man to attend the first lecture to introduce the speaker, and the last one in order to thank him. More curious still, the lecturer's suggestion that he should answer questions at the end of each lecture aroused a storm of agitated protest at the impropriety of ladies putting questions to a young man. One might have thought astronomy a safe subject, and a company of some fifty women sufficient chaperonage, but this was not so and James Stuart writes: "I solved the difficulty by bringing to the first lecture three or four questions in print, which I distributed with the statement that if answers were sent to me by post, two clear days before the next lecture, I would then return them corrected." Thus all the dangers attaching to personal intercourse would be avoided. These lectures were a great success and news of them spread. A mechanics' institute had just been started in Crewe, and an engineer there invited James Stuart to come and lecture to working men. It would seem that when education was difficult to get it was hungrily demanded by men whose material circumstances were far lower than anything we could tolerate today and this, not in the hope of improving their financial position, but of enriching their minds. James

Stuart had an audience of 1,500 at his lecture. This contact between him and the working men of Crewe was destined to be of great importance to Josephine Butler in the near future.

In other parts of the country the cause of women's education had been slowly progressing. As early as 1848 Queen's College had been founded in London by the Governesses' Benevolent Institution with F. D. Maurice as its first Principal, in the hope of training women to be able to teach in girls' schools. Bedford College followed in the next year. Attacks had been made but so far resisted on the University of London to admit women to its examinations. It was at this time too that Miss Buss and Miss Beale began their work of enlightenment; and in 1862 Emily Davies, with her London Committee, asked Cambridge University to extend its local examinations to girls as well as boys. This prayer was granted in 1865 and was most valuable for girls between 15 and 18. Now, however, more was needed, and in 1868 the North of England Council sent a petition to Cambridge University begging it to "be pleased . . . to make provision for such examinations as shall adequately test and attest the higher education of women". This petition was signed by 500 teachers and 300 other ladies, many urged thereto by Josephine, who herself went to Cambridge to present it.

This visit to Cambridge must have been an astonishing experience both for her and for the University. The old and the young alike came under the spell of her charm and beauty and of the eloquence which came from the profound conviction that she was an instrument in the hand of God. She gave private interviews to undergraduates—as many as forty-eight of them were counted—and many in later years recorded these talks as a turning point in their way of thinking. She talked to older men—to F. D. Maurice, already deeply committed to the woman's cause; to Henry Sidgwick, already sympathetic; to Frederic Myers, who in his Greek dedication to her of his poem *St. Paul* records that he owes to her "his very soul"; to many who were enjoying the seclusion of the University without any thought for the needs of those outside. On all these she made a profound impression.

The Senate granted the Petition, not so much, it is said, because of the weight of opinion behind it, as because of the neatness of the expression "test and attest"; but whether this is so or not, Josephine's visit to Cambridge had not been in vain. Although this must have been most exhausting, she did not then go home. She went first to London to meet Jessie Boucherett, who was grappling with the problem of women's employment. To Josephine it was clear that this was primarily again a matter of education: "At the bottom of the whole question of the employment of women we should always come upon their inefficiency through want of education . . . until we can get technical training for women equal to the apprenticeship that boys get, we shall be defeated . . . the woman's want of training is so generally called *incapacity*." She insists that it is important to make a thorough investigation into the conditions of the employment of women, and to arrange industrial training in suitable trades.

It was at this time that she met Emily Davies, the founder and first Principal of Girton College. Though both desired University education for women their methods of approach were utterly different. Josephine was willing to take what was offered in the way of examinations and to go on quietly, hoping to avoid arousing opposition. In this approach she was warmly supported by Miss Clough and Professor Sidgwick. Emily Davies, on the other hand, was determined to have all or nothing, and to the end of the struggle refused to admit to Girton, students who had not taken the same examinations as those required for the men.

From London Josephine went to Oxford. Her visit there seems not to have been so happy. Perhaps she had faintly uneasy memories of her last days there. Certainly by this time she was thoroughly worn out. She had indeed been overstrained throughout her Cambridge visit, and she was thankful now to creep back to Liverpool to rest in her own home.

Her next immediate activity was writing. In the Introduction to a volume of Essays, *Woman's Work and Woman's Culture*, collected by her and published by Macmillan in 1869, she expresses a determination to lift the subject of women's education from "the flippant and heartless treatment, and from the exaggerated and too passionate advocacy, to which it may have been subjected on the one hand and the other". Her argument is logically stated. It rests on the conviction that nothing that improves the condition of women can do any harm to men, since their interests are supplementary, not antagonistic. Women are instinctively home-makers, so that there is no danger of their being deflected by the possibility of work outside. Society must be improved when the woman, being independent and satisfied with work which is respected, will no longer feel thwarted if she remains unmarried. A home, in which the woman has married the man of her choice and to which both husband and wife make an equally important contribution, must be on a surer foundation than one where the marriage has only been accepted as a refuge for the destitute.

Looking beyond the limits of the individual home, Josephine affirms that the State can only deal satisfactorily with its depressed masses by bringing to bear on them the influence of both men and women. The old "Lady Bountiful way of dispensing alms and patronage" is out of date. . . . "We have had experience of what we may call the feminine form of philanthropy, the independent individual ministering, of too mediaeval a type to suit the present day. It has failed. We are now about to try the masculine form of philanthropy, large and comprehensive measures, organisations and systems planned by men and sanctioned by Parliament. This also will fail." What Josephine desires to see is men and women working together, since in everything to do with the human family the woman's point of view is as necessary as the man's.

It is interesting to notice that a large part of her introduction to these Essays is taken up with an account of the state of women's education all over Europe. To secure the material for this, Jose-phine corresponded with educational leaders in Europe and America, and she now projected a periodical called *Now-a-days*, which should keep everyone in touch with these movements. The first number of this periodical appeared on July 1st, 1869. There may have been subsequent issues, but none seems to have survived. That she herself wrote no more on this important

JOSEPHINE BUTLER
In later life

JOSEPHINE BUTLER IN OLD AGE,
from a drawing by Miss Emily Ford

subject is not surprising, since within three months she had embarked on her crusade against the Contagious Diseases Acts.

As one ponders on what Josephine has written on education, it is difficult not to regret that the compulsive force of a new vocation drew her away from this work. Had she remained to guide it, the movement would most certainly have proceeded more rapidly and on more generous lines. For she had advantages denied to the other pioneers in this field. Where they were obliged to tread delicately, seeking to conciliate the other sex and the more conservative of their own, she could walk confidently, secure in her own eyes in the knowledge of her husband's support, and by it guaranteed in the eyes of the world. Her influence was increased by the fact that her husband was George Butler, a well-known head master—for what could be more suitable and womanly than to be working beside her husband in his own domain and depending on him at every step? Besides this advantage of circumstance, she brought to the problem a wide and liberal conception of education, regarding it—as few have done—as opening doors and ministering to the needs of all mankind, without distinction of race, colour, sex or nationality. Her wide knowledge of the needs of women and the opportunities for them all over Europe and America and her ability to interpret one man to another combined to give her a power for the lack of which the education of women has advanced haltingly and not as an irresistible flood. In 1870 with great reluctance she gave up the Presidency of the North of England Council for the Higher Education of Women and devoted herself to her new and more exacting work.

CONSUMING FIRE

CHAPTER SIX

THE CONTAGIOUS DISEASES ACTS
1866—1869

"That which it is wrong to do it cannot be right to regulate". (J. B.)

WHILE they were in Liverpool, the Butlers always made much of their summer holidays. In Liverpool, they missed the natural beauty which had surrounded them in all their earlier homes. Josephine did her best for the family by making rapid expeditions to the Peak District or to the English Lakes. There is a pleasant picture of them written by Miss Emily Ford, and given in the Hay Cooper Biography: "Mrs. Butler and her young sons once stayed at the island home of the Marshalls on Derwentwater at the same time that we did. I shall never forget the vision of her after dinner sitting on a sofa with her sons close by her, with their arms round her, and one on the floor, talking together in low voices with little bursts of happy laughter, more like a girl with her lovers than a mother with her sons." For longer holidays they made a practice of taking a foreign tour every summer so that they could refresh their souls in the beauty of the mountains of Switzerland or Italy, or the rivers of Germany or France. They planned each holiday with great joy and saved up their money for it; and the thought of the pleasures in store for them helped through many a dreary day of the winter.

In 1869 the holiday was more than ever welcome and exciting. Josephine was worn out and badly needing the rest and they had planned a re-union with Hattie and her family in the Meuricoffres'

Swiss home. La Gardonne was a spacious house near Geneva, with a garden that ran down to the lake; it offered a great variety of joys to all the members of the party. The Butler and Meuricoffre boys made excellent companions; together they tumbled about the garden, bathed in the lake, made a raft which should make them independent of hired craft—the fact that it floated a few inches below the surface of the water was immaterial. There were more strenuous exploits too; the Butler boys shared their father's enthusiasm for geographical and geological science and the boys of both families made expeditions with their fathers into the mountains, climbing, geologising and sketching with great enjoyment. George Butler held that it was not possible to draw a mountain without some knowledge of its geological formation, a theory which won commendation from no less an authority than Ruskin, who saw some of the sketches when he visited the Butlers at Liverpool and said: "Your outlines of these peaks are perfectly true; they are portraits. Very few people are able or care to represent the forms so correctly." While the boys disported themselves, their mothers sat together in the garden and talked; memories of the past, problems of the present and hopes for the future, all reinforcing the close intimacy that had always existed between them. It was wonderfully restful, and the summer weather was perfect, and Josephine gathered strength to meet the situation to which she knew she must return.

For the past three years she had had a secret anxiety. The subject of her concern was the question of the government regulation of prostitution. The system had been instituted by Napoleon in the French armies and had thence spread over all Europe; it was based on the theory that continence is impossible for men and that if the exigencies of public service necessitate long separation from their wives, it is the responsibility of the government to see to it that the women with whom they consort are free from disease. Regulationists affirmed that thus alone could the forces of any country be kept healthy and prevented from spreading infection through the rest of the population. Early in the 1860's there were those who advocated the introduction of this system into Great Britain and in 1863, Harriet Martineau, that stalwart and independent Victorian spinster, intelligent champion of the rights of women, wrote four remarkable articles in the *Daily News*. In these she affirmed that in fact there was no proof at all that the regulations actually led to any diminution of disease and challenged those who favoured regulation to produce statistics to prove their contention. Such statistics were not produced, but the faith in the value of regulation was apparently not diminished. She argued further that the recognition of vice as a necessity must have a deleterious effect on the morals of the Army.

On the Continent it was possible to appoint special police and to carry out the system by decree of the Army Command. In England the duties of the police were strictly defined and before the system could be imposed it was necessary to obtain parliamentary sanction. Whether electors would approve of this was considered doubtful, but the promoters were determined to achieve it and showed some cunning in getting the Contagious Diseases Act applying to certain military districts passed through Parliament in 1864. The title of the Bill was ambiguous; there had been a series of Contagious Diseases (Animals) Acts and to many Members this seemed just another such regulation; the thing was done at the end of the Session and there was no publicity. Every man knew, of course, about prostitutes; there always had been such and no doubt always would be; the less said about them the better. The important thing was to ensure that his wife and daughters should hear nothing. They were far too pure and innocent even to know of the existence of vice. So, in silence, the laws were enacted.

In the summer of 1864 Josephine, deeply immersed in private grief, failed to notice this event. It was not till 1866 that she read in *The Times* the report of the debate in the House in which, in spite of protests made by J. W. Henley, a Conservative, and A. S. Ayrton, a Liberal, the Acts were re-enacted and extended to cover other districts. The Acts horrified her. They established a corps of special police, not in uniform, centrally appointed and not, as other police, under the control of the local authority. To these men was entrusted the business of making and keeping a list of licensed prostitutes, who must submit to regular medical examination. To secure the names for this list they were empowered to arrest any woman whom they had "good cause to believe" to be a common prostitute. There was no definition of prostitution, and since the police were not required to prove the "good cause", it put into their hands immense and corrupting power.

Josephine read the report of the debate with a sinking heart; she had seen the system at work in Paris, the power there of the "Police des Moeurs"; the degradation of the unhappy women and the general lowering of the standards of decency which followed. She could not bear to think that this should be imposed on her own country; a horrible presentiment came upon her that she would be involved in this thing, so ugly and so vile that the light of the sun was darkened and a cloud of black depression overwhelmed her. She describes how she went into the garden, hoping that the sun and the flowers and the brilliance of the sky would help her and she watched the sparrows, envying them because they could know and care nothing for the sins and follies of mankind. As she threw herself into her work, the blackness lifted; in thinking and writing about education, in caring for the women in the Home of Rest, and in watching over the girls in the Industrial Home, she could to some extent forget that deeper evil, and as the weeks went by and no call came to her to take new work, she began faintly to hope that the Lord would perhaps accept this from her, instead of calling her to so much more difficult a task. But as a child she had pledged herself to go wherever the Lord should send her, and even while she threw herself into her work and her duties in Liverpool, she was half-consciously waiting for and dreading the call. It came in 1869.

Things had moved since 1866. Regulationists abroad had become more insistent on the importance of having a uniform system for the whole Continent. To secure this, an Association for the Control of Prostitution by Government Regulation was formed and pressure was put on the British authorities to come into line with the rest of Europe. This propaganda was so far successful that in 1866 an English branch of the Association was formed and so zealous was the Secretary, Dr. Berkeley Hill, that forty-three branch Associations were set up in this country, and petitions were sent to Parliament asking for the extension of the Acts to other districts. It is probable that many of those who joined the Associations and signed the petitions did not realise the nature of the Acts; few people will wade through the verbiage of an Act of Parliament and the great majority will accept as true the contents of it as represented by its promoters. The purpose of the Acts—the preservation of the health of the armed forces of the Crown and more especially the protection of their wives and children from a loathsome disease—was one to which no one could take exception. The medical profession, including the newly qualified women doctors, were whole-heartedly in favour of the Acts, and at that time the prestige of the man of science was very high. Whereas, a generation earlier, the words "The Bible teaches" lulled hearers into a comfortable state of acquiescence, obviating the need for thought, now the phrase "Science teaches" fulfilled the same soothing function. This must largely account for the adhesion of many men of undoubted good-will to the Regulationists. F. D. Maurice was a supporter, and Dean Stanley as well as many others of the clergy; the Heads of Oxford Colleges were on that side and, more remarkable still, John Morley, that wise and clear-headed statesman, who wrote in the *Fortnightly Review*: "To sacrifice the health and vigour of unborn creatures to the 'rights' of harlotry to spread disease without interference is a doubtful contribution towards the progress of the race. . . . This sentimental persistence in treating permanently brutalised natures as if they still retained infinite capabilities for virtue is one of the worst faults of some of the best people now living. . . . How long are we to go on sacrificing the future with all its hopes to this most cruel tenderness for the worst elements of the present?"

Actually the opposition to the Acts was not based on this emotional ground. The first to come out publicly in opposition was the Rev. Dr. Hooppell, the Principal of a Nautical College at South Shields, and the ground on which he protested was simply that the Acts did not do what was claimed for them and that the amount of authority put into the hands of the special police could by no means be justified. Dr. Hooppell found an ally in Dr. Bell-Taylor of Nottingham, and these two opened the campaign against the Regulationists. It was difficult, because the Press, except for the *Daily News* and one paper in Newcastle, refused all publicity. A select Committee of the House, enquiring into the workings of the regulations, refused to call Dr. Hooppell to give evidence, though he had experience with the Navy, which enabled him to speak with knowledge. The Committee was determined to take no evidence from anyone who would not say what it wanted to hear.

Some support for the Abolitionists was, however, forthcoming. In the North Miss Wolstenholme, who had been working in the woman's cause for some time, brought in some helpers especially from the Society of Friends. In London, Daniel Cooper of the London Rescue Society enlisted the help of all the societies with which he co-operated. Every M.P. and all the London beneficed clergy were circularised. But the result was disappointing. In 1869 a Congress for Social Science was held in Bristol. Dr. Hooppell offered to read a paper on the subject of the Acts and this offer being refused he, together with Dr. Bell-Taylor, took a large hall in Bristol in the same week and had a meeting devoted entirely to the subject. The meeting was a great success; it was very well attended, enticing many members of the Congress, and a resolution condemning the Acts was passed by a large majority. It was thereupon determined to make a National Association for the Abolition of the Acts. So far so good, but if the whole country was to be converted, there was much to do. Perhaps Miss Wolstenholme remembered George Butler's exhortation to women to fight their own battles; certainly it was she who proposed that Josephine should be called upon to take the lead in the campaign they saw before them, and it was her telegram begging for an interview which met Josephine at Dover, when she arrived fresh and invigorated from her holiday.

She went, of course; she had no doubt what the answer must be. There could be no question of refusing to do what was asked of her, but it was only human that she should count the cost. This was indeed heavy. It must involve long and frequent absences from the home she so dearly loved. That was the least of the sacrifices she must make. Far worse, she, a woman, must be prepared to stand up and speak in public, to men as well as women, about a subject so painful, so shocking, that she must seem to some extent at least degraded by it. She knew well that the ladies of Liverpool already thought her rather odd, but at least they knew her also as a person who, though she might unfortunately have a bee in her bonnet, was yet on the whole acceptable. She was going to make herself notorious to those who would know her only as an agitator. She would undoubtedly alienate many acquaintances and wound many friends. Worst of all, there was her husband. Her heart failed her when she thought of him; she knew of course that he would be with her heart and soul; indeed without him and his strong masculine support she could not have ventured. But it would be the end of all his professional prospects. He was doing well at the College, universally respected and making his mark, not only there but in the whole educational profession. How would it seem to the world, when his wife acquired such unenviable notoriety? In an age, which assumed the man's right and duty to control and direct the activities of his wife, would it not be thought discreditable to him that she should be involved in so sordid a business? He loved his work so much and did it so well; could it be right for her to hamper it? All this and more passed through her mind on her return home. She relates movingly how incapable she felt of saying all that was in her heart and how, while he worked in his study, she wrote him a letter putting the whole case to him. She took the letter to his study and before going in she stood outside, leaning her head against the door, while she prayed that she might not hurt him

75

too deeply. George Butler's attitude was characteristic. Without thought of his own position, or of anything else except the rightness of her work and her need of him, he said: "Go and the Lord go with you." Of the anxious days that followed, in which they faced together the ugly journey before them there is no need to speak.

It was with relief that Josephine turned from her agonising self-communing to the business of the war she was to wage. She was always a fighter, and now that the trumpet had sounded there was a certain exhilaration in making the response. Her first step was to make a tour of the subjected areas under the guidance of Mr. Cooper of the Rescue Society. She describes a visit to a brothel in Chatham, where she was horrified at the youth of many of the soldiers. She spoke to the lads who told her they were there "because there was nowhere else to go and everyone went". She was shocked by this experience, which was repeated in one place after another, and her detestation of the whole system increased. She went back to the North, where she was already well known as a social worker, and where she found those who had joined her in the North of England Educational Council ready to co-operate in this new venture. The Society of Friends in Leeds offered a meeting place and there Josephine made her first public speech on this subject to a small gathering of women. Among her audience were Mrs. Jacob Bright and Miss Wolstenholme and these, with all the others, recognised in Josephine not only their obvious leader, but an inspired speaker who could exercise unique power over her hearers.

From Leeds she returned home to direct the campaign. The first thing was to secure publicity. Both Houses of Parliament and the country generally must be made aware that the women of the country were in revolt against the proposed injustice to their sex. It was necessary to communicate with everyone influential in politics, education and the Church. To this work she set her hand; she had many allies, foremost among them James Stuart. He had become much attached to the Butlers and he had a real affection for Josephine. Indeed he was almost like a son to her, understanding her point of view, in full sympathy with her thought, and always caring for her with great tenderness. To the day of her death he worked with and for her devotedly. As the answers to their letters came in and one after another was unfavourable, if not positively hostile, it became sadly clear that support from the privileged was not forthcoming.

It was then that James Stuart suggested a propaganda campaign among the working classes. He had lectured to working men in several Northern towns and he was confident that their reaction to a talk about the Acts would be sound and encouraging to Josephine. He felt it to be important for her that her first talk to men should be a success. Accordingly he planned her first meeting to be with his friends the railwaymen at the Mechanics' Institute in Crewe, and having prepared everything he escorted her there to address them. Josephine went with some trepidation. Now she was to talk to working men, on a subject not only contentious, but to a woman of her generation almost impossibly distasteful and embarrassing. An immense audience awaited her; she said afterwards that she had no idea what she would say, but as she looked at the sea of faces below her—simple men, so like the working men she had known in Northumberland—she forgot everything but what she wanted to say to them. The words came naturally and the men listened in utter stillness. Benjamin Scott describes the impression she made:

"It was surprising and refreshing to men to find themselves spell-bound by the passionate eloquence of a gentle sweet voiced woman, who lifted their minds out of the commonplace political controversies. . . . Their imaginations were aroused. They felt themselves called into a heroic and historical struggle for religion and liberty. They responded with enthusiastic acclamations to her appeal."

This meeting in Crewe, so frightening an experience for her, so surprising for her audience, was a triumphant success. She was so lovely to look at, so gentle, and her voice was not to be resisted. Moreover, about the main issue she spoke very simply and they understood. "We understand what you say, Madam," they said at the end. Some of them—engineers—had done part of their apprenticeship in Paris; they had seen how the Acts worked there and they dreaded the idea of their introduction into England; after all, it would be their daughters and womenkind who would be in danger from the police. With thankfulness in her heart and the conviction that she had not misjudged her fellow countrymen, Josephine went on to other Northern towns. Everywhere the result was the same. English working-class feeling was sound and since the Reform Act of 1866 had enfranchised just this class of man Josephine's spirits rose. James Stuart had judged rightly. Public speaking was never again so formidable a prospect.

Josephine went back to Liverpool and got to work. It was decided that there must be a Ladies' National Association for Abolition and that a Manifesto should be published in the Press, giving the reasons for opposition to the Acts and announcing the formation of the new Association. The next business was to draw up the Manifesto and get as many prominent women to sign as could be persuaded to do so. In view of the arguments against the Acts put into the mouths of Abolitionists by their opponents, it is worth while to consider what they themselves declared their objections to be. They were not primarily concerned with what is nowadays called "social purity", though the condonation of immorality by the State was condemned in the fifth of eight objections:

"Because, by such a system, the path of evil is made more easy to our sons, and to the whole of the youth of England; inasmuch as a moral restraint is withdrawn the moment the State recognises, and provides convenience for, the practice of a vice which it thereby declares to be necessary and venial."

This, however, came after the primary objections, which were that the Acts deprived one half of the population of its constitutional rights under Magna Charta and the Habeas Corpus Acts. By these measures every citizen was granted freedom from arrest except on a clearly defined charge and freedom from imprisonment or any punishment except by the judgment of his peers. The law insisted that everyone must be regarded as innocent until proved guilty. All these rights were contravened by the C.D. Acts, which allowed a woman to be arrested on a charge not defined at all and regarded her as guilty unless she could prove herself innocent. Further, it was manifestly unjust that in an offence—if offence it was—which by its very nature involves two persons, only one should be liable to punishment. This, and no sentimental pity for a degraded woman, was the main basis of opposition.

The Manifesto drawn up, the task of collecting signatures was begun. Before the day of publication 124 had been secured, including those of most of the prominent women of the day: "Harriet Martineau, Florence Nightingale, the sisters and other relatives of the late Mr. John Bright, all the leading ladies of the Society of Friends, and many well known in the literary and philanthropic world." The draft Manifesto, in Josephine's writing, still exists. With the signatures at the foot of the names is a note in her hand: "There are more who would like to sign, but they are afraid of their names being known—dear gooses!" The inclusion of Florence Nightingale's signature on this Manifesto is interesting, for it is recorded in Geoffrey Faber's Life of Jowett that she consulted him on how to answer a letter from Mrs. Butler, whom she knew to have been his friend in Oxford. Jowett replied "I would answer shortly, refer her to Army reports, say you have no time for it. She is thought to do good, but she is very excitable and emotional, of an over-sympathetic temperament, which leads her to take an interest about a class of sinners whom she had better have left to themselves. She is quite sincere and has a touch of genius."

The Manifesto was published on December 31st, 1869, in the Daily News, and on the following day in all the other papers. There was a pause of shocked silence, then the storm burst. No motive was too base to ascribe to these hardy women. They were so miserable in their own homes that they had to find an outlet elsewhere, they desired at all costs to be noticed, they took real pleasure in a "hobby too nasty to mention". Having delivered themselves of these enlightened views, the Press fell silent, boycotting the subject. For four years it was impossible to get a word on the side of abolition into any national paper. No meetings held in favour of it were reported, no resolutions passed against the Acts recorded. To meet this situation the National Association for Abolition founded an organ of its own, *The Shield*, which appeared first in South Shields edited by Dr. Hooppell, but was later transferred to London where it continued to flourish. It kept the Abolitionists in touch with one another and made a forum from which Josephine could address her public. She used it often. The silence of the Press could not prevent the movement from making an impact on public opinion. Resolutions were passed and petitions signed, largely by women, and were sent to Members of Parliament. These, at least, could not pretend that there were only a handful of sentimental and ignorant women opposing the Acts. Josephine was greatly cheered when a friendly M.P. wrote: "Your Manifesto has shaken us very badly in the House of Commons; a leading man in the House remarked to me: 'We know how to manage any other opposition in the House or in the country, but this is very awkward for us—this revolt of the women. It is quite a new thing; what are we to do with such an opposition as this?'"

In the North, the movement was making marked headway; working men, stimulated by the contact with Josephine, had at once begun to make local societies and to hold meetings to enlighten their fellows. The South moved more slowly, but the first by-election triumph of the National Association was in Colchester. The Government, being now faintly anxious about the opposition to its policy, desired to have a strong man at the War Office and it happened that General Sir Henry Storks, a soldier of eminence, who had been Commanding Officer at Malta, had retired and wished for a seat in Parliament. He was exactly the man the Government wanted; in Malta he had administered the Acts to his own complete satisfaction, regretting only that it was not possible to bring under them the wives of serving men. Colchester was a "protected" town, having been added to the schedule of garrison towns included in the last revision of the Acts. Storks had thought to stand at Newark, but opposition of the Abolitionists led by Dr. Hooppell had obliged him to withdraw. Colchester, however, was reputed to be a safe Liberal seat and he gladly accepted the offer to stand there. The Abolitionists took counsel together. Here was a chance to make a demonstration. They did not think they could win the seat, but they hoped that by putting up an Abolitionist candidate they might split the vote and inflict a damaging defeat on the Government. Dr. Baxter Langley agreed to stand, and the Abolitionists gathered their forces with some trepidation but with considerable exhilaration.

Elections in 1870 had outgrown the Eatanswill stage, but they were very far from the decorous—not to say dull—affairs with which we are today familiar. A great many voters were newly enfranchised and for them voting was a thing to be taken seriously. The Abolitionists established headquarters in Colchester and Josephine was there, billed, boldly enough, to speak to a meeting of women. When the nomination meeting was to take place, those responsible agreed that she should not be present; they had judged something of the temper of part of the electorate and were not prepared to expose her to it. She waited therefore at the H.Q., guarding the wallets of the candidate and his friends. When they returned to claim these, she could not but admit that they had been right, for they returned in a filthy state, having been stoned by a mob and pelted with all sorts of refuse. Josephine had been doing a certain amount of canvassing in a quiet way in working-class streets and was sufficiently tired when she returned to her hotel. She was just thinking of going to bed when an embarrassed landlord appeared very apologetic but saying that he must regretfully turn her out. He explained shamefacedly that a band of roughs were threatening to burn his hotel down unless he expelled her. He was sorry, but—the hotel was his living. He added that he had secured a room for her in a very respectable working-man's house just round the corner, and thither he led her, most thankful that she accepted the situation so calmly. She was a great success as a guest in her lodging, which though primitive was spotlessly clean.

On the next day, led by back ways to avoid encountering the enemy, she addressed a meeting of women. She was unmolested, presumably since, as women had no votes, it mattered little what anyone said to them and it was simply not worth while to break up their meetings. But as Josephine sat in her little room before she went home, she was amused to hear a very small woman, walking beside an immensely powerful man, say to him: "And if you don't vote like she says, I'll KILL you." Whether there were many women prepared to go to that length and whether, if there were, they were able to intimidate their husbands is immaterial, but it may well be believed that, three days later, when she was thankfully resting at home, Josephine was elated to receive a telegram from James Stuart reading "Bird shot dead".

After the strain of the Colchester election, it was good to be home in Liverpool. Josephine was tired, but she had no time for idleness; she gave herself to the business of writing for the cause. The contribution she made to the movement in this way was very great; an immense number of books, pamphlets, reports of speeches, articles, open and private letters has survived, and one is moved to wonder how, in a life so full of physical activity, so much can have been committed to paper. Among all the writings of this period, none is more significant than *The Constitution Violated* an essay in which she states clearly and forcibly the grounds on which the Ladies' National Association opposed the C.D. Acts. The position had been stated clearly enough in the Manifesto, but what is published in the Press is in its nature ephemeral, and since it was constantly misrepresented by opponents, Josephine felt it worth while to re-state it as simply as possible. This she proceeds to do. Disclaiming all intention of discussing moral or medical aspects, she deals simply with the constitutional issue. She enlarges, as it was not possible to do in the Manifesto, on the rights secured to every British citizen in what Lord Chatham called "the Bible of the British constitution" —namely Magna Charta and the Petition and Bill of Rights, which guaranteed that no man should be imprisoned or in any way "destroyed" except by the judgment of his peers. She quotes Blackstone among English constitutionalists and de Tocqueville, de Lolme and Lieber among European writers on government and law, to prove that this "destruction" includes any sort of interference with the person. Having thus expounded the rights of the individual, guaranteed by a constitution which is "the pride of all Englishmen, the envy of all foreigners", she turns to the Acts, showing how English women by them are being deprived of their rights and "destroyed" in Blackstone's sense, by Acts which can compel them to undergo medical examination. This examination is a violation of human dignity so gross that it would be indignantly repudiated by everyone if it were not that "society in its present state seems to judge an indecent action to be less reprehensible than the plain words which would be needful to bring that indecent action to light and judgment. . . . The hardest part of this whole controversy is, that the deepest wrong among all these wrongs is unmentionable." She goes on to consider how this situation has been allowed to arise and concludes: "It cannot be expected that due attention will ever be paid to the interests of any class which is not duly represented in the government of the country. If women had possessed the franchise, the Contagious Diseases Acts could not have been passed."

To the argument of those who believed that Josephine was a hysterical neurotic woman, basing her opposition to the Acts on a perverse emotion of pity for degraded women, *The Constitution Violated* was a complete refutation. They probably avoided reading it, but had they done so they would have discovered an energy of expression which characterises all she wrote; a dispassionate examination of historical fact; a line of argument followed clearly to its logical conclusion and an entire absence of anything that might be described as hysteria. There is, indeed, a certain amount of indignation towards the end. After her clear exposition of the dangers she turns to the assurances offered by the promoters of the Acts that there is no danger to any innocent woman. For who are they who offer these assurances? It is those who drive through the streets in their carriages, whose privileged position makes them immune. They do not think about the girl trudging to her work and protected by no wealth or position. This is what rouses her indignation. Brought up under her father's influence to believe that those who inherited privileges OWED a debt to society, she was shocked to discover so many among the "aristocracy" who, recognising no debt, could go their way without making the imaginative effort to understand what the laws, about which they spoke so lightly, meant to the under-privileged. This unimaginative optimism, based on a belief that officials were infallible, was a doctrine anathema to Josephine. She ends her essay with an exhortation to newly enfranchised voters to consider carefully the principles of those who present themselves for election, and not be blinded by party labels or to allow themselves to be manipulated by the party machine.

It cannot be too plainly stated that Josephine, in this campaign, was not fighting primarily for social purity. To her it was simply the old war against slavery, between Abolition and the Slave Trade, between North and South America. It was a war for justice and she claimed for every woman the right of every individual— to be given the education and training she could comprehend, the work she could undertake, the right to determine, together with other individuals, the conditions under which the common life should be lived.

CHAPTER SEVEN

WESTMINSTER 1871—1873

"We shall never rest until the system is banished from our shores".
(J. B. in evidence)

THE result of the Colchester election filled Josephine and her friends with exultant hope. Their achievement had indeed been remarkable; in less than a year they had so aroused public opinion against the Acts as to make them an issue at a by-election and to bring a flood of petitions and resolutions to Westminster. The response of the Government was to appoint a Royal Commission. This was really a triumph for the Abolitionists; the Government, which had been promoting a Bill for the extension of the Acts to the whole country, was now prepared to call a halt and look at them again. Josephine did not recognise this as a victory. She was bitterly disappointed. She had had no experience of politics. For all her forty-odd years she was curiously unsophisticated; she was apt to see things as black or white; and of the shades of opinion within a political party, of the shifts and compromises necessary to hold it together, she had no conception. She felt the appointment of a Royal Commission was simply an attempt to escape from the clear duty of repeal. An enquiry into the working of the Acts seemed to her irrelevant; whether they worked well or ill was a matter of supreme unimportance, since they ought not to work at all.

The Commission was announced in May, but not appointed till November 1870: its twenty-five members were carefully chosen to represent both sides of the controversy.

Its terms of reference were "to enquire into and report on the administration and operation of the C.D. Acts (1866–1869) with the power to suggest whether the same should be amended, maintained, extended or repealed".

It met first in December 1870 and Josephine was called to give evidence on March 18th, 1871. It was a fierce ordeal. Her letters to her husband, who could not leave the College to be with her, show how acutely she felt her position as the only woman among so many men, obliged to speak about a subject inexpressibly painful to her. It was the secret of her power that her nature was never "subdued to what it worked in". To the end of her life she suffered acutely at the contemplation of evil. She stood not above but beside an unhappy sister, moved not by pity seeking to raise the fallen, but by true compassion—sharing the burden. This alone is redemptive suffering. Furthermore, she was most unhappily conscious of the hostility of many who were questioning her. The Commission was no judicial body trying dispassionately to discover the truth. About half its members believed that the opposition to the Acts was no genuine popular sentiment, but an agitation worked up by religious fanatics, who did not know real life at all. These had been enraged by the Ladies' National Association's campaign, and they tried to discredit Josephine, to entrap her into contradictory statements, to make it appear that there was no substance in the accusations she had made. They did not altogether fail, for Josephine had no cunning; her opposition to the Acts rested not on this incident or that, but on their fundamental iniquity. She underrated the importance of being able to produce supporting evidence. She had given instances of abuse in some of her speeches and these were brought up against her and she was asked for proof of them. She could not supply this, saying: "I have only had a few days' notice to come to this Commission. I was not told . . . I should be called upon to substantiate everything that reporters have said I have stated in public speeches. If you had given me proper warning . . . I should have gathered together all my speeches, and seen which of them was reported correctly and which not, and then should have prepared my answers, which would have been satisfactory both to you and myself. As it is, I consider it scarcely fair, without any notice . . . to be called on to substantiate statements of reporters which may or may not be correct." That was fair enough, but it left an uneasy doubt. In the Report of the Commission a severe paragraph shows the effect of Josephine's attitude of indifference to these accusations.

"Among the means adopted by some of the opponents of the Acts to bring them into public odium, had been charges of misconduct or gross negligence on the part of the police in putting the law in force against common prostitutes. Cases have been brought forward in publications and speeches at public meetings, not only of cruel insults offered to innocent women through the agency of the Acts, but of repeated wrongs to the unhappy women who have been or are subjected to them. We have made enquiry into every case in which names and details were given. We have requested the persons who have publicly made these statements to substantiate them. In some instances the persons thus challenged have refused to come forward; in others, the explanations have been hearsay, or more or less frivolous. The result of our enquiries has been to satisfy us that the police are not chargeable with any abuse of their authority, and that they have hitherto discharged a novel and difficult duty with moderation and caution. The charges thus rashly made and repeated have contributed much to excite public indignation against these enactments. Even if it had been proved that they had in some instances made mistakes, or exceeded their duty, such errors might have rendered it necessary to make provision for the more careful administration of the Acts, but it would have been no valid argument for their repeal."

In justice it should also be noticed that Mr. R. B. Williams, of the Rescue Society, had evidence against the police and was willing to bring witnesses in support of his statements and the Commission refused to hear them. Mr. William Shaen also suggested that a Sub-Committee should visit the subjected areas to investigate this evidence. This too was declined. It cannot therefore be said that all the indifference to factual evidence was on one side.

On the essential facts Josephine was unshakeable. Asked what she meant by the buying and selling of girls she replied with complete frankness: "I have seen girls bought and sold just as young girls were at the time of the slave trade . . . Are you not aware that there are gentlemen among the higher classes who will pay so much? When a gentleman sends to a professional brothel for a girl he pays for her. Is that not buying?" This was the first opportunity she had of bringing to the notice of Parliament an evil she had long deplored. The age of consent was 12 and this made possible the sale of quite little girls into prostitution and indeed a lucrative trade was carried on. She had tried through various gentlemen of her acquaintance to get the subject discussed in Parliament in the hope of change. She had hoped, perhaps believed, that so gross an injustice must be redressed, once Parliament realised its existence. It was fifteen years before this end was achieved. It was no wonder that, feeling as she did the in-difference of her hearers to so shocking an evil, she spoke of the necessity of "letting in a floodlight on your doings". She was asked what she meant by "*your* doings". Was it the members of the Commission she was referring to, or the whole of the male population? Unflustered, Josephine replied: "No, I mean the immorality which exists among gentlemen of the upper classes. I will give an illustration of it if you like." It was the last thing the questioners wanted, and the matter was allowed to drop.

But that was not the end of her questioning. If the Acts were abolished, what could be substituted to achieve the desired ends? Here again, Josephine made her position absolutely clear. No legislation could achieve any satisfactory end, since the only worthy end was the cure—not of the disease, but of the moral corruption which caused it. Certain alterations in the laws were desirable; the laws against solicitation, against procuring and the public flaunting of vice. These laws must apply equally to both sexes, but the work of reclamation, of curing the evil itself rather than the disease which came from it, must be left alone by the State. The work of reclamation could be done only by individuals or by voluntary bodies which must at all costs avoid taking a grant from the Exchequer, since that gave the Government the right to interfere. She spoke a little of her own experience in Liverpool.

She was asked tauntingly whether she really believed there were enough individuals to cover the whole country in this work, and she admitted frankly that there were not at the moment, for it asked much of the doer, and not all the privileged were ready to make the necessary sacrifices. But she still believed that interference by the State did more harm than good.

When one of the Commission asked if she really believed that a fallen woman had any sense of shame left, which should make it possible to redeem her, she expressed surprise at the question. When a young *man* had been known to visit brothels regularly, the question of redemption was never raised, he had merely "sown his wild oats". It was with this popular opinion that the Commission concurred. In its Report we read: "There is no comparison to be made between prostitutes and the men who consort with them. With the one sex the offence is committed as a matter of gain, with the other it is an irregular indulgence of a natural impulse."

Josephine had brought letters from her working-class friends in the North, expressing their insuperable hostility to the Acts. These she laid before the Commission, who asked first if they came from genuine working men, and then remarked: "We may as well see them, for no doubt that class takes some little interest in the question." This attitude of superiority to her working-class friends enraged Josephine and she was not sorry to be given the opportunity of saying that she had found a far higher standard of morality among the working classes of the North than among the "Gentlemen" with whom she had discussed the matter. She showed that their opposition to the Acts was due not merely to its power of harming their own daughters, but still more on account of the general degradation of moral standards to which they led. She quoted the words of a Rochdale man: "I should fear the influence of these Acts more for my sons than for my daughters." One working man especially expressed his dread of the power the Acts would put into the hands of an unprincipled foreman, who could utterly destroy the reputation of a girl who worked under him, by false accusations. At once those who resented Josephine's attacks on the upper classes leaped at her.

Here was a chance of exposing the inconsistency of this intolerable woman. If the working classes were as moral as she had suggested, what danger could there be in giving them power? Her answer came carefully: "Because the influence of this Act on the population generally is so subtle and powerful that slowly, in the course of years, the moral standard of these men whom I love and admire, will be lowered, and they will be capable of those villainies which they are not now capable of; when I hear that no mistake can be committed by a policeman under these Acts, I am led to contrast that boastful, confident expression with the deep humility of these men, who say 'God knows, if such a power was in my hands, I could not say I might not, in an evil moment, use it.' They are very much more humble. They do not say they could not make a mistake; but these policemen, I believe, contend that they never can err." Some of those sympathetic to Josephine gave her an opportunity to state her fundamental position perfectly clearly: "The elevation of impure and unlawful intercourse, to the dignity of a recognised traffic under legal regulations exercises a most baneful influence on the community."

Asked if she had any general statement she wished to make, she made one, which must slightly have startled the Commission. "Allow me to say I should not be doing my duty to myself, nor to that very large association which I represent throughout the country, if I left your presence without very clearly declaring to you that all of us who are seeking the repeal of these Acts are wholly indifferent to the decision of this Commission. . . . We have the Word of God in our hands, the Law of God in our consciences. We know that to protect vice in men is not according to the Word of God. We hold that the practical working of an Act, which is vicious in principle, is not fit subject for an enquiry, and therefore we do not require your verdict any more than if it were to tell us whether there is a God or not. You may be sure that our action in this matter will continue to be exactly the same, even if the Commission pronounce the Acts highly moral. We shall never rest until this system is banished from our shores. I am able to speak with calm confidence, yet with humility, because I believe in the power of prayer. There are tens of thousands throughout this country, men and women, who are daily praying to God that this legislation may be overthrown. . . . The Acts are doomed for this country and for the colonies. . . . This legislation is abhorred by the country as a tyranny of the upper classes against the lower classes, as an injustice practised by men on women, and as an insult to the moral sense of the people. It is this stern resolution which I speak of, which must be fairly faced and grappled with, by any Government, and by any medical or other clique which shall determine with a high hand, or plot in secret, to maintain and force upon us an iniquity which is abhorred by Christian England." It was perhaps not very politic.

The Hammonds, in their biography of J. B. Stansfeld, suggest that she would have served her cause better if, instead of treating the Commission as the enemy, she had been more conciliatory and tried to get from them some concessions to her point of view. This may be a sound judgment. We have all known from childhood that the hare would have done better if he had emulated the tortoise, but few of us attempt to persuade any hare of our acquaintance to change its tactics. Josephine acted according to her nature. Compromise was impossible to her; the thing was evil and no one must think his spoon long enough to enable him to sup with the Devil. She felt she had spoken for and through the Holy Spirit and she had no choice in this matter. Even those who were opposed to her recognised her sincerity and courage, and one of the Commissioners, Mr. Peter Rylands, wrote to a friend: "I am not accustomed to religious phraseology, but I cannot give you any idea of the effect produced except by saying that the influence of the Spirit of God was there." There were solid gains, too, in the conversion of two or three prominent supporters of the Acts: the Rev. F. D. Maurice, who, advised by medical men, had actually signed a petition in favour of the Acts, became convinced of his error and published a full retraction; and Mr. Charles Buxton, M.P., who had been a Vice-President of the Pro-Act Association, resigned this position, saying the Acts had been an utter failure.

Josephine had hardly got back to Liverpool before she was obliged to come south again to present a monster petition against the Acts, signed by 250,283 women. The Commission was still sitting, but a letter to her friends in Bristol showed she had not been so much flattened by her ordeal as not to get some enjoyment out of this episode.

Ap. 4th, 1871. "I must tell you a little about the presenting of our great petition. . . . I went up with the great fat baby, and was very glad to land it safely at Mrs. Pennington's on Wednesday evening. Its railway ticket cost me 17s. 6d. and it required two or three men to get it hoisted on the top of a cab at Euston. Its weight was very considerable . . . Mrs. Pennington, Mr. McLaren and I drove, *with* our petition to the House with her two fat horses and strong men servants.

"The petition was carried into a small room near the lobby for a while where M.P.s came swarming in to look at it. Blind Mr. Fawcett said to his boy who leads him 'Take me to the large petition, I want to *feel* it', and he felt it all over! Dr. Lyon Playfair bustled in and said 'May I look at this wonderful petition?' and poked it as if it had been a fattened pig for a show, muttering something which was meant to be friendly about 'the opinion of women on this subject being very important'.

"Mr. Cowper Temple and others of the Royal Commission were there and came up to me . . . to talk about it. Mr. C. Temple said . . . 'No doubt it was a nervous thing for you.' I replied 'Not at all sir, I was not nervous, but my soul was deeply troubled at the sight of so many men with so base and low a moral standard as you seem to have, and such utter scepticism both about God and human nature.' He bit his lips and looked at his boots and said 'Ah, I fear it is too true.'

"It was a full house . . . when Mr. McLaren and Mr. Candlish (a most hearty adherent to our cause) went to the little room to fetch out the hero (or heroine) of the day! . . . Only one side of the folding doors of the house is opened at other times, but as it was found impossible to get the Petition in, both sides were flung open, and Mr. McLaren and Mr. Candlish with the monster between them, staggered in and up the House."

The Commission ended its sittings in May and the Abolitionists waited eagerly for its Report. When it did not come they were convinced that the delay was deliberate in order to put off dealing with the question at all. The Report was published on July 7th. It was a curious document. It was signed by every member of the

Commission, and instead of a Minority Report, groups of members wrote Minutes dissenting from one or other of its findings. It did recommend the discontinuance of compulsory medical examination, and that the special police should be in uniform. For the rest it was difficult to discover what was the mind of the Commissioners. Benjamin Scott completely condemned their efforts:

"All these inconsistencies, gropings in the dark, desperate shifts of the struggling reason, hideous and mangled relics of incessant divisions and interminable dissensions, were of themselves enough to stamp the Report as one of the most discreditable specimens of political workmanship to which this country has given birth."

The National Association at once called a conference to consider the Report and this was held in Westminster Palace Hotel on July 19th. Representatives from every part of the country attended. It was unanimously agreed that a deputation from this meeting should be sent to wait on the Home Secretary next day and that the conference should be resumed on the return of the delegates. Josephine was among those chosen, and she has left an interesting account of the meeting with the Home Secretary, Mr. Bruce. She describes how someone had sent a "grand blue satin open carriage" to take her to the Home Office. "We mustered from 50 to 60 people at the Home Office—about 8 ladies, the rest men. There were 14 Members of Parliament." They all arrived at the Home Office and were kept waiting for an hour, during which impatient delegates ramped up and down the passages. When she asked Jacob Bright how far she might safely go in her speech he replied: "So long as you put the requisite number of Right Honourable Sirs into your speech, you may say anything; you may arraign him before Almighty God as solemnly as you please." At length they were shown into the sanctum. "At last the redoubtable Bruce arrived. I never saw a man look more sullenly defiant than he did the whole time. He stood up with his tall stout figure and his coat tightly buttoned over—what in the Bible would be called, I think, a 'proud stomach'. I never disliked Mr. Bruce until I saw him, but I was most unfavourably impressed, and so were others. Nothing could be more haughty, and he

93

several times attempted to browbeat members of the deputation. . . . He looked all flesh and blood and official haughtiness, though he was nervous too. He shuffled his hands about. . . . It was a very quiet, solemn deputation, well ordered. Every speaker had prepared his say, and the order of speaking had been prearranged." Professor Newman spoke first, followed by Josephine and others, some of them working men. Bruce in reply was unyielding, saying that what the Government wanted was *facts* not sentiment. Dr. Bell-Taylor thereupon provided facts—not at all in accordance with those on which Government was depending and which "a little bamboozled Mr. Bruce".

Directly the deputation was dismissed, the members hurried back to their interrupted conference, at which, to Josephine's great satisfaction, a letter from her husband was read and was received with great applause. After this, instead of going home, she was carried off by Jacob Bright and others to address a meeting at Woolwich, where the opposition to the Government was fierce. The Ladies' National Association at the same time determined to send a protest against the Commission's Report to Mr. Gladstone, the Prime Minister. This runs: "We hold Mr. Gladstone to be personally responsible for the policy of his Administration in this matter; and for every outrage committed on every woman under the enaction of laws which his authority upholds. We demand from the Prime Minister, in the name of sixteen millions of Her Majesty's subjects to whom he refuses the protection of Constitutional Government, total, immediate and unconditional repeal of the Contagious Diseases Acts." His reply is extant: July 24th, 1871, from No. 10 Downing Street, signed by a Private Secretary: "I am directed to request that Mr. Gladstone may not be held to be committed by any impressions, which may prevail in any particular quarter, as to his opinions or tendencies on the important and difficult questions to which you allude."

This answer was most disappointing to the Ladies' National Association, for they had hoped much from Mr. Gladstone and with reason, for no one could doubt his sincere concern for the whole problem of public morality and for the welfare of the prostitute. His work in this field was well known; very soon after his marriage he had begun rescue work, devoting not only considerable sums of money to the foundation of "Homes for the Fallen", but also giving himself to the work of reclamation, walking the streets of Soho to the peril of his own reputation, to seek and save the lost. It could not therefore be indifference to the problem which dictated the masterpiece of evasion which came from Downing Street.

In the following year, December 1872, Josephine had an opportunity of forming her own judgment on this inconsistency. It was at a College function which Gladstone was to address. As the College Governors, violently Tory, refused to entertain the speaker, it fell to the Butlers to give him luncheon. Josephine had determined, contrary to the wishes of some of her friends, not to broach directly to her guest the subject so important to her, "never having considered it a wise thing constantly to introduce 'in season and out of season' any subject which may be near one's own heart. It is as often out of season as in season that zealous advocates are led to press their views on others, and I have never felt assured of good being done in this way." She begins a letter describing the ceremony, "I am not able to write at length," and goes on for an immense number of pages: "I had much more conversation with Mr. Gladstone than I expected, and on very deep subjects. I led him as *close* as I possibly could to the subject I had at heart. . . . He looked at me very hard, and showed some surprise at some of my most serious remarks, pausing before he gave his answer. . . . Poor Gladstone, I felt as I sat by his side, a feeling of sorrowfulness on his account. . . . Though so able, there is the perverseness of a child about him—he has no sense of proportion. His mind was full of Strauss and his unbelief. It was easy for me to lead him on from this, to that *moral* unbelief which denies the possibility of virtue in man. . . . He seemed struck, and took fire, as it were, as I spoke. Then, as his hostess, I felt it would not be in good taste to draw him on to the very heart of the subject, though inwardly I prayed every moment he might have light. We had some most interesting talk about centralisation and local government, and he intentionally showed me how carefully he had read some of our publications. Well, what is the verdict on all this? After careful thought, I feel it my duty to say 'hope nothing from Gladstone as Prime Minister in respect of our cause'. I say it with grief. I feel almost sure that under proper influence, he could be brought to look this question straight in the face, and I feel *quite sure* that doing so he *would curse the evil thing*. He is full of passionate horror of evil. . . . I fancy that Mr. Stansfeld is the only man who has spoken to him faithfully, and plenty of '*good men*' whisper to him lies on the other side. He said to me himself how difficult it is to arrive at the truth when the *best and purest* of men tell you of the excellence of what your own conscience may not approve. My husband did a nice thing. Mr. Gladstone proposed my health coupled with George's at the 'Banquet'. In reply, George said that he felt it a *great honour* to have his name coupled with mine, and to be identified with me in a great social and public movement by the Premier. I can't remember his exact words—Mr. Gladstone shouted 'hear, hear' when George said this. . . . Some of our friends . . . looked mightily pleased and knowing, for it was impossible that he should not have *understood*."

Further light on the conversation and on Gladstone's motives in the matter of the C.D. Acts comes from a letter from Gladstone to Stansfeld, quoted in the Hammonds' life of the latter. J. B. Stansfeld was a member of his Government, and though at heart an Abolitionist, his loyalty to his colleagues had prevented him from coming forward. He had, however, projected a private meeting between Gladstone and Josephine, which the former had declined. Gladstone writes:

"I was about to write to you respecting Mrs. Butler, for I did not state properly to you my reason for declining, as I perceived when I came to reflect on it. It was in the main this. There is no use in an arrangement by which the leader of a movement warmly presses his views on any member of a Government who is already in the main well disposed towards them; unless he can, which I cannot, become a propagandist of them in the Cabinet. The interview would only have tended to mark the differences of opinion which exist among us. And the subject if bad for public discussion is still worse for free private exposition between a woman and a man. I had a good deal of conversation with Mrs. Butler and was greatly struck and pleased with her. Knowing her feelings about *the* topic I appreciated her perfect abstention. Also I was struck with the force of her mind, and I thought her perfectly and rather remarkably feminine, notwithstanding the said material which under a strong impulse of conscience she has had to handle."

It now remained to be seen what action the Government would take to implement the Report. This was announced on February 6th and the Bill, commonly known as Bruce's Bill, was introduced by him on February 13th, 1872. Its title was "A Bill for the Prevention of certain Contagious Diseases and for the better Protection of Women". It had certain satisfactory features— provisions for the better protection of girls, the age of consent to be raised from 12 to 14 but, though it proposed the abolition of the C.D. Acts, it substituted other regulations which still permitted police to arrest women on suspicion, and it was to extend over the whole country instead of only to special areas. Bruce, who was a convinced Regulationist, in his speech introducing the Bill made no attempt to hide his detestation of Abolition, and to compensate his supporters for the concessions he was making to the enemy, he assured them, "I believe we shall have powers, with regard to the whole country, such as we never had before. The mesh may be somewhat larger, but the net will have a far larger sweep; and although many who are now taken will escape, many more will be taken than is now the case under the existing law." Nevertheless, the Bill did go some small way towards fulfilling the wishes of Abolitionists, and the National Association, which included all friendly M.P.s, believed that if it passed its second reading, amendments could be made in the Committee stage which would remove its objectionable features.

At a conference held by the National Association on February 29th, attended by representatives from all over the country, a resolution was proposed that the second reading should not be opposed. Speaker after speaker supported this proposition, but the women present took a different view. First Miss Becker for the Ladies' National Association, then Mrs. Butler, spoke against the Bill, seeing in it the re-introduction of wrongs and abuses to women and "the old vicious principles of the protection of men in the practice of vice". In spite of this opposition, a resolution generally supporting the Bill was carried, though its last clause said: "This Conference is . . . of opinion that the Bill contains several clauses which are immoral, unconstitutional and needlessly severe, and deems it essential that these objectionable features should be remedied in Committee."

So the unity of the Abolitionists was broken. How sadly Josephine felt this may be seen in her letters to Henry Wilson in which she complains of those who "all swallowed Bruce's Bill and are *bitter* against me because I dared to point out its dangers. They sneer at my 'hatred of Bruce' and 'suspicious temper'. . . . I learn our so-called friends in the House are disgusted with our opposition to Bruce's Bill and lay it upon the absurd fanaticism and suspicion of the ladies. . . . What broken reeds most of them are to be disgusted because we would not accept a *compromise*!" She had worked so happily, feeling that all were united against a terrible enemy. Now here was a breach in the ranks. It was tragic because all were on the same side really, detesting the injustice of the Acts, but Professor Amos put his finger on the point when he said he did not himself think that the Association would surrender any principle in supporting the second reading. It was a matter of policy, not a matter of principle, and opinions might well differ. For Josephine *nothing* was a matter of policy. If the thing was wrong, it was wrong, and must be fought. When her friends remonstrated with her, using the proverb "Half a loaf is better than no bread", she replied grimly "not if it is poisoned". It was partly at least her encounter with Bruce himself and the strong dislike and distaste he had inspired, which convinced her that he had framed the Bill with extreme cunning on purpose to disrupt the Association. It was a bitter and an anxious time. She collected a few like-minded friends, who worked, wrote, spoke and prayed about the situation. Their labours were not in vain for before the end of April the National Association had come round to her view. The battle raged in the Commons, the women repealists coming in for much abuse, Sir James Elphinstone even declaring that "he looked upon these women who have taken up this matter as worse than the prostitutes". The Press, which had been completely silent since the Manifesto, now opened its columns again to the Regulationists and the whole movement was reviled and derided, the women being called "indecent maenads", "shrieking sisters, frenzied, unsexed, and utterly without shame". The Regulationists complained that the Bill was giving in too much to the faddists. Clearly it pleased nobody. It was dropped.

CHAPTER EIGHT

TESTING THE COUNTRY 1873—1874

"Seek men and women first, before any machinery". (J. B.)

WHILE this controversy was raging at Westminster the movement was spreading and gaining force all over the country. The inspiration which had stirred the working men at Crewe and in the other Northern cities had not been allowed to evaporate. Associations had been formed and great meetings held and it was from these that the letters and resolutions had come which Josephine had presented to the Royal Commission. Working men too had taken part in the deputation to the Home Office, where they had warned the Home Secretary that the spirit of Wat Tyler was not dead in England. The Commission had been startled by the expression of opinion of these working men. They were a new feature in the political scene, having become important there only since they had been enfranchised. They represented the most able of the working class, believing in education and eagerly attending the Mechanics' Institutes, University Extension Lectures and the Working Men's Colleges; ardent Trade Unionists, they could see beyond the immediate horizon of their daily lives and were concerned with something more than the necessity of earning enough to live on. They were an immense potential force in any movement.

The opposition to the C.D. Acts was of course not confined to the working classes. From the beginning Dr. Hooppell of South

Shields had fought against them and he had organised an Abolitionist Association in Newcastle; Dr. Bell-Taylor in Nottingham
had made another, and other local Associations followed in
Sunderland, Liverpool and Belfast. In Birmingham the Mayor
and Corporation were on the side of Repeal, and after a large
public meeting there with the Mayor in the Chair, another was
arranged for women, to be addressed by Josephine. To this meeting came two ladies, members of the Society of Friends, who had
determined to raise the banner in Bristol. They came to find out
for themselves "whether Mrs. Butler was really one whom we
could fearlessly follow in the dark path we had entered on. . . .
The door opened, Mrs. Butler came in, slight, graceful, almost
young and very beautiful. As she moved to the table she raised
her eyes, weighed down with a look of infinite sadness, as if the
world's sin and sorrow rested on her innocent head. Surely here
was a Christ sent to save us from despair was the involuntary
thought that came into my heart." One of these two ladies was
Margaret Tanner, who with her two sisters the Misses Priestman
of Bristol became among Josephine's closest friends, working
with her with the utmost devotion till death separated them.

Another of the earliest recruits to the cause was Henry Wilson
of Sheffield. Like so many who were drawn into this campaign—
like Josephine herself—he was born into an atmosphere of bitter
hostility to slavery; his father, like hers, had been an uncompromising fighter in the war of emancipation, and like her, he
responded instinctively to the call to oppose this new form of
slavery. He was the owner of a smelting works in Sheffield, well
respected, a religious man and liberal in outlook as well as in
politics. He was ahead of his generation in regarding his wife not
only as a housekeeper and the mother of his children but also as a
companion who would take a share in his political and business
activities. They had read the Women's Manifesto and at once
recognised its validity. They set to work to get support for the
Abolitionists, holding meetings, circularising their fellow citizens
and collecting signatures for petitions against the Acts. Henry
Wilson and his wife Charlotte had been at work for some little

time before they invited Josephine to address a meeting in Sheffield in April 1871, without any certainty that it would attract a sufficient audience, even though it had been meticulously prepared. Charlotte determined that she ought to sit on the platform to save Josephine from being the only woman there. Long before the time fixed for the meeting the room began to fill, and so enthusiastically was it supported that it was agreed that a woman's meeting should be held on the following day. The success was repeated. This was the beginning of a warm personal friendship between Josephine and the Wilsons.

The importance of Henry Wilson's adherence to the cause cannot easily be exaggerated. He was a business man, clear thinking and methodical; he supplied to the movement a solid foundation of good sense and kept it from excesses to which at times some of the more ardent were tempted. After the conflict was over, he made a chronological list, which he called "A Rough Record" of all the events in the campaign. This and his valuable habit of dating and docketing every letter he received from Josephine, adding where he could the place from which it was written, make it possible to thread a way through the maze of her correspondence. For Josephine herself thought the day of the week a sufficient heading for any letter, "Dear Friends" a sufficient beginning; and many of those who corresponded with her adopted the same habit.

After the withdrawal of Bruce's bill Josephine went back to Liverpool with war in her heart; determined that petitions and resolutions should continue to flow to Westminster to support the friendly M.P.s who on every possible occasion were bringing in bills for repeal, for reform of the criminal laws, for raising the age of consent, only to have them talked out, counted out or negatived. The withdrawal of Bruce's objectionable bill had created a new situation. She rejoiced in the prospect of a General Election, and it was clear that this could not be long delayed. The immediate task therefore was to get the Abolitionists ready for the approaching campaign. There was much to do. Agents must be appointed all over the country, therefore money must be

collected with which to pay them. She sent out a circular to all
branch associations. "Friends, do not start—I want £500!"
There was a great deal of good-will towards the movement, but
it was necessary that the numerous local associations should be
given some sort of coherent organisation, to prevent overlapping
and waste of effort. For this business of organisation, recognising
her own limitations, she turned naturally to Henry Wilson. "You
know I have not a good head for organisation; and am not fit to
give advice on matters of arrangement. My one gift, if I have one,
is to breathe a little fire and courage into *individual* workers and
so gradually to influence a good many. I can never see my way
clearly in a great campaign." Wilson responded at once, and the
two made a wonderful combination.

The work could not always run smoothly, for Pegasus is never
an easy yoke-fellow, and to work on a planned basis was practically impossible to Josephine. She did her best to keep in step;
she saw the importance of following a prearranged course, of
economising effort and fitting details into a master plan. But
conformity was very difficult to her. "The wind bloweth where it
listeth and thou hearest the sound thereof but thou canst not tell
whence it cometh nor whither it goeth. So is every one that is
born of the Spirit." Josephine was emphatically one of these; she
had dedicated herself to His guidance and this gave her at once
her unique power and a certain unpredictability. While others
were pondering on a problem, weighing pros and cons, she could
suddenly see into the heart of it so clearly that she could not wait
to convince others. It was this which gave her her sure touch in
dealing with the wretched and degraded and filled her with fury
against the oppressor; it was this which gave her the gift of
eloquence so that she could move any audience she addressed. It
made it impossible for her to identify herself with any denomina-
tional body. Loyalty to her husband made her worship normally
in the Anglican Communion, but she was impatient of all ex-
clusiveness, believing that all forms and ceremonies were unimportant and that every man must seek for himself the guidance
of the Holy Spirit and communion with the Lord. She was a

mystic and did not perhaps realise that the consciousness of the Presence of God is not vouchsafed to all even of those who believe; it is a gift, a kind of genius bestowed no more commonly than other kinds.

In spite of their mutual trust and affection, Josephine and Henry Wilson could not always see eye to eye. Her sense of values was subtly different from his. This difference was shown over the organisation of a Working Men's Association for Repeal, under a working man as President, which was set up without any reference to the National Association. Henry Wilson felt this separate organisation, cutting across his own, could only do harm and asked Josephine to discourage it. She replied that she had had no hand in the formation of it and would on no account interfere. "It is the most spontaneous movement I have seen." She went on to say that it was a much more valuable and important movement when organised entirely by the working men themselves, rather than being imposed on them, as it were, from above. The Working Men's Association continued to flourish.

With patience and good-will and enthusiasm for the cause on both sides, the work of organisation proceeded apace. It was clearly necessary to have some central body to co-ordinate all the local associations and the first regional body was the Northern Counties League. Josephine, naturally enough, gave her own beloved North her best attention and she wrote to Mr. Wilson: "I look upon the Northern League rather as my child. I hatched it with much cackling and care." The Northern League was followed by the Midland Counties Electoral Union, which took the place of the Birmingham Association. The National Association had established its headquarters in London and the organisation in the South was mainly in its hands. There followed the appointment of paid agents, often working men, to any local branch that could profitably use them. Henry Wilson's files bear witness to the amount of time and trouble Josephine expended in seeing that the right man was appointed and that he was stationed in the place where he could be most useful. She studied the reports sent in by the agents and assessed each one's capacity

as canvasser, public speaker, money raiser or contact maker. She
was not easy to please but she was just. There were some agents
whom she could not bear to have on the platform when she was
speaking, but these were not men who offended by want of
education or a bad accent, but rather by a certain want of sensi-
tiveness which jarred on her. About one man she wrote: "His
manners are against him. He is a vulgar man, in dress, walk and
Cockney accent—but I like vulgar people, when they are not
vulgar in heart like so many of the aristocracy. Yes, I like them.
I am so sick of the refined 'better' classes, my sympathies are so
wholly with the non-privileged, even when they drop every 'h'."

All this dealing with agents was sufficiently exacting, but it
was only a secondary activity. Her main work, as she herself had
suggested, lay in kindling in the hearts and minds of her hearers
that fire which should "burn up the evil system". None of her
colleagues could touch her in her gift of eloquent speech, and
she moved from one centre to another as she was called for.
She went to Glasgow, where 200 medical students, who determined that no one should hear Mrs. Butler, broke up the meeting;
she went to Leeds, where a large audience in the Corn Market
listened with deep attention to a moving exhortation from a
veteran of the War of Emancipation; she went to Bristol, to
Plymouth, to Woolwich. At a town in South Wales she concluded her speech by quoting with great effect one of the de-
nunciatory passages in Isaiah, described by a scandalised reporter
in the local paper as "a tirade of language which we would rather
not reproduce in print". Mrs. Fawcett, in her life of Josephine,
calculates that in one year she addressed 99 meetings and four
conferences and travelled 3,700 miles in the course of this
campaign. The fact that her poverty made her travel third class,
in conditions hardly conceivable today, makes her achievement
even more remarkable.

In August 1872 there was a by-election at Pontefract, where
the sitting Member, H. C. E. Childers, sought re-election on his
appointment as First Lord of the Admiralty. He had held the seat
for twelve years and was well liked. Though there was an Oppo-

sition candidate, Childers confidently expected to have a walkover. The Abolitionists decided that this should not be so. They welcomed the opportunity of proclaiming to a Cabinet Minister their opposition to the C.D. Acts as well as of practising their electoral organisation. They arrived at Pontefract in force and to the astonishment of Childers and his supporters the C.D. Acts became the real issue in the election. There were riotous scenes at a meeting addressed by Childers from the windows of the Buck Inn, where Henry Wilson was protected from physical violence only by a band of working men who made themselves into his bodyguard. When on their way to a meeting at the Town Hall some of Josephine's friends offered to conduct her and the other ladies by back streets, to avoid possible trouble, the working men exclaimed, "Never go by a back way. Come along through the middle of the crowd and before their windows; we will protect you", and their "progress to the Town Hall was thus converted into a sort of triumphal procession, Mr. Wilson walking first with the Blue Book of the Royal Commission under his arm, attended by Mr. Edmondson and others, and loudly cheered by the crowd of men and women. . . . It was not an encouraging scene for a Parliamentary candidate."

When Josephine and Charlotte Wilson determined to address a meeting of women, things became even more melodramatic. The meeting was planned for a time when it was thought the enemy would be fully engaged elsewhere. When Stuart reached the room which he had managed with great difficulty to secure, he found the floor heavily strewn with cayenne pepper. He set to work himself to help wash this down "with nothing better than a broken pot and a newspaper used as a sponge" and the meeting began in good order. The room was over a disused stable, approached only by a step ladder through a trap door. It was full of women. They had not gone far before smoke began to creep through the floor boards, bundles of straw having been lighted in the stable below. This was disconcerting, but worse was to follow, for through the trap door appeared a number of rough men, who approached the speakers with menaces. Josephine and Charlotte stood perfectly still facing the men, who probably did not really mean violence, for they went no further than threats. This was, however, sufficiently alarming, and while they were wondering what their next step should be, a working lass made a bolt for the trap door and rushed for help. Mr. Stuart came instantly, and there followed a free fight in which Stuart, though hopelessly outnumbered, fought valiantly, offering to explain himself and answer questions whenever he could find breath to speak. Josephine and Charlotte, rightly perceiving that their presence made things more difficult, flung themselves down through the trap door and escaped to their hotel, pursued, not by assailants, but by a crowd of working women, eager to hear what they had to say.

The day before polling day they carefully planned a canvass of the whole town, ensuring that every house should receive their leaflets. In this work they were helped by a working man who tramped from Leeds—a distance of some twenty miles—delivered literature all night and walked back to clock in at his job next day. This enthusiasm was very heartening to the Abolitionists. The result of the election was even more so, for though Childers was returned, his majority was substantially reduced. He himself was so much impressed by their arguments that he never again defended the Acts and subsequently voted for their repeal. Josephine's comment on the whole campaign was characteristic: "Several who heard of the conduct of the men at Pontefract have been *convinced* by it of the wickedness of the Acts and have sent money. This shows us that it may not be wise to conceal the venom of our adversaries, though I confess it goes against my feelings to publish what one sometimes has to go through. It is so *nasty*."

Naturally enough, Josephine had always looked for her main support from religious bodies: "My great hope is from the Christian Churches, setting aside all differences and combining against a *moral* heresy which threatens the foundation of religion and virtue." From the beginning the Society of Friends had been strong supporters: "They are so pugilistic and so obstinate and so gentle and calm ... I delight in them" and some of the Free Churches had joined them, but in spite of some outstanding exceptions, the Established Church had been woefully backward. Indeed, at Nottingham Church Conference, when George Butler endeavoured to read a paper on the subject of the Acts he was prevented by his brother clergy. "We had heard, many times before, rude and defiant cries and noisy opposition at crowded meetings, but never so deep and angry a howl as now arose from the throats of a portion of the clergy of the National Church." This violence defeated its own ends and reaction set in in favour of the Repealers. The Dean of Carlisle and others came forward in support, and there were frequent petitions to the House of Commons; in June 1872 the General Assembly of the Free Church of Scotland; in August of the same year 700 Wesleyan Ministers in conference; and in May 1873 1,500 Clergy of the Church of England all sent in petitions and memorials for Repeal.

As the approaching fall of the Government became more obvious, the Abolitionists met in conference to make their position absolutely clear to themselves as well as to their opponents. A great many able business men had been brought into the movement; some of these, like Backhouse of Sunderland and Thomasson of Bolton, were wealthy and most generous in their financial help; others, like Edmondson of Halifax gave service rather than money. James Bryce was another. Of him Josephine remarks, "A sort of pupil of mine. He came to my room privately to be taught a little. He is an *enquirer* in religious matters, a good, earnest, able man." It was very important that these allies should be clear on fundamentals. Their instincts were right; they were repelled by the injustices perpetrated by the Acts, but they had not considered the whole social problem and the principles involved. They looked to Josephine as mediaeval scholars did to their tutors, laying their problems before her, anxious to secure her approval. She for her part spared no pains to ensure that their views should be sound, for it was of extreme importance that they should speak with one voice.

Abolitionists were constantly accused of being merely des-

tructive in their criticisms, of offering no alternative to the Acts
they wished to abolish. The answer to this accusation is so
important that it is best given in Josephine's own words. She
wrote to Henry Wilson:

"My motto is *no* legislation at all on prostitution, for all such legislation
will press on women only. But even if it did not, I have no faith in it.
For our legislative programme I would ask *only repeal*. No alternative,
no substituted legislation, but let it be understood clearly that our
social programme is not the same. As private or associated workers,
societies, etc., we are bound to do all we can to attack and heal the
vices and miseries of society, and to reclaim the fallen, and prevent
immorality. The very fact of leaving the State to do it by its laws will
lessen the sense of personal responsibility and weaken the fervour of
charity in all, the best of us, so that our hands will hang down and we
shall leave it to the State to do this deep, difficult, holy work."

At the Conference she reminded them all: "We are not met to
discuss principles; there is a call to battle, and for that we have
to get our guns and earthworks ready, there is no time for mere
talk. . . . We are here to plan *work*, and not for *jaw*."

Outside the Conference Josephine continued to instruct. The
distinction between sin and crime, between moral and legal
responsibility was very clear in her mind and central to all her
thought about the problem of prostitution. For this reason she
resisted the pressure from those who believed that the law could
usefully be invoked, as long as it dealt equally with men and
women. Josephine was at pains to convert them. She begged them
to look into the history of the subject: "Dufour's *History of
Prostitution*; Rabuteaux *de la Prostitution en Europe*; Herold and
Jozou *Manual of Individual Liberty* . . . any history of the Church
in the Middle Ages would tell a good deal about it". . . . The
punishment of both sexes had been tried again and again and
had always been most unfortunate in its result. The immediate
effect had been a reaction in favour of the sinner and hence a
toleration of vice. She urged them to consider what an attempt
to deal with prostitution by law would involve, for while it
would be possible to find and punish those who patronised
brothels, the evil would go on outside them and could only be

brought to justice by an elaborate network of espionage—since neither offender would inform on the other. This establishment of a system of authorised espionage, which would destroy all mutual confidence and make decent society impossible, would be a far greater evil than that which it professed to cure.

Parliament was dissolved in January 1874. The Abolitionists approached the election full of happy confidence. Josephine had exclaimed: "My heart burns with wrath and shame when I think of these men in power permitting these abominations to go on for another year", feeling certain that the coming election would put an end to all that. A great revolution was already on the way. The deputation of 1872, knowing that the mass of working-class opinion was on its side, had threatened Bruce with a rising of the working classes. "Irish land bills and the like will not hereafter be the engrossing matters for Parliament to deal with," Josephine wrote jubilantly to her husband. No army of Israel ever faced a Canaanite tribe with more confidence. But elections do not happen like that, for a moral issue which cuts across party affiliations is by the leaders of both parties pushed out of sight, so that each may present a united front. It was on the Irish and financial policy of the Government that it was handsomely defeated, and in such a book as Philip Magnus' *Life of Gladstone*, the crusade against the C.D. Acts is not so much as mentioned.

CHAPTER NINE

FIRST EUROPEAN SALLY 1874–1875

"This conflict is not for England alone". (J. B.)

THE election results had a depressing effect on the Abolitionists. All over the country, throughout the election, groups of their supporters had been meeting to pray for a successful issue to their efforts and now a Conservative Government had been returned, more firmly convinced than its predecessor of the necessity for maintaining and extending the system of regulation. In the preceding year, while the National Association had been working hopefully for an electoral triumph, a Medical Congress had met at Vienna and had passed a resolution declaring Regulation to be the only possible way of controlling disease, and calling on every port in Europe and indeed the world, to adopt the same measures and enforce the same regulations. A book by Dr. Jeannell of Bordeaux published about this time called on Great Britain to co-operate in this movement and it seemed only too likely that the new government would respond cordially to this appeal.

The Ladies' National Association called a conference in June 1874 at York. It was not very well attended and the delegates were suffering from a reaction from their earlier confidence. They still believed firmly in the righteousness of their cause, but their adherence was dogged rather than ardent; they would do whatever could be done but, for the moment, their hopes of success were dashed. Josephine knew only one answer to this. They must meet and pray. They had prayed for success, and if God had not answered in the way they had hoped, it could only be because He had some better thing to give in His own time. As she meditated in silence she began to realise how this defeat could serve a greater purpose. "I think it is better for this country and for the world that this struggle should be prolonged and should become hotter—until this seven times heated fire has more completely separated the dross and the gold, and purified the moral atmosphere. This conflict is not for England alone. The eyes of Europe are upon us, and the spirit manifested among us is full of significance to many who have long mourned on this evil in other countries. The longer and more earnest our struggle is, the more effectually will it loosen the chains of wickedness in other parts of the world."

Josephine had long known from her friends on the Continent that there were many who, like the English Abolitionists, detested the system against which they were fighting, and she was now convinced that the next step must be to co-operate with them. The threat was international and must be met internationally. This was the view she put to the meeting, and the delegates responded, as people always did, to her fire. Reassurance came; they could not be defeated ultimately, and since the end was certain, the rigours of the way could joyfully be endured; immediate hope was deferred, but there was work to be done and a prospect of a long struggle offering infinite opportunities of achievement to any who took part in it. The conference dispersed with the understanding that correspondence with possible supporters abroad should be initiated and, as soon as enough information had been received, the members should meet again to determine the next step.

The Society of Friends had been long concerned with this work and had many contacts on the Continent. The Free Church of Scotland also supplied a list of sympathetic Pastors. To all of these Josephine sent a circular, setting forth the policy of the Ladies' National Association. Then she waited for the replies for which she had asked.

In July a very important and most heartening event occurred. This was the adherence of J. B. Stansfeld to the cause. Stansfeld, the Member for Halifax, held the office of President of the Poor Law Board in Gladstone's Cabinet. Until 1871 he had not seriously studied the problem of the C.D. Acts, but had accepted the assurances of the medical profession that their imposition in certain military and naval districts was absolutely essential to the health of serving men. When, in that year, a strong deputation of Abolitionists among his constituents put the case against the Acts to him, he said he would keep an open mind on the subject until the Royal Commission had reported. His subsequent study of the question led him to become a wholehearted opponent of the Acts, and in 1873 he voted for Fowler's Repeal Bill. The fall of the Government released him from all party obligations. He was now a private individual, free to take his own line, and in July 1874 he allowed his name to appear as Vice-President of the National Association for Repeal. His first of many addresses on the subject was to the Ladies' National Association in Bristol in October 1874. Josephine was present and wrote to her husband: "This was ... Mr. Stansfeld's first appearance publicly in our ranks, and it was a striking and pathetic appearance. He had been alone in his room almost the whole day, and looked pale and nervous when he appeared on the platform. He passed on to me a little note, on which were several memoranda—among them this: 'I am so thankful for the women's prayers.' The newspaper report gives but little idea of the effect of his manner. An old clergyman said to me, as we were leaving the hall, 'It was like a confession of faith. He seemed to invoke the presence of the Divine Being as he stood with his hands uplifted.' This is true. It was felt to be the utterance of feelings long pent up, and was like a trumpet blast to call us afresh to the battle, as well as the key-note of the future—full of courage and confidence."

Stansfeld knew he was sacrificing his political career when he took this step. He was an important leader of the Radical group among the Liberals and there was little doubt that he was destined for high office. These prospects he deliberately jettisoned when he espoused a cause described by the *Sheffield Independent* as a "hobby too nasty to be touched" and, as the Hammonds say in their biography, "he stepped out of his place as a Radical leader to join a ship that looked as if it was sinking".

"I have taken a course lately", he wrote in a letter, "which . . . very much modifies my political position and probable future . . . I have done what I thought right, deliberately, with my eyes open to the possible consequences, and shall go my own way now in this and in other things."

Stansfeld's assumption of responsibility in the Abolitionist Cause is second only in importance to Josephine's acceptance of its leadership in 1869. *The Times* sincerely regretted "to find a statesman of Mr. Stansfeld's eminence identifying himself with this hysterical crusade", but the very fact of his doing so raised the crusade's status, so that it could no longer be derided or ignored. The Hammonds have ably summarised the debt the movement owed to Stansfeld. "An eloquent speaker, a master of debate, he could hold his own with experts, and he was enabled by his lucid mind and his patient industry to make statistics intelligible to a plain audience. Above all, he saw where the agitation lacked power. He knew enough of the conditions of parliamentary life to realise that having failed to carry the position by storm the Repealers must settle down to the hard, unexciting discipline of a siege." Of this siege Stansfeld took command in the House and Josephine trusted him as she had trusted no other Member. He also trusted her to deal with rousing and maintaining public opinion outside the House. They could work together harmoniously because each recognised in the other the same religious convictions, the same sense of vocation to a cause from which both alike instinctively shrank—repelled by its sheer sordid ugliness. Looking back at the end of the battle Stansfeld wrote: "I revolt against the task . . . I loathe its details . . . no man knows, or ever can or will know, what to me has been the suffering, the burden and the cost."

In the months following the York meeting, as the letters from correspondents on the Continent came in, it became increasingly clear to Josephine that she must investigate the whole situation on the Continent herself, to see what co-operation could achieve. When she made her decision known at a meeting of colleagues it was received with mixed feelings. One of them wrote: "This announcement fell like lead on our already heavy hearts, that our leader, our guide, our mainstay should be called to leave us *just now* was sad indeed." The prospect of such an expedition was not inviting to Josephine herself. She was acutely sensitive to cold, and separation from her husband was difficult to face. But it had to be. The Friends summoned a meeting at Birmingham in November to wish her God speed, and she wrote to a friend about this meeting: "As we sat, during those calm silences which I so much love in Friends' meetings, when God seems even more present than when any voice of prayer is breaking the hushed stillness, I did not think any more of the cold winter, long journeys, cynical opposition and many difficulties I was going to meet." The text came into her mind "Behold, I have set before thee an open door, and no man can shut it", and this text remained comfortingly with her throughout her journey.

Josephine left for Paris early in December 1874, carrying with her letters of introduction, including one from Lord Derby the Foreign Secretary, to men of authority in Paris. It was bitterly cold, there was a biting wind and the streets were covered with the slush of half-melted snow. The outlook was bleak. Paris was still reeling from the shock of the Franco-Prussian War. Thiers, the first President of the New Republic, had been succeeded by MacMahon, who with a majority in the Cabinet was grappling uneasily with a much divided government. Josephine had known Paris of old, she could not be ignorant of conditions there, but hitherto she had been able to ignore the distasteful evidences of moral disorder in the streets. Now it was her duty to see all she could and to examine all the evidence that presented itself.

She sought at once an interview with Lecour, the Prefect of Police. The unsettled political conditions had given him more power than it is good for any official to possess. It was reported that the head of Government in France could do nothing without the consent of the Prefects of Police, "permanent officials stronger than Government itself", and that MacMahon sent for them daily to take his instructions from them. Josephine's mind flew instantly to historical precedent. "Is it not a good deal like that wretched time in Rome, when the Praetorian Guards elected, deposed, or dictated to the Emperor of the time, and became themselves the most oppressive of tyrants?" Josephine described Lecour's office—designed to exalt his importance—its white marble staircase, the guards and uniformed flunkeys in attendance, the gold letters above the door proclaiming the "Service des Moeurs"—in her opinion an outrageous title for an office which should more fitly have been described as designed for the service of "Débauchés". She was shown into the sanctum with impressive ceremony and given a paper to read while Lecour was concluding an interview with an earlier caller. As she sat and listened, behind her paper, the man's arrogance and self-satisfaction became more and more apparent and by the time he was at leisure to attend to her she was blazing with suppressed fury. She rose to her feet, disdaining the proffered chair and looked him fully in the face throughout the interview. We need not be surprised to learn that he appeared to quail before her. When she asked him a question the answer came in a flood of talk, designed to prevent her from saying more. When she asked him if vice in Paris had increased or diminished in the preceding three months, he replied eagerly, without realising that it condemned his own system, that it increased all the time and added hastily that this was due to the "coquetry" of the women. As the interview proceeded he became somewhat flustered and made statements that she was able to refute from one of his own books; whereupon he attempted a diversion by declaring that he was as earnest a Christian as she was, to which Josephine replied that that might be so, but she was there to talk not about Christianity but about justice. She was sure, she added in the letter describing the interview, that he would see no connection between these two.

She left the Prefecture with a permit from Lecour to visit St. Lazare Prison and any other establishment under the control of the police, but she was sad at heart. She knew she had failed to make any impression on him. He had no doubt been surprised and vexed to find a woman whom he could not frighten, who answered him calmly in perfect French—which was insufferable since he could speak no word of her language—who failed to be impressed by his declamations and histrionic exhibitions, but he had not been in the least shaken in his self-esteem or made to doubt the perfection of a system in which he had acquired so great a vested interest.

Josephine next visited St. Lazare, a huge fortress-like "prison, hospital and general depot for all the unhappy women of Paris, both for the vicious and for those accused only of vagabondage, or who were seeking work and had no friends". Armed with her permit she approached its grim entrance and on the grudging advice of a sentry, knocked to attract the door-keeper. She made not the slightest impression on the heavy iron door for her hands were not strong enough. Despair seized her; for a moment she faltered, then remembering the "open door" she looked round and seizing a stone from the roadside she hammered with all her might and this produced the desired effect. A nun was directed to show her round the establishment. Josephine described her visit to the yard where some of the prisoners were taking their compulsory exercise, walking round and round. She was not permitted to speak to them though she yearned to do so, for while some of them were obviously well used to the routine and hardened to it, there were others, quite young—children almost—who were still unspoilt and only on the threshold of their miserable lives. Josephine thought some of them looked at her wistfully and slowed down their walk as they came past where she stood. She was taken over the rest of the place, but of this there is no record. She wrote long, detailed, and interesting letters to her friends at home. She depended so greatly on their support and felt bound to draw them into all her experiences. However tired she may have been at the end of a day's work, she never failed to retail to them all that had happened. But of St. Lazare she could not write. What she saw there was so inexpressibly painful that she would never speak of it. She remained silent; only when she was ill and half delirious in a dream of horror she saw gigantic men sweeping women into a furnace and woke herself by crying out "Oh be merciful, they are more tender than you think."

Josephine had learned all she needed to know and she turned with relief to meet her husband who, with their sons and Stuart, came out to join her for the Christmas holidays. She could now deal with the more constructive part of her mission. Here there was encouragement. "The best men and women in Paris" welcomed and helped them, and they were received "by Victor Hugo, Baroness de Stael and by the whole body of the Protestant pastors and Protestant society of Paris generally". Meetings were arranged with sympathisers and Josephine had a private interview with the veteran Jules Favre "the eloquent advocate and member of the National Assembly", who had been one of the Triumvirate to make the Government of National Defence after the disaster of Sedan. He sympathised warmly with Josephine's objects, but felt sadly that, with the existing government, there was very little chance of reform. Vested interests in the system were immensely powerful, one of its features being that the Police des Moeurs was paid so much a head for every girl put on the register. At the same time encouragement of every sort was offered to young men, who were invited to balls and banquets and discovered only when they got there that the purpose of these entertainments was simply to introduce them to prostitutes. So indiscriminately were these invitations made that even so sober a young man as Stanley did not escape. Jules Favre believed that the education of public opinion on the subject was the most hopeful immediate objective in France. Cardinal Manning, who had already shown his sympathy by sending a letter to George Butler to be read to a meeting in Liverpool, now helped Josephine by "a very warm and beautiful letter of recommendation to any and all the Catholic clergy of Europe with whom we might come in contact: 'This lady,' he said, 'has undertaken a difficult and very needful mission. I beg you to give her such assistance and encouragement as you can in her work of charity, and to recommend her to persons who may have any influence in the matter of the reform which she seeks to promote. No Catholic who fears God can refuse to give his allegiance to the sacred cause which she has espoused.' "

From Paris the Butlers went on to Lyons: "eleven hours in a train, wrapped in a large rug; with foot warmers, and *no responsibility for eleven hours*! I almost laughed to myself for joy", and from Lyons to Marseilles. Everywhere the position was the same; the system was warmly approved by those who administered it, bitterly resented by those who suffered under it, and uneasily tolerated by the great majority, whose consciences, already somewhat troubled, needed only to be stirred into activity. Before she left France Josephine wrote to Mr. Stansfeld: "I should like our friends to know how much the little faithful band of sympathisers in Paris recognise our mission as from God. . . . There was among some a feeling of suspense, of expectation . . . in the belief that aggressive action ought to follow. . . . It is not enough to meet and pray . . . there must soon be a call to battle."

From Marseilles the whole family went happily to Les Antibes for a few days' holiday. Josephine, in that bitter winter, had never been warm since she left England. "It was perfectly horrible in Paris", she wrote to her sister. "I could not get warm night or day. . . . The travelling does not try me so much, for one can get plenty of foot warmers and rugs; but in the hotels they give us tea half cold, and the uncarpeted rooms and sunk-back fires make one feel the cold horribly." The cold wind pursued them even to Marseilles, but at Les Antibes the Mediterranean sun shone and they were able to bask in its warmth.

It could not be a long holiday, for Josephine still had much to do. She went to Genoa, where she left her sons with her niece Mme. Leupold, then to Rome for a few days' sight-seeing with her husband. After that he went home, while she travelled to Naples, meaning to enjoy the great pleasure of her sister Hattie's society and to take a complete rest. She found, however, that the news of her coming had preceded her and there were many people in Naples eager to hear her speak. She could not resist so promising an opening, and she allowed them to arrange a large meeting for her. She wrote of this to George: "At the meeting we had no expressed opposition, but I was aware of an opposing current of thought and opinion in the room, which we were able to trace to its source, namely, an English doctor. I thought he looked ominous as he entered with a great bundle of the *Lancet* under his arm; and I observed him whispering impatiently to his neighbours on each side as I spoke. It almost makes one smile to see that miserable *Lancet* brought forward as an authority in a great moral and humanitarian question like this." And again in another letter she says, "The only vicious, unfair, stupid opposition I have met is from English doctors, who come with bundles of *Lancets*."

Then she went on to her serious business in Rome. Italian opinion was divided. The system, imposed there by Cavour, had never been really approved by public opinion. Pope Pius IX had protested against it and had written to Victor Emmanuel denouncing it, but the Government had none the less upheld it and it was actually flourishing. When Josephine reached Rome she found friends at once. The most important of these was Giuseppe Nathan, an able and intelligent young man, socially and politically influential. He had married an English wife, who had died very suddenly after a brief period of extreme happiness. The shock had undermined the health and spirits of her widowed husband so that his friends feared for his recovery. To him Josephine presented her mission as a new call to life and service, something which should give a purpose to his existence. He responded and gave himself, as she demanded, to considering how best the cause could be served in Rome. He took her to the Italian Parliament. In Rome, as in England, the public had the right of access to the lobbies of the House and could ask to see any member. Nathan took Josephine there and introduced her to Deputies who were likely to be interested in her crusade. Many of these encouraged her warmly and she worked hard addressing a succession of meetings where plans were laid for an Association to forward the movement. Josephine asked Nathan to secure for her an interview with the Minister of Justice and Police. He gladly complied with her request, though she noticed that he smiled a little sardonically when she made it. Here again, as in Paris, she found a grand official establishment, marble staircase and much pomp, and the Minister, though less odious than Lecour, equally impressed with his own importance, equally contemptuous of any point of view other than his own. The only satisfaction Josephine got out of the meeting was the pleasure of foiling him when he tried to find out from her which of the Deputies had given her encouragement.

When she left Rome Stuart was with her and Nathan accompanied them. They went first to Florence. She had been given a list of people likely to be sympathetic and in the short time she had there she called on them all. Apparently in Tuscany the regulations were ineffective as the Tuscan peasantry resisted by force any attempt of the police to register their daughters. It was characteristic of Josephine that, in spite of having many calls to pay and much hard work to do, she yet found time to visit the Duomo where she noticed among the worshippers "several dear familiar cats, who rubbed themselves up against people's legs; pious well-behaved cats! no one thought of turning them out"; the Uffizi and the convent of St. Mark's, where she "remained a good while alone in Savonarola's cell. . . . It was pleasant to be in his silent room and to remember the source whence he derived his power to endure to the end, combatting evil and wickedness in high places." From Florence they went on to Milan, where Nathan had contacts in the University. While he was busy arranging a meeting for her, she took the opportunity of visiting orphanages, hospitals, technical schools and a crêche, and having talks with various groups of women. Nathan invited to his great meeting some people known to be in favour of regulation, and specially asked them to speak. There resulted an interesting debate, at the end of which a most satisfactory resolution was passed and reported next day in the Press. "That this assembly, having heard the wise, noble and virtuous address of Mrs. Butler, recognises with her the urgent duty of endeavouring to do away with 'tolerated prostitution', approves her ideas and declares itself ready to assist her in her holy purpose."

It was just at the end of January that Josephine left Italy. She had been less than two months out of England. When one contemplates Josephine Butler's accomplishment—the journeys she had made, the places she had visited, the long sessions of conversation as well as the calls and interviews she had conducted, the vivid and detailed accounts of all these activities which she had sent in her letters home—and when one remembers that in addition to all this she was constantly making and delivering speeches to large mixed audiences on a most difficult subject in English, French or Italian, as circumstances demanded, one feels vicariously exhausted and can only wonder that she had energy left to exclaim joyfully as she left Italy: "The Italian newspapers are already fighting about our cause; the fire is lighted, it seems."

Josephine went on to Geneva, a place which always troubled her. With its religious and cultural past, she felt that it should be a centre of light and learning. Its beauty appealed to her; the Meuricoffres' Swiss home on the lakeside had always been so happy a place. She meant to like and enjoy the city too and yet, from the beginning of her crusade to the end of her life, it brought her unhappiness and anxiety. So it was on this first attack on it. She made some good friends. It was here she met Dr. Hornung, Professor of Jurisprudence at the University, and Mme. de Gingins, widow of an aristocrat, who became a loyal and devoted colleague. But the religious leaders in Geneva were on the wrong side. The attitude to regulated vice was unlike that in Italy or France. There was a great deal of rather sentimental talk about the highly beneficial moral effect of the special police, their zeal in reforming "fallen women", the gratitude and affection these felt for their reformers—but it did not ring true. The official voice spoke with much more conviction of the importance of punishing the women who persisted in sin and of the utter impossibility of safeguarding health by any means other than regulation. The brothels flourished and the brothel keepers, "tenanciers" as they were called, were so powerful that they practically ruled the Canton and were applauded by the local papers for their wisdom.

At a large meeting, which Stuart arranged, Josephine was particularly asked to deal with the legal aspect of the question. This was difficult enough, for it was more natural for her to speak of its moral and religious sides. But with the help of a pamphlet by Professor Hornung, she prepared her speech very carefully, beginning by dealing with all expected objections, and she was able to silence her opponents, even though she was speaking in a foreign tongue. An American present, who had come to Geneva for the education of his children, warned the Genevese that "they could not expect Geneva to continue to be a centre of education, unless they got rid of this corrupting system," an important warning, as Stuart remarked, "since educating children is one of the 'industries' of Geneva, and they had better look to it, or their gains will be gone". In spite of the success of this meeting, the general feeling was discouraging, and sick at heart, Josephine wrote to Hattie: "I felt so *angry* with Switzerland. There had been such sinister influences, to prevent me having a meeting, to injure my plans, to stop my mouth or frighten people from coming near me . . . Geneva is the one place (so far as I know) where these poor women (children many of them) are most *cruelly* treated. It is the combination of the greedy lust of Paris with the cold, heavy Old Testament repression to 'thrust her through with a dart' spirit of Calvin." . . . "There is never a woman of bad character to be seen in the streets of Geneva. Never seen—how beautiful! They are carefully *locked up*. Nevertheless the moral corruption of the male population is not less, but rather more, than before. There may be evils *even worse* than our wretched London streets. No individual solicitation can possibly have so soul-corrupting an influence upon the young, as the State-offered, State-sanctioned, State-protected solicitation of that organised and regulated vice which the State thereby assumes to be a necessity."

It was a relief to go from Geneva to Neuchâtel and her first letter from there to her husband shows the lightening of her spirit.

"I am safely here, in a most lovely room, high up overlooking the lake. . . . The view before me is strangely beautiful. . . . There are numberless fleets of snow white gulls floating on the blue waters. . . . An hour ago there was a heavy fall of snow. The flocks of gulls sat motionless on the water while it lasted; the soft snow gathered in a little mound on the back of each, till they looked like perfectly round balls of floating snow with a beak and bright eyes. When the sky cleared they all rose, apparently at a given signal, and wheeled round and round in the air with joyous cries, shaking the masses of snow from their wings and making a second little snow-storm. I think they have a sense of humour and fun about it."

In Neuchâtel she was welcomed by M. Aimé Humbert. Her first contact with him had come about in a curious and to her very encouraging manner. In her search for possible supporters on the Continent, she had come across a little book containing names and addresses of people connected with international benevolent organisations. Among them was a M. Humbert of Neuchâtel. The postman, by "what we call chance", delivered it, not to the addressee but to a M. Aimé Humbert. "He was no stranger to the question. He had for years said to himself 'When I am more free from other public work, I must turn to this terrible subject.'" He had responded warmly to her circular, recalling that many years earlier he had seen the need to make an international body to fight government regulation of vice, and rejoicing that now English Abolitionists were prepared to act. "England alone can take the initiative," he wrote, "but remaining alone she would not arrive at a successful issue. . . . Bring among us then the fire of that faith that can remove mountains. . . . May we see you here in Neuchâtel in the spring." Josephine felt an instantaneous affinity with the Humbert family. Mme. Humbert was as instinctively reluctant as Josephine had been to tackle this painful subject, but recognised an impelling call to take her part; and the whole family, including two daughters, dedicated itself to the work with a sense of vocation.

The law in this Canton was at least even-handed. Prostitution was illegal and for both sexes equally punishable In fact, however, brothels existed unmolested and public opinion tacitly approved them. The industrial town of Chaux de Fonds, situated high on the slopes of the Jura, was especially notorious. Mme. Humbert escorted Josephine there, travelling both ways by sleigh. As they mounted higher and higher they were alternately exalted by the beauty and majesty of the snow-covered mountains, and petrified by sheer physical cold. They were encouraged by their reception and held a great meeting at which many local worthies declared their adherence to the cause. From Neuchâtel she went on to Berne and Lausanne with satisfactory results, a Berne paper reporting one of her meetings, commented on the part Englishwomen had taken. "These Englishwomen are remarkable; they unite with their great freedom a dignity seldom seen elsewhere. . . . We have not dared to associate women with us, as is done in England, in this work of moralisation. Mrs. Butler, an instrument prepared by God Himself for this combat, brings to us troops of female auxiliaries whom many men will fear to meet, and with good reason."

Now Josephine was on her way home. She left Switzerland and travelled to Paris, where Humbert met her. After consultation with his wife, he had finally decided he must give up all other work, at whatever loss to his material prosperity, and devote himself to this cause. He put himself entirely at Josephine's disposal. Together they took counsel. Coming from Switzerland, he had no idea of the state of things in Paris, the cynicism of the officials, the indifference of a large part of Parisian society and, what Josephine found hardest of all to bear, the hopelessness of those men of good-will who wished for reform but had no faith in the possibility of its achievement. "The despondency of *good* people," she said in a letter to Edmondson, "is worse to bear than the opposition of our opponents." She felt that M. Humbert should know the worst, so she sent him to call upon the Prefect of Police. "After this interview," she wrote, "I found him with his face covered by his hand, groaning '*Ah! c'est une dure croisade— une dure croisade.*' He had been arguing, for me, for two hours with the incorrigible Mettetal, Lecour's predecessor as Prefect of

Police. I sent him to the Louvre and told him to look at the wonderful painting of St. Marguerite, the patron saint of purity, trampling down the hideous dragon and looking so calm and peaceful. He went and the thoughts he had therefrom were strengthening." They had some encouragement. At a public meeting attended largely by the working class a speaker in favour of the Regulations "proceeded to say all the untrue and cowardly things which men generally say when defending the enslavement of women, for they use the same arguments all over the world. Before he had gone far . . . I was pleasantly surprised by the furious burst of scorn and anger, which proceeded from all the women and almost all the men present . . . the women hissed and moaned, and protested so energetically that his voice was drowned. . . . When he declared that the unhappy women for whose civil and natural rights we had pleaded, were the vilest of creatures, scarcely human, and justly expelled from and scorned by society, the women sprang to their feet, and almost with one voice demanded, 'But the men! What about the men! Are they not equally guilty, base and despicable?'"

With these shouts echoing in her ears, Josephine crossed the Channel and reached home on February 22nd, 1875. She was very tired and would have much liked to feel that she could go home to Liverpool, and rest for a long time. But the demands of the situation did not permit this. She must first report on her journey to the Association which had sent her. She wrote to Henry Wilson: "I feel it a very urgent duty laid on me to settle as soon as possible with our friends at home what are to be our relations with the Continental Committees. I promised to do this as soon as I could and for the cause's sake it is well that we should not delay, but should meet soon and decide, while the fervour on the Continent is so great, and to engage people in practical work before this feeling has time to die away. . . . I have a sketch of what it seems advisable to do . . . but we *must have* a friendly conference about this matter, at which conference I would give my report of foreign work done and of money spent and would explain my proposals. . . . Our friends abroad wish to be *openly connected* with the English Societies, and to feel that they are working with us and under our eye."

The meetings were arranged as Josephine wished. A small informal gathering of those who had financed the journey, in which she reported her experiences and her hopes for the work in the future, preceded the full meeting of the National Association. Stansfeld was in the Chair and speeches were made by him and by Harcourt Johnston on their prospects in the House. Josephine spoke briefly about her tour, insisting on the widespread desire on the Continent that England should take the lead in the crusade. An account of the meeting which survives from one of the delegates says: "Mrs. Butler looks much worn with her winter campaign, but always graceful and dignified, possessing herself so calmly that no harm can touch her." It was unanimously agreed that an international society to abolish regulated vice should be formed and to this end delegates from local associations all over Europe were invited to a Conference at Liverpool on March 19th. It was obvious that if an International Association was started Josephine must be its mainspring, and it was equally clear that she could not both take on this new work abroad and continue to be responsible for the Ladies' National Association at home. Of all those who worked with her none were more zealous and intelligent in the work than Mrs. Tanner of Bristol and her sisters the Priestmans. It was to Mrs. Tanner that Josephine handed over the Ladies' Association and when the former spoke deprecatingly of her own powers, contrasting them ruefully with Josephine's brilliance, Josephine replied: "It is all very well to have comets flashing about occasionally, but their value is not great in comparison with the steady planets which never err from their orbit!" So that was settled.

The first international conference met in Liverpool, and formally constituted the British and Continental Federation for the Abolition of Government Regulation of Prostitution. Stansfeld became its President and Josephine Butler and Henry Wilson its joint Secretaries. The Conference dispersed feeling that an important step had been taken in a very serious campaign.

CHAPTER TEN

THE INTERNATIONAL FEDERATION
1875—1877

"England alone can take the initiative but remaining alone, she would not arrive at a successful issue".   (Humbert to J. B.)

JOSEPHINE, described by a friend as "sitting in Liverpool with a finger on each part of Europe", set to work on her new task. In this she gratefully recognised the help of her co-secretary, Henry Wilson: "Dear Mr. Wilson, What a man you are! It is delightful to me to find my wheels greased and my coach rolling on so quick and easily, and all without much effort to myself." But in spite of this competent colleague, now that she tried to get down to business, she realised how tired she was. She wrote rather pathetically, "I have not felt *warm* since July 1869. I can echo Jeremiah's lament 'My leanness, O my leanness!' " She struggled on against pains in her head and presently constant attacks of giddiness. She was always reluctant to summon a doctor, but she recognised that she could not go on and sent for Dr. Carter, who had from the beginning been one of the profession who resisted the policy of the British Medical Association and had done his utmost for the cause. He took a serious view of Josephine's condition and insisted that she must at once give up all the work she was doing. She was in no state to resist these orders; she had a sense of numbness in her limbs, she was constantly so faint as to be barely conscious and no restorative gave her more than a very little relief; she could not sleep and the pain in her head was acute. It was difficult for her not to worry about the work and she fretted at her enforced inactivity. Her friends and colleagues were appalled. Mrs. Tanner wrote to Mr. Wilson: "The bare thought of her being ill paralyses some of our workers, who almost exist by her inspiration." Fortunately the acute stage did not last very long; the complete rest had the desired effect, and although it was long before she could return to the battlefield, Dr. Carter was soon able to report that he had every hope that she would make a complete recovery.

Meanwhile there was the ticklish question of what should be said to those outside the close circle of intimates. With Josephine's approval, a circular letter was sent to all workers in the cause; it is worth quoting for it breathes her indomitable spirit and her indifference to her own suffering, as long as it was not allowed to hinder the work. The circular ran: "Our beloved and honoured leader Mrs. Butler is, as many of you are aware, compelled to rest for a time to recruit her strength which has been too heavily taxed in her recent work both at home and abroad; but lest the news of this should discourage any of you, she is anxious that you should know that though faint *she* is not discouraged and she begs that you will not let your courage fail. She desires to communicate to you if possible the hopeful feeling she has as to our great work. She is full of thankfulness to God for the indications of progress and the foretaste of victory that He is granting, and she hopes that while she is compulsorily withdrawn for a time from the heat of the battle, we shall all be 'strong and of a good courage' knowing that the battle is not ours but God's." As one reads the letters of this period, one cannot fail to be touched by the tender concern of those who had been working with her, the Wilsons and Stuart doing all in their power to help George through this time of difficulty, Henry Wilson warding off the importunate, and Charlotte visiting girls in trouble, in order that Josephine should not have them also on her mind. Stuart, in spite of domestic difficulties of his own, came to be with her in Liverpool, wrote letters beginning "Mrs. Butler would like you to know . . ." went with her to Rothbury when the time came for convalescence, and sat with her on the moor expressing her views and opinions and writing to correspondents who had appealed to her. From April to the end of June she was obliged to leave everything to other people and she heard only as much about the work as they could not keep from her.

While Josephine was slowly struggling back to health, the seeds she had sown were germinating and the first signs of a harvest were appearing. Under Henry Wilson's active organisation, the Northern Counties' Association was extremely energetic in holding meetings in all the large towns. Even the doctors were beginning to move. As has been seen, the British Medical Association was a convinced supporter of the Acts, and though from the beginning there were doctors on the side of abolition, like Dr. Bell-Taylor of Nottingham, for some years official medical opinion had spoken with one voice. The doctor who played the most important part in the conversion of medical opinion to repeal was Dr. Nevins of Liverpool. He was on the staff of a teaching hospital, and finding himself obliged to teach about venereal disease, he determined to make a very thorough investigation into the effectiveness of the Regulations. To this end he proceeded to study the statistics. He confined himself to making a careful examination of all the returns issued by naval, military and mercantile marine authorities. He had no preconceived ideas and ignored the propaganda both of Regulationists and Abolitionists. When therefore, as the result of this scientific study of the question, he came out against the Regulations, declaring that he could find no evidence that they had in any way diminished the disease, he was an immensely valuable ally to the Abolitionists. He founded the National Medical Association (for Abolition), and when the *Lancet* and the *British Medical Journal* refused to publish articles or letters discussing the Regulations objectively, he started a new journal, the *Medical Inquirer*, whose first number appeared in March 1875. The belief in the beneficial effects of Regulation was thus rudely shaken.

At about the same time the credit of those who administered the Regulations received a heavy blow. This came from the case of Mrs. Percy. It was a sordid and disagreeable story. Mrs. Percy was a widow, who with her daughter Jane maintained herself and her two little boys by singing at concerts in the camp at Aldershot. The police wished to put her name and her daughter's on the list of registered prostitutes and when the mother absolutely refused, they tried to force her hand by denying her a permit to enter the camp to sing, and by spying upon her in her lodgings. Then they summoned her to Headquarters, and interrogated her with such brutality that she became desperate and, seeing no means of escaping from their clutches, she committed suicide. It was true that she had sought the protection of a man to whom she was not married, but she had never been a prostitute and the child was completely innocent and only bewildered by the questions put to her. The case received much publicity, as Mrs. Percy, before she took her life, in a last effort to get help had written a letter to the *Daily Telegraph* and though that paper did not move in time to save the unhappy woman, it did publish the facts after the event. A tremendous storm of indignation was aroused. The National Association held a meeting of protest at the Westminster Palace Hotel, and confidence in the discretion and wisdom of the special police, which had been one of the articles of faith most frequently affirmed by Regulationists, was severely shaken. The Butlers took Jane Percy into their own home, caring for her until she was fit and ready to be launched into a new life.

The changed attitude of the general public engendered by these events and by the educational work of the Repeal Associations was most strikingly illustrated when Harcourt Johnston moved the second reading of his Repeal Bill in June 1875. Though the motion was defeated, the whole tone of the debate was entirely different from that of earlier occasions. The subject was treated, not derisively, but seriously, and even the principal opponent, the Judge Advocate General, in the course of his speech disassociated himself from the vulgar attacks of his predecessors on the ladies. Benjamin Scott reports him as saying about them: "I say all honour to them for it, and I should be the last to join in the outcry which has been raised against these who have so devoted themselves." A significant feature of the division list was that Gladstone himself, as well as many members of the previous Liberal administration, voted for repeal.

On the Continent the same process was taking place. Public opinion against the system, which had been latent, was becoming vocal. The conspiracy of silence about an abuse which people were unwilling to tackle had been defeated, and now the Press of Italy, France and Switzerland constantly published reports of odious acts of injustice to girls and young women, which aroused widespread indignation. Josephine had written a pamphlet in French called "*Une Voix dans le Désert*", and this, under Humbert's direction, was translated into Italian, German and the Scandinavian languages. The demand for it grew steadily. On the Continent, too, medical evidence was being sifted. Humbert organised the collection of medical statistics about the supposed efficacy of the Regulations in checking the disease, on which the whole case for them depended. This aspect of the question did not really interest Josephine, who held that even if it could be proved beyond doubt or question that the Regulations could eliminate disease, they would still be inadmissible, since it is manifestly unjust to secure the health of the community by the destruction of some of its members. But she did recognise that statistics had their place in the campaign. There can be no doubt that the gradual realisation of the ineffectiveness of the Regulations played a large part in the ultimate victory of the repealers.

By this time Josephine was on the mend. In the spring of 1876 Wilson and Gledstone, a Free Church minister, were sent by the National Association to New York, in response to an appeal for help against the threatened imposition of Regulations there. Josephine was at the quayside to see them off and she kept Henry Wilson in touch with events at home. The immediate important event was the first International Conference of the Federation, which was to be held in London. Since the League of Nations, international leagues, conventions and conferences have become so common a feature of our social and political life, that it is difficult for us to realise that this Federation, founded by a small group of English people and led by a woman, was an innovation. This first Conference therefore was very important; it was to be held in London and delegates came from all the branches in Europe; the speakers chosen were distinguished in their own countries, Stansfeld was to act as Chairman and a large attendance was expected. On the night before the Conference a conversazione was held and it would seem that in connection with this, Stansfeld arranged a dinner party at which plans for the future were laid. Henry Wilson heard from Josephine about it and wrote to his wife:

"New York. 31.5.76. A letter from Mrs. Butler has completed my joy today. To think of her *dining with half the ex Cabinet* and *our* question being the one question before them! I am *so thankful* for that too. I see day break on the mountain tops. It is an enormous gain to us, in fact inexpressibly valuable. We are comparatively safe against 'compromise' now. They have met and discussed this thing with women—they are bound to be impressed by Mrs. Butler—they will consult her and Stansfeld on future action—the Lord has given us the victory! No one thing before or since Stansfeld insisted on the Cabinet being free to vote individually in 1873 is comparable with it in importance, and this event is greater than that by far."

The Conference lasted two days and fulfilled its purpose, which was to bring together people from all parts of Europe so that they might feel themselves members of a great fellowship, united by a common ideal. Some of the speeches made a great impression on the hearers, but the eloquence of past generations, on an issue which has ceased to be a live issue, has not much power to move its descendants; the idiom is different and the underlying assumptions have changed. The Conference dispersed, determined to hold a congress for the whole International Federation in Geneva in the following year and if possible to hold such congresses triennially in different cities, with smaller local conferences in the years between.

Josephine now felt herself entitled to a holiday, and with her husband and sons betook herself to Switzerland. They had not meant to do any work while there, but on their way back from

Grindelwald they found in Berne that Nathan had arrived from Italy, and their friends were anxious to consult about the coming Congress in Geneva. Josephine described these consultations. After the freshness of Grindelwald, they found the weather of Berne very heavy, a heaviness reflected at the meeting: "A very useful one. I think the Swiss—especially the Bernese—like dullness, and would probably consider a meeting a failure if they did not infuse an element of dullness and slowness into it; this they are, however, generally successful in doing. But there is great reality among them, and not a word said more than is meant." George Butler made a short and moving speech in his characteristically gentle manner, expressing the conviction, "that men should be ready, not only to hold women as their equals, but to let those of recognised experience be at times their guides in moral and spiritual matters. . . . He said all this . . . his hand on my chair, and standing over me like a guardian angel. They saw in his face and manner, a noble honesty and humility which does not particularly characterise men of the German race in their relations to women."

After this meeting, George was obliged to go back to Liverpool. Josephine's holiday was also over. She stayed a few days with her sister, and in Geneva addressed a large meeting of working-class people who effectually silenced a brothel keeper, "a man with a most hideous expression of countenance resembling a vulture greedily scouring the face of the earth for prey", who tried to interrupt proceedings. Then she started for home, visiting and holding meetings at various German and Belgian towns by the way.

At Liége she first encountered the White Slave Traffic: "Poor girls are being sought for everywhere to be enslaved in this diabolic service, waggons full of them arrive by train from other countries under the care of the police, crowded *comme la bétaille*." This horror was to haunt her for the next few years, though at the moment she could see no useful action to take. She went on to Brussels, and met Pastor Annet who, in her early days in Liverpool, had entrusted to her care English girls he had rescued from the brothels. He told her that a strong tide of public opinion in Belgium was turning "against this evil tyranny and vicious institution". She wrote to Harriet: "How wonderfully God . . . directs our steps. I am really an almost *passive* instrument now in His hands—like Balaam's donkey, just made to walk in a certain path and to speak words of rebuke to the wise!"

Meanwhile, a curious situation was developing in France. Lecour and his Police des Moeurs reacted against criticism of his department by more drastic action. The excesses of the police began to cause serious public indignation. The more liberal part of the Press published one account after another of outrages against innocent and respectable women. The Municipal Council of Paris became uneasy, and M. Yves Guyot, a Councillor who had previously been Minister of Public Works, took the lead in demanding action against the police. He recorded in his paper the attempted arrest by one of the police of a respectable and very popular young actress, who being lusty and able to defend herself, flung the policeman on to the pavement. This incident created so much ill feeling that Lecour felt bound to take action and accused Yves Guyot of publishing false information, on the grounds that the assailant was no policeman but someone masquerading in that character. To keep up appearances, this young man was tried and given a short sentence—no doubt behind the scenes also a considerable sum of money—and Yves Guyot was condemned to a six months' term of imprisonment—a sentence for some reason not immediately carried out.

The Municipal Council, however, was seriously disturbed, and in spite of efforts to prevent it made by Lecour and backed by MacMahon, a Commission was established to enquire into the whole system, and experienced people from other countries were invited to give evidence. Here was a wonderful opportunity for the Abolitionists. Nathan from Italy, Humbert from Switzerland, Stansfeld, Stuart and the Butlers were all invited. The enquiry took place in the Palais de Luxemburg, in a stately and beautiful room which impressed the Butlers. The Committee was serious-minded and really wished to arrive at the truth rather than to score debating points. Josephine, comparing the whole thing with her experiences over the Royal Commission in the House of Lords, felt ashamed of her own countrymen. When the enquiry was over, a large meeting was held in the Salle des Écoles. It was of necessity a "private meeting", since no public meeting was allowed without the consent of the Government, which, with its tenderness for the Police des Moeurs, it would certainly have withheld. All therefore came by private invitation; nevertheless the hall was packed and blue-bloused workmen as well as the aristocracy were present. M. Yves Guyot introduced the foreigners. George Butler spoke with his usual quiet dignity. All the speakers were conscious that it would have been very easy to arouse the audience to fury, and deliberately kept the emotional temperature low.

Back in England George Butler had to face bitter criticisms in the English Press, which protested that no clergyman of the Established Church had any right to address a Republican meeting in France! He did not as a rule answer attacks, but on this occasion he did so, pointing out mildly that any meetings in France were likely to be Republican, and stating that his standpoint was not political but moral.

After George's return to England, Josephine stayed on in Paris. She had become well known among the poorer classes and women of all sorts flocked round her. She stayed in a little hotel and warned the manager that he was to forbid no poor or shabby-looking man or woman who wanted access to her—and they came in streams. In the story of these few days in Paris one is struck not only by her compassion for "the fallen" but even more by her understanding of those who had contrived to remain respectable—the desperately poor, but also the lonely, the unsuccessful in any walk of life. As she met each one she offered the best thing she had to offer—the opportunity of sharing in a great work of humanity. Speaking of a poor actor in a very inferior theatre she wrote: "I often think how sweet must be the sudden sense of companionship in a good cause to such a solitary being. He does not mind now the very feeble applause given to his poor

singing on the stage, for he has found an interest and treasure of
which the audience know nothing." In a letter home she described, with that artist's gift so much a part of her mental
equipment, a random collection of her callers. The Marquis de B.,
"young, with yellow hair starting back from a fair face, which
wears a very innocent expression. He always has the most ex-
quisite lavender kid gloves and shining boots and belongs to an
old aristocratic family, and he wishes to be a servant of the cause.
. . . Some time afterwards I was touched to see him addressing a
group of poor men and a few porters and students and odds and
ends of humanity. They were laying their heads together to think
what they could do. . . . On this occasion the young Marquis had
taken off his lavender kid gloves and put them in his pocket, and
had become simply Citizen B." Then there was the little faded
elderly schoolmistress, who had started a small school to teach
the girls little handicrafts and to watch over them and keep them
from temptation; and "Victorine S. a washerwoman, tall and
gaunt, with bright red hair and a small, shabby, black velvet hat
on her red head, with a very old feather in it, a feather which has
a look of misery, as if it had been plucked from a very indigent
bird. I love and revere her. You are impressed in talking with her
by her calm, womanly strength and good sense. And slowly you
see also her profound pity for her unfortunate fellow women.
Though big and bony, she has a remarkably soft and gentle voice;
she does not gesticulate, but holds her arms stiffly and ungrace-
fully by her side. Her hands, seamed with washtub operations,
do not fit well into her poor brown cotton gloves. She made a
speech at the Working Man's Congress. It was a masterly speech,
filled with statistics and facts illustrating the misery of the Paris
workwomen. She will do; one trusts her."

All these and more came to her privately, met her in the streets
and flocked to her meetings, which were held in a variety of small
private halls, sometimes attended by the police, who resented
and were infuriated by the whole business. She records one
meeting at which, "towards the close of my brief address, during
which were present several police officers of high rank, I alluded

to what had been said by one of Lecour's agents shortly before, i.e. that parents of young girls sometimes came themselves to the Prefecture and requested to have their daughter's name placed on the register, and 'How', he asked, 'could the Prefect refuse in such a case?' 'Let us suppose' I said, 'that a father came to the Prefect and said "Cut my daughter's throat for me"; if he consented to do so, would not the Administration by such an act render itself the accomplice of assassins?' " The officials present immediately closed the meeting by putting out all the lights and summoned its promoters to the Prefecture, where they were examined and re-examined in an effort to prove something damaging to the movement—Mrs. Butler having been reported as having said that M. Lecour was an assassin. When this failed the police took refuge in a stony silence and when summoned to give evidence to the Municipality replied, "If you think we will give you information, you are mistaken; you shan't have any at all." As Josephine remarks: "The Prefecture regards itself as an irresponsible Pashalik, which, though it has a right to receive money from the Municipal Council, is not bound to render any account thereof."

There was a sequel to this visit to Paris. In February 1877 the City of London had founded a Committee for Repeal with Benjamin Scott, Chamberlain of the City, as Secretary, and this body invited a delegation from the Municipality of Paris to London to discuss Regulation. The Lord Mayor invited all the delegates to a banquet. Yves Guyot was, of course, among those invited, but at this moment the Prefect of Police of Paris discovered how dangerous it was that he should be at liberty any longer, and he was called on to serve his deferred sentence of six months' imprisonment, in order to prevent his visit to London.

The following months were fully occupied with preparations for the great Congress at Geneva. These were most thoroughly organised. It was agreed there should be five Sections, dealing respectively with Hygiene, Morality, Legislation, Preventive and Rescue Work and Economics. A Committee was made for each

Section, and groups met in all the countries to discuss what should be brought up under each heading. During this process of preparation, important questions emerged. One came from some Swiss women, who wrote to Josephine asking that certain sessions in the Hygiene Section should on the grounds of delicacy, be confined to men alone. Josephine would not for a moment entertain that idea. She believed profoundly that *no* social question could be adequately dealt with by men or women alone. Since it was ordained that human beings lived in families, any question affecting the well-being of the family must be tackled by men and women together. This conviction was no doubt founded on her own happy marriage and was basic to all she did for the woman's movement. On the question of delicacy, Josephine's opinions had long been firmly established. The standpoint of those who thought it more indelicate to *mention* the oppression and the evils arising from the Regulations than to suffer them to go on, exasperated her. It seemed to her that to take refuge in sensibility rather than to face facts frankly was one of the main contributory causes of the existence of the system she was fighting. When the question arose of the propriety of ladies attending debates on these subjects in the House of Commons, she wrote to an M.P. saying that with her it was a matter of principle that women should *always* be present when any matter concerning women was discussed.

"These Acts were passed in a Parliament of men, no woman knowing anything about them. At the very base of the Acts lies the false and poisonous idea that women (i.e. ladies) have 'nothing to do with this question', and ought not to hear of it, much less meddle with it. Women unfortunately have accepted this dictum for generations past, have retired and left the matter in the hands of men, have drawn a veil, so to speak, over their faces, and have cravenly shrunk from giving pain to their male friends by taking any part in discussions of the social evil; have quietly left the room (as they are now requested to leave the House) whenever the subject was mentioned. This has been called propriety and modesty. We are asked to continue to exercise this propriety and modesty, which have been the cause of outrage and destruction to so many of our poorer fellow women, by keeping away from the House of Commons. . . . I cannot forget the misery, the injustice and the outrage which have fallen upon women simply because we stood aside, when men felt our presence to be painful . . . I think that if men were capable of enacting such an outrage against women, they ought, in justice, to give an account of their action in the presence of those women—for we are the representatives of those women actually oppressed and insulted by the Acts . . . so long as any woman is obliged to suffer that outrage I should be ashamed to speak of the pain to myself in hearing of it."

She replied therefore to the Swiss ladies that none of the Englishmen in the Abolitionist camp would consent to attend any meeting from which women were excluded, and she expounded her general principles to them. At the same time, as she hated the whole subject so greatly herself, she sympathised with their feelings and agreed that if any individual could not bear to attend, she was of course free to stay away, but there must be no acceptance of the principle of the exclusion of women as such, since if the possibility of this attitude were once admitted by the Federation, the pass would have been sold.

The next question was more serious, though here again Josephine was perfectly clear as to principle. It arose out of a letter written by the man proposed by Humbert to be the President of the Hygiene Section. He wrote, with the concurrence of other members of his group, saying that while they were of course opposed to the present system of registration and to the excessive powers of the special police, and to discrimination against women, yet he could not contemplate the abolition of Regulation without the introduction of some new rules to take its place. Prostitution in both sexes alike must be punished, and to effect this some form of police supervision must be instituted. Medical examination of women must be continued, though of course not with the present brutality. This again was a position Josephine had long contested. Again and again she had affirmed that the State could do nothing in this field. It was very important that this compromise should be rejected and she sent a circular letter to all friends and begged them to be sure to attend and to vote against it. Stansfeld went at once to Geneva to meet Humbert and to ensure that the views of at least the Presidents of each Section were sound.

The great Congress opened at Geneva with a service in the Cathedral on Sunday, September 17th, 1877. There were over 500 delegates representing 15 countries and the general public was admitted to all meetings. People of all nationalities flocked in. This was very valuable. The Sections had been planned to cover every aspect of the problem, and to combat the fatally easy tendency to ignore what is unpleasant and to accept things as they are because they have always been so. Discussions and papers in the Economics Section, for example, compelled a large number of people to recognise the appalling position in which women were placed by current economic conditions—the desperately low wages, the exclusion from nearly all trades and professions and the resultant steady increase in prostitution. That a large international conference should recognise and repudiate these things must be of value.

Discussions in all the Sections were free and frank and women were not always on the same side. Josephine at one moment, "felt obliged for once to oppose my own countrywomen" . . . But she then records triumphantly: "The young advocate who had opposed us called yesterday to say he had come round to our views, chiefly influenced by that desperate little impromptu legal discussion among the ladies. He had imagined, he said, that we were a number of 'fanatical and sentimental women', but 'when he heard women arguing like jurists, and even taking part against each other, and yet with perfect good temper *like men*(!), he began to see that we were grave, educated and even scientific people! He came afterwards to every meeting and, as he said, weighed all our words."

It was hard work, and often exciting. In the Legislative Section, after a long and heated session in which delegates stood up simultaneously all over the room, with finger raised, crying "Je demande la parole", the Chairman at last, at about one o'clock, when they were all feeling the need of food, rose to propose the resolution. Instantly an Italian delegate leapt to his feet declaring there had not been sufficient discussion. While the Chairman stood with his mouth open in consternation, Josephine perceived that the German and Swiss delegates were contemplating a break away for refreshment. She described what happened next in her letter home: "Half the meeting would have gone out, and so damaged the worth of the voting. So I ventured to shut the door and set my back against it, declaring that no one should have any food until he had voted! This half startled and half amused the assembly, and they all sat down again obediently. After another half hour of discussion, it was agreed that we should meet again for a final voting at half past six the next morning." The postponement of the vote to 6.30 the next morning seems a severe measure, and it was perhaps on the same evening that young George witnessed the scene he afterwards described: "A long row of ladies, *all sound asleep*." "But," says Josephine, "they had appointed a watcher, Mrs. Bright Lucas, who sat at the end of the row and whom they had charged to keep awake, and to give them the signal whenever voting began on each clause of the resolution. Mrs. Lucas was wide awake, with eyes shining like live coals!"

The resolutions passed by the various sections were submitted to the whole Congress and Josephine and the other promoters were very anxious that these should be unanimously adopted. This unanimity was achieved largely because of "Professor Stuart's tact and patience in talking to the different presidents individually".

The report of the Congress with most of its speeches and all its resolutions was published in two large volumes. It is unlikely that they are read today, or that the modern reader would find much inspiration in them. None the less, it was an achievement to get from so large an international body a complete repudiation of the system of Regulation, a demand for its total abolition, and for equal treatment of men and women before the law and in economic opportunity. It is no wonder that Josephine reports herself and her friends to be "tired and stupefied for want of sleep, but at the same time inwardly giving thanks to God".

CHAPTER ELEVEN

HOLIDAYS ABROAD 1877–1879

"I will pour water upon him that is thirsty, and fresh springs upon the dry ground". (Isaiah XLIV. 3.)

AFTER the hard work at Geneva, a holiday was imperatively necessary. Dr. Butler, of course, had to go back to his College at Liverpool, but the Universities were still in vacation, and young George was able to look after his mother. They went to Provence, and there remain delightful letters describing the pleasures of their days. Sometimes they jogged along behind horses, sometimes they walked, taking a lift now and again from a friendly passing driver; they went to Grenoble, still full of evidences of the Franco-Prussian War; from there they visited the monastery where the Chartreuse liqueur is made. This depressed Josephine, for the great building, sited so magnificently, is so built as to shut out from the monks the inspiring views of mountain and valley which lie around them. Josephine grieved that they should turn their backs on the beauty which is one of the best gifts God makes to His creatures. George did not share this feeling. He wanted to see the inside of the monastery, so he was admitted by a door which opened mysteriously and clanged behind him, leaving his mother sitting, a little sadly, on the hillside. It seemed very delightful to her, after this, to be jogging down the mountain road with George beside her, feeling the warmth of the sun on her back. From Valreas she wrote in October 1877:

"This country would delight you. It is not grand like Switzerland, but it is picturesque in the highest degree. The colouring is quite ravishing, especially in autumn, as now, and the sunlight brilliant and clear. The people are very primitive, and we pay almost nothing for our modest shelter and food in the curious old inns, which are sometimes ancient castles, half in ruins. The lower hills are covered with a short growth of sweet lavender, wild sage and many aromatic plants which scent the air delightfully. There are no fences to the vineyards, and the purple grapes are now all fully ripe, and the vintage beginning. There are immense bunches of ripe grapes hanging over the road. I have sometimes gathered a bunch, shaken the dust off and eaten the grapes as I walked. There seems to be no objection made to this. They are of very fine flavour. One sees them scattered about out of the waggons and baskets of the grape gatherers, just as hay is out of the carts at home."

It was a most happy expedition, but the end of the vacation came and George had to go home.

Josephine went on alone by quiet stages, sketching by the way such scenes as attracted her, enjoying the silence and peace, the complete unimportance of time. So she came in due course to Sestri, near Genoa, the home of her niece Edith Leupold. Genoa was in the grip of a heat wave; even at night the temperature did not drop and when Josephine, unable to sleep, crept out on to her verandah in search of a breath of air, she saw on every roof and terrace in the village others in the same plight. It was too much for her. She was taken ill and after a time of considerable anxiety to her friends was removed to Turin, whither, since she became worse instead of better, her husband was summoned. As soon as she recovered sufficiently, he took her into the hills and they stayed at a little inn recommended by Edith Leupold in the Waldensian country. Here Josephine soon revived; her fame had gone before her and the pastors from all the villages along the valley came to La Tour to see her, and to offer their support in the cause. When the time came to go, the landlady declared herself incapable of taking money from any compatriot of Oliver Cromwell, to whom Waldensians owed so deep a debt of gratitude. "When I said I was not responsible for gathering in debts due to Cromwell, she did not reply, but waved her hand and left the room." They travelled slowly home, resting by the way, and in the following year again took a tour, this time in Germany. Such expeditions were delightful to both of them, they were ideally matched companions, both sketched, walked and rode with the keenest enjoyment, both delighted in mountains and mountain scenery. If he could move more quickly and cover greater distances than she could manage, he was always happy to wait for her, geologising, sketching, or simply enjoying the beauty of his surroundings until she rejoined him. There is a pleasant picture of one of these joyous meetings:

"I saw him sitting on the hillside. He had given up the thought of my coming, on account of the storms and damaged roads. He was sketching. I shall never forget his face of joy when he recognised me coming up through the woods. I thought he would have broken his neck, bounding over the rocks to meet me."

There are many such descriptions in Josephine's letters to her sons and her sisters of this and other holidays. They all reveal her quick artist's eye, her enjoyment of every incident, and her quite surprising physical toughness. Once in the little village of Moselkirn they asked for a room:

"They took us up a sort of little hen-ladder, which they called stairs, to a dark, low-roofed room, in which were two little straw mattresses . . . I never slept on anything so hard in my life. They were simply coarse sacks filled with straw, and flung on the top of the stone floor. However, we made the best of it, and managed to laugh at everything."

Then, when they wanted to visit the 'famous Schloss-Elz' they found the only way they could get there was by way of a stony river bed. George got hold of

"a man who had an ox waggon, and hired him to take us. . . . It was a curious new experience for me in travelling. The waggon was . . . drawn by oxen, and made simply of two trunks of trees, with rough wooden ladders placed at the sides, looking like a trough or hay rack. They put a sack with some straw for me to sit upon. The jolting you can hardly imagine. We were often obliged to hold on hard by the sides in order not to be pitched out. But the drive was curiously beautiful."

Even the most delightful of holidays is apt to be tedious when described to other people. These extracts are enough to show the spirit in which the Butlers entered on theirs. Josephine herself felt that it was only the refreshment of spirit that she got on these expeditions that made it possible for her to carry out her work—so often ugly and distressing—and to keep her sense of proportion. Her letters are copious and full of interest, but she by no means confined herself to the writing of letters. She wrote quickly and easily and in her old age, when she could no longer do so much, she remarked that she had been accustomed to write for as many as six hours a day. Even so, her literary output is remarkable.

Between 1868 and 1878 she published innumerable pamphlets as well as four books about her crusade—*The Constitution Violated*, *Une Voix dans le Désert*, *Sursum Corda* and the *Hour before the Dawn*. But this was not all. She edited and wrote the introduction to *Woman's Work* and *Woman's Culture* (1869) as well as a *Memoir* of her father, which came out in the same year. This last, now unfortunately for many years out of print, is one of her more revealing books. It is based largely on the recollections of her father's talk, his memories of childhood, his parents, sisters and country neighbours, his work for agriculture and his political struggles. All this remaining in her memory, is easily and vividly described and made its mark on all her writings. More particularly her father's enlightened application of new and scientific ideas to the treatment of land—harrowing, salting, leaving fallow—constantly recur as similes in her references to the development of the human soul. But there is much more. The book shows a real understanding of the political and economic history of the early part of the century and gives a moving account of a way of life now entirely passed away. John Grey of Dilston stands out as a remarkable North of England countryman, greatly respected and loved by his neighbours, and through his love and understanding of the common man able to interpret public opinion, and to influence those in power at Westminster. His habit of writing immense letters—to his cousin Lord Grey among others—and his energy in collecting large petitions are simply repeated fifty years later by his daughter. It is interesting to note that when in 1872 a second edition of this book was called for, Josephine's name was in such ill repute that no publisher could be found to issue it.

In 1878 Josephine published a *Life of Catharine of Siena*. It is a little difficult to know when she found time to write this remarkable book. It seems hardly possible that it could have been in the hectic days of preparation for the Congress of Geneva; but in the six months following the Congress she was away from home and from access to reference books. In the Introduction to her Life she remarks: "There have been more than forty Lives written of Catharine of Siena—in Latin, Italian, French, German, Dutch and Spanish." She herself, however, has consulted merely five Italian and one French book. Even this, together with Catharine's "Dialogue" which she must have had, seems rather a formidable load for the traveller, but her references to many more sources and the familiarity which she shows with the history of the City States of Italy in the 14th century, of their revolutions and internal constitutions, make it quite impossible that she should have written the book while out of reach of libraries. She makes the whole complicated story of revolution and counter-revolution readable, and her strong passion for liberty, her indignation against tyranny, illumine the pages. But the point of the book, of course, is not the history, but the personality of the Saint. In Catharine of Siena Josephine Butler found a congenial character. It was not only the humble background of the dyer's family that appealed to her, but more than that, the combination in Catharine of the practical reformer with the contemplative mystic. Like Josephine herself, Catharine was conscious of a direct call to costly service. Like Josephine she did not flinch nor give up under disappointment and she learned from hope deferred. Josephine was surely writing about herself when she said that Catharine,

"like many other reformers, at first hoped for a more quick return for her labours; but as the years went on, she learned, as they have learned, that God had greater designs in view than any which came within their human calculations . . . the time of reaping was not yet."

In Catharine's mystical experience we can trace Josephine's. Both knew the desolation of losing the consciousness of the presence of God, and both knew the answer. It is given in the answer to Catharine's question: "Lord, where wast thou when my heart was so tormented?" "I was in the midst of thy heart," He replied. She asked further how this could be, when her heart was so full of detestable thoughts? And He replied: "My presence it was which rendered those thoughts insupportable to thee." Here we have one mystic portrayed by another. Josephine was aware that many of her readers would be sceptical about the reality of Catharine's experiences. To them she says:

"If you are disposed to doubt the fact of these communications from God, or to think that Catharine only fancied such and such things, and attributed these fancies to a divine source, then I would give you one word of advice, and one only: go you and make the attempt to live a life of prayer, such as she lived, and then, and not till then, will you be in a position which will give you any shadow of a right, or any power, to judge of this soul's dealings with God."

With her public work and her writings, it might well seem that Josephine had as much on her hands as any one woman could manage. But she was also the wife of a Head Master and the mother of three sons. She was, moreover, by disposition and upbringing, hospitable. It would have been impossible for her not to welcome to her home her sisters and their children, her son's friends, her own colleagues from overseas, or anyone else who came to the door. She enjoyed this aspect of her life immensely. Twice the old American abolitionist Lloyd Garrison came to stay with the Butlers in Liverpool, the last time during his last visit to England in 1877. She rejoiced to have him, remembering that when he had first come to England and had found women excluded from a meeting to which he had been invited, he refused to take the seat of honour prepared for him and had insisted on joining the ladies in their banishment. He was old now and very frail, but Josephine glowed under his appreciation of her work.

One December she went with George to a meeting of the Head Masters' Conference at Eton. The invitation, issued to wives, was something of an innovation and in a meeting of some 200, only 9 wives were present. Josephine writes with appreciation of a very grand dinner party in the College Dining Hall—so grand that "Mrs. Harrow", Josephine's sister-in-law, felt like the Queen of Sheba, thinking how far less glorious any party at Harrow would be. Josephine, knowing that the Conference would never contemplate a meeting at so distant a spot as Liverpool, was not tempted to make comparisons, and gave herself up to the enjoyment of the beauty of the occasion:

"We all dined in the Great Hall at Eton, such a grand place, with three immense fireplaces each large enough to roast an ox, and with banners, armorial bearings and ancient portraits around the walls. We ladies sat at the High Table with masses of gold plate presented at different times by Kings and Queens to the College, and such splendid flowers. There was a boar's head with a wreath of camellias! Each couple of us had a tall flunkey at our backs. The nine ladies sat of course alternately with gentlemen ... Mrs. Eton with Mr. Harrow for example, Mrs. Harrow with Mr. Eton, Mrs. Liverpool with Mr. Rugby ... Jex-Blake, Head Master of Rugby, remarked to me 'We are an ugly lot, but there are some good heads amongst us!' "

The Conference on the following day discussed the relative importance of the study of modern languages and the classics; a subject which has not gone altogether out of fashion in the intervening eighty years.

The Butlers went on from the Conference to spend Christmas with her eldest sister, Mrs. Masson. It was a family gathering and George was the only man. In the evening they played games, "You would have been amused to see how George laid himself out to do his duty"—acting charades in which George made a hit as the music master in a girls' school, playing the fiddle with a poker and tongs and dancing the while with neatness and precision. Josephine wrote a full and amusing account of these parties to her sisters abroad. However busy she was, however worried or tired, she could always find time for this, for her family roots went so deep, her sense of fellowship with those who had shared her first home was so strong, that to leave them out of what she was doing, either in work or play, was unthinkable. It is to these epistolary habits of Josephine that we owe a knowledge of the lighter side of her strenuous life.

CHAPTER TWELVE

WESTMINSTER AGAIN 1879–1883

"It was half past one in the morning and the stars were shining in a clear sky". (J. B. 1883)

THE Federation held its Annual Conference in Liége in 1879. It was a happy affair. Josephine describes it to her Bristol friends in a letter which covers eighty-four sides of quarto paper, in which every line breathes exhilaration. At Geneva there had all the time been a sense of strain; anxiety lest some of the delegates should not be sound in their opinions, lest some of the resolutions should be defeated, and all the time the consciousness of "tenanciers" in the background, supported by the local Press, hoping and perhaps intriguing for the failure of the Congress. It was quite different at Liége. The delegates who came were all of one mind and speaker after speaker insisted that the fundamental issue was simply that of liberty and justice for all alike. "You are not free," said Mr. Benjamin Scott to the citizens of Liége, "Liége is not free; Brussels is not free; and Paris is not free, though she has battered down the Bastille and placed the statue of Liberty on the column of July. . . . It could never be said that the United States were free so long as they held four millions of negroes enslaved. Paris, Brussels and your fine city of Liége are not free so long as any woman may be deprived of her civil rights at the caprice or tyranny of a police agent, or through the denunciation of a scoundrel." Liége was a friendly little town; Josephine received a bouquet of roses every day while she was there. The Headquarters of the Conference were established at the principal hotel. The delegates were enjoying a new experience, for here men and women, English, French, Dutch, Danish, German and others; Catholics, Protestants, Free Thinkers; men of the working class and members of the aristocracy met in uninhibited friendliness—a thing unheard of in those days—pooling their ideas, recognising each other's quality and enjoying all that fellowship in a great cause gives. Among all these Josephine moved with a sure step, interpreting one to another, using perfect French and Italian and rather more doubtful German as occasion demanded, steering conversations round awkward corners, always able to lift differences to a level above personal feeling, and at the same time infusing a spirit of gaiety into the whole thing. She speaks of dining in the hotel:

"We always sat in one group and we always laughed so much that the people in the hotel must have thought that moral reformers were the merriest people in the world."

It was a great pleasure to her to see M. Humbert acclaimed as an indispensable organiser, for it was she who had sponsored him as the chief officer of the Federation on the Continent. There was a great public meeting in the principal hall of the town:

"Humbert took his place as President, he amused us all a little by introducing us all by name to the meeting, one by one, and giving a brief description of each while he pointed to each like a showman with a wild beast show. It was very difficult for *us* to keep our countenances, but the audience seemed to think it a very serious and interesting proceeding. M. Guyot was obliged to hide his face, he has such a propensity to laugh and goes off like a soda water bottle, sometimes at inconvenient occasions."

Benjamin Scott, Chamberlain of the City of London could only apologise for being unable to speak in French, the language of the Conference. His weighty speech was read for him. Yves Guyot enjoyed himself thoroughly "preparing a scourge of scorpions for the police des Moeurs".

There were other meetings too, one for women, about which Josephine was warned to expect practically no audience, since it was to be held in a Protestant hall which no Roman Catholic would enter. She went along, therefore, prepared to give a homely chat to a handful of women, but arrived to find the place packed to the doors, with people outside listening through the windows. It was as she came away from this meeting that she saw

"close beside the carriage a group of about a dozen very poor ragged little girls from about 5 to 11 years old, standing perfectly silent, just of the class who will be the victims of the future to the evil we are fighting against. I heard one of them say, standing in front of the group, with her hands clasped and in a tone of reverence 'O-o-oh qu'elle est belle, cette Dame Butler' and then gave a deep sigh. Please to observe that it was dark and that they could not see anything except the faint outline of a lady. But the idea of something beautiful had entered their poor little heads in some way, and might justly be applied to the work we were doing."

It is more probable that, after the way of little girls, they were simply repeating their elders' remarks, for Josephine's striking beauty always moved her audiences and was a great reinforcement to her words.

Besides the regular meetings there were informal ones— Josephine was always liable to be caught by them. She describes how, on returning to her hotel one evening, she was met by

"a group of poor women, some with babies in their arms. This was a deputation which had waited for more than an hour to see me and presented to me a formal and neatly written petition, evidently prepared with extreme care and slightly ornamented. It was a request that I would address them in their own People's Hall. It was not in me to resist such an appeal. . . . At the end of the meeting they all crowded to the platform. There was quite a little mountain of pennies and little soiled notes on the table . . . a contribution towards the Federation's work."

At one of her meetings in Liége Josephine caught sight from the platform of "an earnest looking young man in the audience", and set to work to write pencilled invitations to a party at her hotel, which she handed at random to suitable looking young men. The result was a tremendous influx of visitors who were hard to provide with refreshment, but not hard to entertain, and were eventually only got rid of by what Josephine described as "a hint" from Professor Stuart, who, well used to helping awkward undergraduates on their way, said to the largest group: "Now, gentlemen, Mrs. Butler wishes you good night!" The people of Liége were very hospitable, and there are many charming descriptions of other parties, but the work of the Conference was over and the delegates dispersed. Josephine went to Brussels.

Here it was quite another task she had in hand, and there was no gaiety in it. From the time when in Liége three years earlier she had been told of the waggon loads of girls brought into Belgium *'comme la bétaille'* she had been haunted by the memory, and now in Brussels she had time to pursue the subject. The Society of Friends had sent two emissaries, Alfred Dyer and George Gillett, to make enquiries into the subject and a Dr. Alexis Splingard, a Belgian barrister, was investigating on his own behalf. He had been begged by an English girl of his acquaintance to try to find out what had become of her sister. He had searched in vain, but in the course of his enquiries he came upon much that horrified him. In Brussels Josephine met these men and with Pastor Annet studied the evidence they offered her.

The Belgian law sanctioned prostitution, and brothels were recognised and taxed. The penal code, however, did forbid the admission to them of girls under the age of 16. Dyer and Gillett, in the course of their investigations, discovered that there were, without doubt, little girls of all nationalities, aged between 11 and 15, enslaved there. The children, being illicit, were kept shut up so that none should see them—except most favoured and trusted clients—and were treated with great cruelty. The brothel keepers and the police worked hand in hand. Dyer and Gillett made a statement to this effect to the Procureur Général and to the British authorities, and the Procureur invited the British police to come and see for themselves. Two detectives were sent from London to examine the situation, and the Brussels police, with the greatest show of frankness, took them to the brothels, having first warned the keepers to remove all the young girls from the place. Scotland Yard went home fully satisfied that all was in order, and reported in this sense to the British authorities.

When Josephine got home, she was summoned by Colonel Vincent, the Director of C.I.D., to the Yard to see the report, but was by no means convinced by it, being absolutely certain that there was no show of doubt as to the traffic, but wondering anxiously what her next step should be, as the whitewashing by Scotland Yard made the whole situation much more difficult. That Belgian official circles were deeply and profitably concerned was to her abundantly clear; she was convinced that many of her own countrymen in high places were also involved. It was a case in which a false step might do more harm than good.

While she was in this doubt, a great meeting to be addressed by Yves Guyot and others, called her to Paris. There she met a Belgian detective, who had become so disgusted with the corruption of the Belgian police that he was prepared to reveal all he knew. He said that Messrs. Dyer and Gillett's assertions that there were very young girls in the Brussels brothels had caused uneasiness to the Procureur du Roi, who had

"sent for Schraeder and asked 'Is it true that you allow very young girls, and English &c. &c.?' Schraeder said 'Oh, non, non Monsieur'. Then he rushed off to Lenaer's house (Lenaer is head of the whole police) and said 'M. le Procureur asks *have we any minors?*' Lenaer turned livid and sank back in his armchair. After a bit he jumped up, and ordered two carriages. In ten minutes these carriages 'brulaient les rues de Bruxelles' flying along. They called at such and such infamous houses and carried off the minors who were there, and sent them with a detective *across the frontier*. Then the detective went back in a couple of hours to M. le Procureur du Roi and smilingly said 'Perhaps M. le Procureur would come himself and walk through all the houses and see if there are any minors.' M. le Procureur *did so*, and next day, says Josephine, 'he wrote to our *Times* and *Standard* saying that our statements were entirely false."

This gave Josephine the evidence she wanted, for the Belgian detective had given her definite names and addresses of all the people concerned. With the consciousness that she could prove her case up to the hilt, she published on May 1st, 1880 in *The Shield*, a perfectly plain statement declaring that in the brothels in Brussels there were—contrary to Belgian law—quite young English children aged between 11 and 15, that these children were often treated with great cruelty and that they were shut in and never allowed to leave the house. This statement was at once translated into French and published in French and Belgian papers.

A storm of rage broke out. Belgian police authorities furiously denied the truth of these assertions, and the English papers deplored so intemperate an attack on friendly neighbours. None the less a good deal of uneasiness was aroused in Belgium among public men, and public pressure on the Belgian authorities was so strong that they were obliged to act and the Procureur Général sent a formal demand to the Home Secretary in London that, under the law of extradition, Mrs. Butler should be required to repeat her allegations on oath before a magistrate.

There followed a curious outburst. A determined attempt was made to prevent Josephine from making this deposition. It was natural enough that those who had an interest in concealing the truth should take this line. The violent abuse and the threats as to what would happen to Mrs. Butler if ever she showed her face on the Continent again are clearly the utterances of fear. What is difficult to understand is that she was inundated with letters from her friends and supporters imploring her to let the matter rest— to withdraw, to do anything to avoid opening "the gates of Hell". "If you declined," they said, "it would be worth everything to the cause for you to suffer the full legal penalty of refusing to answer. This would arouse the public as nothing else could." Benjamin Scott became almost melodramatic about it, sending a messenger through the night to Liverpool, who arrived and knocked up the household before 5 a.m. "It was quite dark. I lighted my candle to see to read the letter, and Jane made a fire downstairs and prepared some tea etc. for the messenger who was shivering with cold. He was to return to London again by the first train. I felt a little confused in the cold and dark morning, reading a mysterious letter from the Guildhall, which contained also a telegram in cypher from Brussels, warning me that there was some trap being laid for us, and probably some collusion between the police of London and that of Belgium."

Josephine found herself in a difficult position. She had made accusations which she was sure were true; she had been challenged and now some of those whose opinion she respected advised her to draw back. She felt she could not take the advice of any of them.

"If I refuse," she said, "the Belgians and our opponents elsewhere would naturally say it was because I had no positive charges to make against them. Moreover, I am longing to make known in the most public way these terrible cases. We wish these iniquities to be known."

Escorted by her husband, she went into Liverpool and made her deposition before Mr. Stamford Raffles, the Stipendiary Magistrate. The deposition was sent to the Home Office and then to Belgium. Josephine waited for Hell to break loose. The sequel, as far as she was concerned, was something of an anti-climax. An enquiry was ordered in Brussels and the editor of one of the Belgian papers asked her for a copy of her deposition which had not been published there. Josephine sent it, thinking he only intended to use it privately, and that it might help the enquiry. It did. The editor published it in full in his paper and in the violence of public indignation which followed the Chiefs of Police were dismissed and various people "found the state of their health required them to visit the South of France" . . . "But," she wrote sadly nearly twenty years later in 1898, "the system of Government-patented and regulated vice *continues to exist*, and the friends of Justice continue to work and to wait."

An immediate result of these disclosures was the formation by the City of London of an Association for the Suppression of the Traffic in Women and Girls. Benjamin Scott was the moving spirit, and he and Josephine agreed that a public enquiry into this traffic would force Parliament to take active measures to repress it. An approach was made to the Government in 1881;

Josephine, from London, wrote to her husband to tell him of her part in the business. She had written to Lord Granville, the Foreign Secretary:

"I shall be in London for three days and will wait those three days *outside your door*, until Your Lordship chooses either to hear our petition, or to order my removal! Lord Granville sent for me at once and said 'No need for your three days' siege—I have already given notice I shall move on May 30th for a Committee of the House of Lords'."

The Committee sat through 1881 and 1882 and issued a report which confirmed all the allegations which had been made. As a result the Criminal Law Amendment Bill was introduced in the House of Lords, raising the age of consent from 13 to 16. The Bill passed through the Lords, but when it reached the Commons it was either talked out or dropped. So the matter rested.

By 1881 a Liberal Government had replaced the Conservative. This was more hopeful for the Federation, though Abolition had not been made a test question for candidates at the Election, and Harcourt at the Home Office, Hartington at the India Office, and Northbrook at the War Office—"lovely trio", as Josephine calls them—were all avowed Regulationists. Stansfeld himself had been given no seat in the Cabinet. This last, though it signified the end of his political career, was definitely an advantage to the cause, for it made it possible for him to take complete charge of the campaign for Abolition in a way he could not have done had he been a Member of the Cabinet.

A Select Committee of the House of Commons had been appointed in 1879 to enquire into the Acts and to recommend their "retention, extension or abolition"; the new House re-appointed the Committee and Josephine was called as a witness in May 1882. This was a very different experience from that of 1871. For one thing the whole attitude of Parliament to the question had changed. There had been a time when the mention of any subject connected with women had evoked shouts of laughter in the House. That had passed, to be succeeded by a period when instead of derision the attitude of the Members was rather one of shocked surprise that any "woman who called herself a lady"—Cavendish Bentinck's phrase—could meddle with any subject so improper. There were still Members who persisted in this attitude, but by most it was recognised that those who were advocating Abolition were serious-minded and conscientious people whose views, however ridiculous, must nevertheless be heard. The composition of the Select Committee, too, was different from that of the Royal Commission. There were only fifteen members and of these six were committed to Abolition. The other nine were inclined to favour Regulation, but only one, Mr. Osborne Morgan, the official Government representative, had an entirely closed mind on the question. When Josephine gave her evidence, therefore, she was conscious of a strong friendly section among her hearers; no doubt also the ten years that had passed had given her so much experience of public speaking, so much familiarity with all the traps likely to be laid for her, that she was less agitated than she had been in 1871. After all, there is something in being ten years older. Her evidence made a good impression; her friends put questions which enabled her to show the strength of the opposition to Regulation among women of all classes and in all parts of the country and to assert the grounds of morality and justice on which the opposition was based; she refused to be disconcerted when those who had studied her evidence of 1871 quoted it to show some discrepancies with her present evidence, or when they tried to make her admit that she could not know anything about the conditions in the prescribed areas since she had not recently visited them. She was less aggressive now than she had been in 1871, but she was not less firm.

"Negro slavery", she said, "was abolished in our British possessions by a body of persons in England who had never seen a negro slave. They took their stand upon the principle that slavery was wrong; we take our stand entirely and purely on the principle that the State must not regulate prostitution; and no results given to us from year to year, as they are, no reports of this present Committee will in any respect or in the smallest degree alter our position, because we take our stand upon principles which are eternal."

Her dignity and obvious sincerity made the impression they always made.

When one reads the reports of the Select Committee, one is tempted to wonder what is the exact value of a Committee of Enquiry. There were nine Regulationists and six Abolitionists at the beginning of its meetings. At the end there was a Majority Report signed by nine members and a Minority Report signed by six. It is true that one or two of the majority wavered on some of the paragraphs, but they all signed the whole report at the end. This Majority Report is a very remarkable document and reveals the astounding capacity of the human mind to exclude from it anything it does not wish to entertain. It declares wholeheartedly in favour of the Regulations, re-affirms without any uncertainty their effectiveness in checking disease and the value of the work of reclamation carried out by the agents. More remarkable still, it re-affirms the finding of the Commission of 1871 that the Special Police "are not chargeable with any abuse of their authority, and have hitherto discharged a novel and difficult duty with moderation and caution". Yet the Committee had had the case of Mrs. Percy recalled to its memory, and in addition some quite unanswerable cases of abuse, one of a girl of 18, who having been accused of prostitution by the police and examined under threat of being sent to prison if she refused, was found by the prison doctor to be a virgin and rather hastily sent home with a present of 6d. from each of two nurses and 5s. from the matron. Yet still the majority could declare that the powers of the police were never abused.

With all this enthusiasm for the Acts, it would have been natural that the Report should recommend their extension, but this it failed to do. In a curious recommendation it declared that while no doubt the extension of the Acts to the whole country would be highly beneficial and would become most popular wherever it was tried, there was none the less a feeling against them which must be respected—and therefore things should remain as they were. Actually, in its exaggerated praise of the Regulations, the majority over-reached itself. The Minority

Report, drawn up by Stansfeld was, as might be expected, a statesmanlike document; it put the case against the Acts cogently and reasonably and in the event it was upon this Report that the House acted. But that time was not yet.

The Report appeared in August 1882. Hartington at the India Office welcomed it joyfully and wrote to the Viceroy, Lord Ripon, who wished to abolish the system in India, that there was not the smallest chance of his being able to do so, since the Report of the Select Committee made extension more likely than abolition. In these circumstances it was clear that, while Parliament pondered the Report, it was necessary for the National Association to make it aware of the strength of public opinion in favour of Abolition. An extensive campaign was carried on all over the country.

Josephine herself went to Oxford, where she was always faintly ill at ease. She had been very happy there, but she could never quite forget that it was also there that she had first discovered and had been wounded by the attitude of men to women. But she had made up her mind to go in order to raise the abolition issue there.

"I had made a promise to my own soul that I would speak on the subject, if only twenty words, to *everyone* I met at Oxford even casually, and I believe I kept my promise except in two cases. It is rather hard work resolving to speak to *everyone* in season and out of season, but life is short and the night cometh in which no man can work."

She already had some supporters in Oxford and it was to them she first went. Canon and Mrs. Rawlinson welcomed her and sent her off in good heart. There followed a chilling experience with a Professor of Law for India. She left him with a copy of *Constitution Violated* and *Government by Police* and "hoped she had done some good". She went on to "my dear friends the Harbords to get cheered. They live down in Paradise Square; he is a joiner and came out to meet me. He was buying a ha'porth of milk for their tea—in his shirt sleeves at the door—and I said 'I am Mrs. Butler' and his eyes gleamed and he said 'I see, I see', and like little Rhoda at the gate who kept St. Peter waiting in her joy, he left me and the milk and ran to tell his wife. . . . Of course as you might expect, the two were like Princes in dignity and repose of manner, liberal and catholic in sentiment, and true and constant in our cause." In her next call she found encouragement again. This was on a Professor of Chinese recently come from Hong Kong, where he had heard nothing but good of the Regulations. The Professor, however, learning from Josephine that there was another side to the question, called his wife and daughters to hear what she had to say and this sent Josephine on her way rejoicing, since a man who could so frankly consider a new point of view and consult his wife and daughters about it, must be fundamentally sound.

She went on to Keble, where Talbot, the Warden, listened to her courteously, but was puzzled at her choosing Oxford as a place in which to discuss this particular subject. Her reply startled him:

"It is fully time, I think, to come to Oxford and to Keble College; when I get letters frequently from men dated 'Keble College Oxford' beseeching me to give them instruction and to guide their bewildered minds to a little light on this great social problem. He started as if he was shot, and said 'What! Do my boys write to you?' 'Yes,' I said, 'they do, and many other *boys* as well. They want some thoroughly truthful and manly instruction on this question, and they claim that they can best get it by writing to a *woman*.' "

Leaving Talbot to ponder on this she next met Scott Holland,

"a saint . . . learned and eloquent and rather subtle. I am not sure about him, though he eagerly listened. He *looked* as if a message from Heaven had been thundered at him and said 'What shall we do?' "

In Mr. Chevasse she met a keen fellow worker; he had an evening service which some 500 undergraduates attended, and he spoke enviously of the work Stuart was doing in Cambridge. Then, somewhat unwillingly, she visited Dr. Acland, whom she knew to be a determined opponent. After an interview in which he displayed venomous hostility, as she left he said that he did not wish her to represent him as one in favour of the Acts—on which Josephine commented "oiling his weather-cock, I suppose".

She had no time to see Jowett, and perhaps she was not sorry about this. He was Vice-Chancellor of the University, and she remarked grimly that "he has forbidden a meeting at Oxford—he is afraid for the morals of his sweet undergraduates!"

As she left Oxford she reflected that the older men had not changed since her day:

"How far back some men are. Fancy Talbot saying to me 'but do you really think that the sin is equal in men and women?' and some Archdeacon said to Rawlinson 'But you know it is absurd to suppose that the 7th Commandment is binding on men as it is on women'. I felt plainly the first few minutes with many of these men that they thought of me like Canon Liddon as 'that dreadful woman Mrs. Butler'. This feeling adds to the pain and difficulty of such interviews."

The journey was bitterly cold and this perhaps added to her depression; the only comfort she had was that she had left behind her "those two good women, Mrs. Rolleston and Mrs. Rawlinson, who will pray and carry on the little bits I began". She had done more—she had made so marked a change in Talbot's outlook that when Ellice Hopkins was founding the White Cross League, early in the following year, he invited her to address a meeting of undergraduates at Oxford and himself took the Chair for the meeting.

The opening of the Session of 1883 found the Abolitionists in good heart; they were full of confidence that this year would see the end of the long struggle. Josephine was heart and soul with the Society of Friends which in January organised a great convention lasting for two days at which the subject of Abolition should be considered and corporate prayer offered for the success of the campaign. The Friends invited Christians of every denomination to join them and there was a large and remarkable gathering at Devonshire House, Bishopsgate, then the Headquarters of the Society. In addition to this convention, there were meetings for men and women separately at the East London Tabernacle, and finally a great meeting presided over by Benjamin Scott at Exeter Hall. A great feeling of confidence was generated and those who had come from the provinces went home to in-

augurate similar meetings for prayer all over the country. It was
known that Hopwood had put down a motion condemning the
compulsory examination of women, which was to follow the
Debate on the Address. Josephine took a room at the Westminster Palace Hotel and organised continuous prayer to be
offered throughout the day and as far into the night as the House
might sit. Clergy of various denominations came in turn to conduct services of intercession, and between these, corporate silent
prayer continued. The room was crowded. There were some men
there, but for the most part they were women, and women of all
sorts:

"Well-dressed ladies, some even of high rank, kneeling together
(almost side by side) with the poorest, and some of the outcast women
of the purlieus of Westminster."

Josephine left the hotel from time to time to go into the Lobby
of the House. She was told that many of the younger Members
were distinctly embarrassed at the idea that "all those women"
should be praying for them, but Cavendish Bentinck, "a man who
foams at the mouth when he speaks of us", was infuriated and
could not contain his anger against those who "patronised that
woman's praying". She met Cardinal Manning, looking "even
thinner than a spider! He said he would do all he could for us
through his influence on the Irish Catholic vote." There was no
doubt that many Members of Parliament were moved by the
strength of feeling against the Acts, of which they could no longer
be in doubt. "It is a strange thing," said one, "that people care so
much about this question. All my leading constituents have
urged me to vote with you." But the Debate on the Address was
protracted, some believed designedly so, so that Hopwood was
not able to introduce his motion. It was a disappointment certainly, but it was only hope deferred, for on April 20th, Stansfeld,
more fortunate than Hopwood, was able to propose the motion
"That this House disapproves of the compulsory examination of
women under the Contagious Diseases Acts." The scene is best
described in Josephine's own words:

"All day long groups had met for prayer—some in the houses of M.P.s, some in churches, some in halls, where the poorest people came. Meetings were being held also all over the kingdom, and telegraphic messages of sympathy came to us continually from Scotland and Ireland, France, Switzerland and Italy. There was something in the air like the approach of victory. As men and women prayed they suddenly burst forth into praise, thanking God for the answer, as if it had already been granted. It was a long debate. The tone of the speeches, both for and against, was remarkably purified, and with one exception they were altogether on a higher plane than in former debates. Many of us ladies sat through the whole evening till after midnight; then came the division. A few minutes previously Mr. Gerard, the steward of the Ladies' Gallery, crept quietly in and whispered to me 'I think you are going to win!' That reserved official, of course, never betrays sympathy with any party; nevertheless, I could see the irrepressible pleasure in his face when he said this.

"Never can I forget the expression on the faces of our M.P.s in the House when they all streamed back from the Division Lobby. The interval during their absence had seemed very long, and we could hear each other's breathing so deep was the silence. We did not require to wait to hear the announcement of the division by the tellers; the faces of our friends told the tale. Slowly and steadily they pressed in, headed by Mr. Stansfeld and Mr. Hopwood, the tellers on our side. Mr. Fowler's face was beaming with joy and a kind of humble triumph. I thought of the words: 'Say unto Jerusalem her warfare is accomplished.' It was a victory of righteousness over gross selfishness, injustice and deceit and for the moment we were all elevated by it. When the figures were given out a long-continued cheer arose, which sounded like a psalm of praise. Then we ran quickly down from the gallery and met a number of our friends coming out from Westminster Hall.

"It was half-past one in the morning, and the stars were shining in a clear sky. I felt at that silent hour in the morning the spirit of the Psalmist, who said: 'When the Lord turned again the capitivity of Zion, we were like unto them that dream.' It almost seemed like a dream."

CHAPTER THIRTEEN

THE WHITE SLAVE TRAFFIC 1882—1885

"Terrible work undertaken for God". (Scott Holland)

JOSEPHINE went home, triumphantly thankful. The words of the Psalmist sang in her heart—"The Lord hath done great things for us, whereof we rejoice." She had "sown in tears", she was "reaping in joy". It was a wonderful moment. The fight was of course not over; the detested Acts were still on the Statute Book, but their teeth were drawn. With compulsory examination abolished and the special police disbanded, Regulation was practically dead. Three years were to elapse before the objectionable Acts were finally expunged and for those three years Stansfeld conducted the campaign, very often with some opposition from those Repealers who were less patient than he, and now that the worst evils had been removed, felt at liberty to take a line of their own. Josephine, however, remained a staunch upholder of Stansfeld; she trusted his wisdom absolutely and the main part she took in the struggle between 1883 and 1886 was to exhort her friends to follow his advice and give him the utmost support.

For herself, she felt now that her first duty was to her husband. He had resigned from Liverpool College in 1882. She had for some time been anxious about him, feeling that the work was too much for him. He was now over 60 and the perpetual association with the young is apt to become wearing to the elderly. There were worries too. The complete confidence he had inspired in Governors and parents had been somewhat shaken by his courageous and constant identification of himself with his wife's work. The Butlers had no money. Teachers have never been overpaid and at that time the emoluments of a Principal, depending on the numbers in the school, provided only enough for a very moderate way of life. The Butlers, moreover, had educated three sons at public schools and University and they were incurably generous and quite incapable of withholding gifts from people or causes in which they believed. Henry Wilson and James Stuart understood the position well and determined to invite friends to subscribe to make the Butlers a substantial gift. This was accepted with warm gratitude, but the future was still somewhat obscure when in June 1882 Gladstone offered George Butler a Canonry at Winchester. This offer pleased Josephine particularly as a public recognition of George made by one whom she greatly honoured, in spite of his often exasperating instability.

They had now to dig up their roots from Liverpool—no small matter when one has lived in the same home for seventeen years. Josephine worked hard. Her home had also been her office and besides the domestic sharing out of furniture and household goods, determining what must be disposed of and what given to the three sons or kept for themselves, there were letters and papers covering a long period and an immense range of subjects. There were other things too: a beloved dog, who being thirteen years old and very blind must be put to sleep, a decision which cost Josephine much agony of mind; the consideration of the proper equipment for a Canon's wife in Winchester and the purchase of a fur cape and muff with money which Hattie had sent her for her better outfitting. Nor was this all. During her years in Liverpool she had acquired a number of protégées—old people, sick people, lonely or unhappy people. Some were in homes of her devising, others in institutions where she visited them. For all these "poor hangers-on", as she called them, provision must be made, since clearly they could neither be moved to Winchester nor left uncared for.

When all this had been accomplished it was a somewhat exhausted wife who joined George at the little village of Cornhill in Northumberland, where he was taking charge of the parish while the Vicar had his holiday. This was a happy time for them both; they renewed old pleasures, revived their acquaintance with old neighbours, and found peace and rest in the familiar scene. They went often to see George Grey and his family at Milfield. George Butler returned with zest to his favourite sport and quoted to his son—"A motto put up over the door here 'Nulla dies sine linea.' I suppose that means 'Wet your lines every day.' " He astonished the gillie by his catch in spite of the wrong sort of weather; he went on to grouse shooting on the moors and bade farewell to that sport, for he was sure that, once installed at Winchester, he would not be able to find time to reach the moors. While George was grouse shooting, Josephine went off to Neuchâtel, where the Federation was holding a conference. George followed her there and together they enjoyed revisiting the Humberts and taking part in the meetings.

They settled in the house in the Close before the end of the year. It was the perfect home for the Butlers' last years of married life. The society of the Close was congenial, the Dean and Chapter worked harmoniously and there was a feeling of cordial friendship among the Canons. The Cathedral itself was to both of them a source of inspiration. Its great walls stood between them and the North wind and within, the noble architecture, the antiquity of the monuments and the subdued light all spoke of peace. It was a place for rest, for meditation, for escape from the frets and worries of daily life and in the Cathedral services both found spiritual refreshment. George increasingly loved the worship there. "When he lost his health it became a real rest and help to him, physically as well as spiritually, to take his part in the services. It seemed to lift him even above bodily pain and weariness and to enable him simply to contemplate the eternal realities and the 'rest which remaineth for the People of God'." Josephine loved to worship with him. She recorded an incident during service one Sunday as an illustration of the help he gave her in time of need. "I suddenly felt faint, the effect of a week of unusual effort and hard work. Wishing not to disturb anyone I crept down from the stalls as silently as possible, holding on by the carved woodwork. A moment more and I should have dropped—when suddenly there passed before my eyes something white as snow and soft as an angel's wing. I felt myself held up by a strong loving arm and supported to the West door where the cool breeze restored me. It was my husband. His quick ear had caught the sound of my footstep and he left his seat unobserved by anyone. The angel's wing was the wide sleeve of his surplice on which the sun shone as he drew me towards him."

Fishing was still possible for George, and though he found "the slow, smooth-flowing rivers of the South" less interesting than the "lively ones of the North", he still enjoyed it immensely and returned often in thought to the streams of Glendale. When it was his duty to attend "some solemn public meeting when he occupied a prominent place on the platform", Josephine, watching him, found herself "unable to suppress a smile" as she saw "the furtive movement of his right hand, the graceful turn from side to side of the wrist, and the far-off look in his eyes. He was fishing in imagination! He was in spirit in dear Glendale, casting for trout. . . . And thus he would beguile the time through some uninteresting argument, or long-drawn-out peroration." This tedious duty over, they would return together to their home.

The house itself was lovely, "with its thick walls, its picturesque gables, its antiquity (dating from the time of St. Swithin, Chancellor to Alfred the Great), its ample accommodation, and its surroundings of fine ancestral trees and flowering shrubs, gorgeous in spring". This "ample accommodation" was enough to satisfy the hospitable desires even of the Butlers, and as in the days of her youth Josephine's home was constantly the resort of people of all nationalities, coming from all quarters of the earth and being refreshed and stimulated by good talk. The faithful Jane still reigned below, glorying in her mistress' work and ready to boast about it should anyone look disapproving; the dogs, always an important part of the Butlers' households, stretched themselves on the hearthrug and got up eagerly to welcome their master whenever his tall spare figure appeared. The Butlers rejoiced in the beauty of their home—above all, they enjoyed its peace and privacy. At night, when the gates of the Close were shut, there was a wonderful silence, refreshing to the soul.

The social atmosphere of Winchester was very different from that of Liverpool; it was partly the difference between North and South, but even more the change from an industrial to a religious and military centre. In Winchester the Cathedral clock and bells alternated with the bugle calls and other noises from the barracks. They found in Winchester society "less breathing space, so to speak, socially and politically, if not intellectually . . . It was often remarked that the society of the Close itself was less conventional and more liberal, in the best sense, than that of the city outside."

When George had finished his first term of residence they made an expedition to the Jura Mountains and then stayed again with the Humberts. It was in the course of this visit that Josephine got involved in a totally unexpected battle which had nothing to do with the work of the Federation. At the end of the preceding year, the Salvation Army had started a campaign of evangelisation on the Continent and early in 1883 a party, led by Catherine Booth, the daughter of the General, arrived in Geneva. It had achieved some success; the leaders had been very careful to conform to all the regulations laid down by the police. Their observance of every rule, however, did not save them, when it appeared that their mission was to some extent affecting adversely the business of the brothel keepers, so influential in that town; and gangs of roughs were hired to break up the meetings. The police then proscribed all meetings of the Army, on the plea that they created disorder. The Salvation Army thereupon confined its activities to meetings for prayer and preaching in private houses. Unable to think of any other way of suppressing the work, the Prefect of Police summoned Catherine Booth to give evidence at an enquiry, and the magistrate, affirming that she had made collections of money contrary to the law and that she had refused to submit accounts, a statement which was not true, expelled her from the Canton.

Josephine in Neuchâtel heard of these incidents. There is no evidence that she had met any of the Booth family before this, but no one who had at that time been engaged in rescue work could fail to know of the Salvation Army—and Josephine had sent girls from Liverpool to Mrs. Booth's Rescue Home in London. There were features in the methods of the Army which inevitably jarred on one as sensitive as she to beauty, and especially to musical beauty. She loved best the peaceful silent worship of the Society of Friends; she appreciated the restrained beauty of the Anglican Liturgy and its ordered dignity; she was at home in the simple homely chapel of the Free Churches, its extempore prayer and congregational singing. But the Salvation Army was very strident, and its quasi-military gatherings lacked the atmosphere of peace. Nevertheless, Josephine recognised the sincerity which animated it and saw that its methods of approach were valid for many of those whom it desired to seek and to save. In any case, injustice was an outrage and the flagrant injustice meted out to Catherine Booth roused all the instincts of battle never long dormant in Josephine. Now she went at once to Berne to protest to the Chancellor of the Swiss Confederation against the wrong perpetrated against an Englishwoman. It was a stormy meeting and produced no result but mutual irritation, so she went back to Neuchâtel. There she met Catherine, whose appeal against her expulsion from Geneva had been rejected. At first the Salvation Army was left unmolested in Neuchâtel, but the peace was of short duration. The Press began to attack it, complaining that these foreigners came to stir up strife in their midst. As in Geneva there were riots and M. Humbert's house was attacked by roughs in protest against his having received "Salutists" there.

The climax to the affair came in September. The immediate occasion was the funeral of a young man who had been converted early in the year by the Salvation Army and had become a zealous adherent. When he was dying, before Catherine's expulsion from

Geneva, she had promised him that she would attend his funeral. This promise she was now resolved to keep, though it involved ignoring the expulsion order. She felt fully justified in taking this step, since her expulsion had been itself quite illegal. Josephine of course encouraged her and determined to accompany her. They went together to the house of the young man, and a procession was formed which the Mayor of Geneva tried but failed to stop. At the cemetery the Mayor re-appeared and insisted that Catherine Booth should accompany him to the police. Josephine went too. In the police station Catherine was led into an office and Josephine was left outside, but the door was open and she saw all that passed. When the police asked Catherine why she had defied the order of expulsion her reply was "First, that her expulsion was illegal, she not having been guilty of any offence which could justify it; secondly, that it was a breach of the Treaty of Friendship, Commerce and Establishment between England and Switzerland (she held in her hands at the time a copy of the Constitution of Geneva, and of the above Treaty); and thirdly that the Chief of the Department of Justice and Police had falsified a Cantonal police regulation in order to furnish an excuse for expelling her." Josephine goes on to say: "The surprise and anger of her questioners on hearing this arraignment of their own acts and of their government were beyond description. For a moment Miss Booth was herself surprised when she saw the effect of her own words. She came through the open door to where I stood and begged me to 'look at these men', asking 'What had I better say next?' I considered the effect on these officers of her just and courageous challenge so salutary that my advice was 'Go in and say the same words over again'." The courage and audacity of these two disconcerted the police not a little, but nevertheless the incident closed with the arrest and imprisonment of Catherine Booth. Since there was then no more to be done, Josephine went off to the Congress at The Hague.

This Congress showed in a remarkable way how great an advance the principles of Abolition had made on the Continent. Here in The Hague the meeting was held in a hall lent by the

Government. "The town was very gay, for the King opened Parliament in this hall on the morning of our opening meeting. As soon as this ceremony was over, we entered, amidst decorations of flowers and banners, and with the sound of the retiring military bands in our ears." The same cordial spirit was shown by the Ministers and Court throughout the Congress; the Queen herself was present at the opening service in the Cathedral and official receptions were given, at one of which the Admiral of the Fleet publicly declared his adherence to the cause. Josephine remarks: "It is pleasant when we think how any allusion to our work is still avoided and disliked in England, to find such a cordial welcome here, and so much respect and kindness from members of the legislature and of the King's household, as well as from the people generally." George Butler read a paper, giving "an account of the adhesion to our cause of the Non-Conformist Churches, who 'stood like a wall of stone', and to the gradual coming round to our side of many thousands of Anglican clergy". He was chosen too to make "the farewell complimentary speech". Then the Butlers returned to their home in Winchester.

Josephine now found some leisure for writing. Immediately, while her heart was still burning with anger, she wrote a vivid account of the persecution of the Salvation Army in Switzerland and the full story came out in 1883, which, considering that the funeral which made its climax only occurred in September of that year, proves that writers, publishers and printers worked more rapidly than is common today. The other book Josephine published in this year is the *Life of Oberlin*. This is a very different kind of book. The Salvation Army is full of the fighting spirit so usual in her. Oberlin shows the contrasting side of her rich personality, for Oberlin, like Catharine of Siena, combined, as Josephine herself did, the contemplative with the active life. He was the pastor of some scattered villages in the Vosges. He had lived through the French Revolution, had been condemned to the guillotine for ignoring Robespierre's order that all worship of God must cease and had been saved from execution only by the timely death of Robespierre. He had found his parishioners wild, uncivilised and primitive; he had changed the countryside by introducing sound methods of agriculture. His intelligent application of science in this direction at once appealed to John Grey's daughter. In his enthusiasm for the land, his patient endeavour to teach the ignorant and boorish and to raise their physical and moral conditions, Josephine saw her own father again. But Oberlin was dealing with much less advanced people than the Northumbrians and he had to do himself all the things he wished them to learn to do. With his own hands he built the bridge across the river and made roads so that intercourse between one village and another should be made possible. He ploughed, he sowed and in time he reaped abundantly the trust and affection of his flock—as well as a material harvest. But all this beneficent activity was but the outward expression of an intense inner life. Oberlin spent hours in his little house in contemplation and intercession for his people, at which times none, as a rule, was permitted to interrupt him. These hours came to be known to all his parishioners, and it was usual for carters or labourers, returning from the field with talk and laughter, to uncover their heads as they passed beneath the wall of his house. If the children ran too noisily, these working people would check them with uplifted finger, and say "Hush! He is praying for us." Josephine enjoyed writing this book. It took her mind off the complexities of the present, back to the themes she had heard her father expounding in the easier uncomplicated Northumbrian days, and her courage was renewed by studying this simple man of prayer, "whose ways were ways of quietness and all his paths were peace".

As always with Josephine, the writing went on side by side with her social work. When the Butlers first came to Winchester it was a prescribed area. The passing of Stansfeld's resolution in the following April aroused the same alarm as it did in the other prescribed areas and every sort of outrage and disorder was foretold by Regulationists. Josephine had heard far too much of that sort of talk to be moved by it. But other people were more disturbed and Vigilance Societies and others constantly complained of the state of the streets and urged authority to do something about it. An attempt was made in this direction by the introduction of a Bill amending Acland's Vagrant Act of 1824. This amendment proposed to give the right to the local police, on the appeal of a fixed number of householders in any district, to declare a street or streets to be a "closed" area and made liable to arrest any who "loitered" there. Some Abolitionists and many Vigilance Societies were prepared to support this Bill, feeling that the rights of the individual were safeguarded by the provision that the police could take action only after residents had appealed to them to do so. Josephine would have none of it. She remembered the beautifully clean streets of Geneva—and the horrors that went on behind closed doors, and she shuddered. She felt the danger of putting undue power in the hands of the police and of penalising women without doing anything really to safeguard the innocent. This, she thought, was only an attempt to re-introduce the C.D. Acts in a different guise. In her opinion such legislation could be justified only if it was perfectly clear that it would apply with absolute equality to men and women and that it would give the police no power to arrest anyone except on a clearly defined charge. These two conditions are perhaps still an essential safeguard.

Some years later the Vigilance Societies again appealed to Josephine on a different issue. This concerned a question of licensing a Promenade in a theatre, admittedly used as a convenient place for making assignations. Her reply gives her principles as clearly as possible:

"The principle of the Federation has always been to let individuals alone, not to pursue them with any outward punishment, nor drive them *out of any place* so long as they behave decently, but to attack *organised prostitution*, that is when a third party, actuated by the desire of making money, sets up a house in which women are sold to men, or keeps any place for his own gain which is a market of vice."

This, she said, was the position here and it constituted an official recognition and a tacit encouragement of the traffic in women.

When they were in Neuchâtel in 1883 Josephine had invited

Amélie Humbert to come back to live with them in Winchester and to help in her work. Amélie eagerly embraced the opportunity. She acted partly as Josephine's secretary, but she also undertook visiting, and when she found a girl sorely in need of both spiritual and physical help, Josephine regarded this as a direction from the Almighty to open a house, where it would be possible to give something beyond the medical treatment offered by a hospital. "In a short time," said Amélie, "we found a house and a good matron, and many girls came. During the first year, from February 1884 till April 1885, we received 40 sick women at the House of Rest. Many recovered and were placed in good situations or returned to their parents." This Home of Rest was a great source of happiness to both Butlers, who spent much time with the inmates.

One of the unhappy women sent here was Rebecca Jarrett. Mrs. Booth sent her. She had had a lurid past and had gone from being a prostitute to becoming a brothel keeper. She was very ill when Mrs. Booth found her in London; she had become a heavy drinker and was altogether in a wretched state. Mrs. Booth had cared for her and converted her. Rebecca really wished to make a break with her past and Mrs. Booth sent her to the Butlers' Home of Rest, knowing that Josephine was more likely than anyone to be able to help her. When Rebecca was sufficiently recovered to leave the Home, Josephine was convinced that she was ready and able to help in the work of reclaiming others. There is no doubt that she had a great gift of winning people; it came from an unusual capacity to love the seemingly unlovable. Josephine was determined not to lose so valuable a helper and she and her husband bought a little cottage, which they called Hope Cottage, not far from the Home, and there they established Rebecca who, from that point of vantage, went out to the most difficult and dangerous spots to bring girls back to a reasonable way of life. Sometimes she brought them back to the cottage and kept them with her till she thought they were fit to leave. The work flourished and she even undertook a mission to Portsmouth which met with considerable success.

Rebecca's inside knowledge of all that went on in such places was no doubt a help.

At Westminster the Criminal Law Amendment Bill got no farther. In 1883, '84 and '85 it passed the Lords but each time it came to the House of Commons it was talked out or dropped. This became intolerable to those who had the imagination to realise that every month they delayed, hundreds of little girls were being bought or stolen and sold for the profit of brothel keepers at home and abroad. Benjamin Scott was sure that if people could be convinced of what was going on among their own countrymen, they would not be able to endure its continuance. First his City of London Committee instigated proceedings against a notorious procuress, a Mrs. Jeffries, who ran several houses in Chelsea for the benefit of what she described as "clients and patrons of the highest social order". The Committee appointed as investigator an Inspector Minahan, whose independence of mind had previously so inconvenienced Scotland Yard that he had been retired from that body. His investigations were considerably assisted by the fact that a letter, intended for Mrs. Jeffries, and delivered instead to a blameless Miss Jeffries of Chelsea, had come into his hands. The writer, a foreign magnate, asked to have a little girl forwarded to him, adding that he had been recommended to apply by the King of the Belgians. On Minahan's report, and in spite of the reluctance of higher police officials, the Committee succeeded at last in getting a warrant against Mrs. Jeffries, charging her with keeping a disorderly house. Mrs. Jeffries arrived in Court in a magnificent carriage, escorted by four Guards officers, and when reporters eagerly thronged round to ask her questions, she replied loftily that, because of the position of her clients, she was in no difficulty. This proved to be a just estimate of the situation, for after consultation between magistrate and counsel, a pre-arranged plea of guilty was made, and she got off with a fine—no evidence being taken in Court and practically no report being published in the Press. She went back to business as usual, and the episode added fuel to Josephine's disgust with the licentiousness she had long known to exist among the upper classes. "If the corruption of our aristocracy were fully known, I think it would hasten republicanism among us", she wrote. Benjamin Scott was left with the question—how could the true facts be brought home to a public more than usually unwilling to be made aware of something it disliked?

Benjamin Scott first consulted Josephine and then in 1885, when the Criminal Law Amendment Bill again hung fire, together they approached Stead. At this time W. T. Stead was a remarkable journalist. He was perhaps the inventor of "newspaper stunts". Like Lord Northcliffe at a later date, he had the instinct to recognise in any incident its potential news value, and also the power to exploit it to the utmost. Let it be said also that he was a man of sound principle, who hated injustice; and that the "sensations" he made, though sometimes in doubtful taste, were always designed to promote what he believed to be right-eousness. Scott put the situation to him. Stead did not believe it possible that small girls of thirteen and under were being sold. The story runs that he exclaimed "It can't be true, it would raise Hell", to which Scott replied "It doesn't even rouse the neighbours". Stead answered grimly "Well, it shall". First he must satisfy himself from his own knowledge that the thing was true. He made what he called a "Secret Commission," consisting of himself and some of his staff, and having consulted Howard Vincent, recently retired from Scotland Yard, and social workers who knew the conditions, they made "an actual pilgrimage into a real hell". They came out sick, but utterly convinced. Now came the question of getting the facts across to the public. Stead took a dangerous step. He determined he would prove how easy it was to procure and sell a child. He turned to Josephine. Could she help him by buying a little girl for him? With horror in her heart Josephine asked Rebecca if she would undertake this part of the job. Rebecca of course could do it, as a person of well-known respectability could not; she was known as a brothel keeper; anyone who sold her a child did so without any illusions. She agreed to do the work, though dreading renewed contact with her old companions in vice. The child, Eliza Armstrong, was bought from her mother for £5 and was handed over to Stead; he took her to a brothel and left her there, under careful protection, for the night. Next day he took her to a nursing home where a reputable surgeon examined her. This part of the thing he did without consulting Josephine, who would never have approved. He then took the child to Victoria Station and handed her over to a woman, actually a trustworthy member of the Salvation Army, but to the eye of the observer just an ordinary traveller, and then she was put into a safe lodging in Paris, again under the protection of the Salvation Army. Stead had thus proved that there was no difficulty whatever in buying a child, using her as one would, sending her abroad and settling her in a brothel or an apartment in Paris or anywhere else.

The agony of mind in which Josephine lived throughout this period may well be imagined. Scott Holland has left a picture of it in his *Recollections*. The day he saw her was immediately before the publication of Stead's narrative—he was going up Holborn when "a face looked at me out of a hurrying hansom, which arrested and frightened me. It was framed on pure and beautiful lines; but it was smitten and bitten into as by some East wind that blighted it into grey sadness. It had seen that which took all colour and joy out of it . . . Shortly after, all European civilisation shook with the horror of Mr. Stead's disclosures. . . . I knew I had seen Mrs. Butler in the thick of that terrible work she had under-taken for God. She was passing through her martyrdom. The splendid beauty of her face, so spiritual in its high and clear out-lines, bore the mark of that death upon it to which she stood daily and hourly committed. There was no hell on earth into which she would not willingly travel if, by sacrificing herself she could reach a hand of help to those poor children whom nothing short of such a sacrifice could touch. The sorrow of it passed into her being. She had the look of the world's grim tragedies in her eyes. She had dared to take the measure of the black infamy of sin; and the terrible knowledge had left its cruel mark upon a soul of strange and singular purity."

On Saturday, July 4th, a leader in the *Pall Mall Gazette* warned readers that if they were sensitive it would be better for them not to read the articles which were to follow. Then on Monday, July 6th, the first part of Stead's narrative, "The Maiden Tribute of Modern Babylon", came out. This was followed by further articles on Tuesday, Wednesday and Friday of that week, giving a detailed account of all the horrors he had witnessed. These are altogether nauseating and since there is no particular point in rousing indignation against those long since dead, it is not necessary to retail them here. Stead had rightly estimated the effect that his revelations would produce. The Liberal Government had fallen on June 8th and the Conservatives were in office with Lord Salisbury as Premier. The Conservatives had been more hostile to all amendment of Criminal Law than the Liberals had been, but now they could not withstand the force of public opinion. On July 9th the second reading of the Criminal Law Amendment Bill passed the Commons and a Committee was appointed to investigate the accuracy of the conclusions of Stead's Secret Commission. While they were enquiring, there were demonstrations in Hyde Park and elsewhere and petitions poured into the House. The Committee found all Stead's accusations substantiated by the evidence and the last stages of the Bill were rushed through Parliament. It received the Royal Assent on August 14th, 1885.

With a sense of relief Josephine went off with George to Switzerland. She badly needed a rest, but she was not destined to enjoy it for long. In September she was summoned home to the help of Rebecca Jarrett. A new trouble had arisen. The Armstrong parents were well satisfied with their bargain; they were able to buy enough drink to lull them into a state of happy indifference as to Eliza's whereabouts—if indeed they had ever cared. It was not until their neighbours, proudly conscious of being in or near the centre of publicity, read in the papers that Mrs. Armstrong was a wronged mother, mourning over the loss of her daughter, that the trouble began. It struck the neighbours as a wonderful joke, and they so greatly derided Mrs. Armstrong that she drove her husband to the police to demand that her daughter should be restored to her. The police, smarting under Stead's strictures, were not slow to seize the opportunity offered to them. A detective, accompanied and somewhat embarrassed by a bibulous Armstrong, went to Paris to fetch Eliza. She came home a little reluctantly and proved quite useless to the police, for she had been in no way molested but spoke with enthusiasm of the kindness of those with whom she had been living. However, the police proceeded to arrest Rebecca Jarrett on a charge of abduction.

Stead was in Switzerland, but as soon as he heard of Rebecca's arrest he telegraphed, claiming that the whole responsibility was his. He at once came home to stand his trial. After stormy scenes at Bow Street Police Court, both Stead and Rebecca Jarrett were committed for trial at the Old Bailey on the charge of abducting a child from her home without the knowledge of her father. For Stead the result was a foregone conclusion. He had hoped he might be charged with slander, or some other offence which would have given him the opportunity of producing evidence for the truth of his statements. But this was by no means the intention of his prosecutors. At the beginning of the hearing the Judge ruled that Stead's motive was irrelevant; the sole point at issue being whether Mr. Armstrong had or had not known what was happening to his daughter. Rebecca had certainly bought Eliza from her mother, without reference to her father, and Stead had taken her without question. He was therefore condemned to three months' imprisonment. This was no disaster to Stead; indeed he himself said that his term in prison was nothing but a rest. His reputation was somewhat tarnished among the more conventional and his wife and family went through a time of social boycott. Bernard Shaw, no doubt, was not alone in his strictures when he wrote: "We backed him up over the Maiden Tribute, only to discover the Eliza Armstrong case was a put-up job of his", but those who regarded the whole thing as simply a "put-up job", an opportunity for self-advertisement, did Stead a cruel injustice. He genuinely suffered. Josephine paid a tribute to him. "That man," she said, "combines the deepest tenderness of a compassionate woman with the manly indignation and wrath of a man—a father, whose feelings are outraged by crimes committed against innocent maidens, the helpless and the young." Though Josephine never lost her conviction of Stead's disinterestedness in this matter, she later recognised in him a certain want of balance which made it impossible for her to follow him in all his enthusiasms. Stead himself was well content to have achieved his purpose. He had the mass of working men on his side and he had made it impossible for genuine ignorance about the White Slave Traffic to persist.

For Rebecca Jarrett the situation was very different and she sorely needed the support Josephine had come back to give her. Stead had nothing to conceal, he wished the whole world to know all that he knew. Rebecca on the other hand dreaded the publicity, lest she might betray those who had been her companions in vice. The Attorney-General, who was Counsel for the Prosecution, in order to discredit the whole transaction, burrowed into her past and cross-examined her on it. Rebecca, confused, frightened, ignorant, but determined not to betray old associates, lost her head, contradicted herself, perjured herself and altogether presented a sorry figure in the Court. She ought of course to have refused to answer any questions irrelevant to the case in hand, and this Josephine, who saw her between the two days of her examination, exhorted her to do. On the second day, when she was again cross-examined, comforted by the sight of Josephine in Court, she spoke firmly, telling the Attorney-General: "*You* forced the lie out of me; you make people tell lies." She received a sentence of a year's imprisonment. The papers, in reporting the case, expressed pity and contempt for Mrs. Butler, who had been so easily taken in, and who should have known the kind of woman Rebecca was. Josephine did not mind being pitied in such a cause, but she did resent the attitude of scorn towards Rebecca and at once wrote a pamphlet called *"Rebecca Jarrett"* which was published by the Salvation Army Press. In this she gave an account of Rebecca's life, not palliating her misdeeds but expressing unchanged confidence in her and admiration for her complete repudiation of her old way of life combined with her steadfast loyalty to old associates.

In the autumn following Stead's trial there was a General Election and Josephine issued *A Woman's Appeal to the Electors*, in the course of which she said:

"I would suggest that each candidate should be asked questions in some such form as the following:

(1) Will he vote for the total repeal of the C.D. Acts?

(2) Is he prepared to vote for a parliamentary enquiry into the reason why the prosecution of Mrs. Jeffries was dropped, and why Inspector Minahan was dismissed from the police force?

(3) Is he prepared to vote for, or to ask a question in Parliament on the subject of a parliamentary enquiry as to the circumstances which have induced the prosecution by the Treasury of Mr. Stead, Mr. Booth and their assistants, to whose labours the Criminal Law Amendment Act has been mainly due; while no prosecution has been undertaken by the Treasury against any single one of the real offenders, whose crimes these persons have done so much to expose?"

There is no means of knowing how many women were brave enough to put these questions.

CHAPTER FOURTEEN

GEORGE BUTLER'S LAST DAYS 1885—1890

"He made no noise, but what an individuality he had".
(Harriet Meuricoffre to J. B.)

AFTER the strain of the autumn, Josephine looked forward with more than common pleasure to the annual spring holiday. This year they were going to the Meuricoffre's at Naples. They went by way of Paris and Avignon. From Paris she wrote of the latest fashions, illustrating them by admirable marginal sketches, while from Avignon she wrote of Catharine of Siena and her mission to the Pope. Thence they went through Cannes and Genoa to Rome, and from Rome to Naples. Of this journey Josephine wrote: "My husband had never been on this line before; and as the name of every station brought up to him some classical and historical association, he became more and more interested and happy—so lively, indeed, that I could not, even if I had wished it, take a nap for five minutes; but I did not wish it. . . . We passed Signi, an old Tuscan town, anciently called Signium. My husband gave some lectures about it long ago at Oxford, when I drew for him a large, rough picture of the Cyclopean architecture of this very place. What mysterious people these Oscans were—so civilised and artistic, and yet we know so little about them. . . . The country from here to Naples is like a continuous garden of fruit crops and flowers, and gives one a pleasant feeling of great industry." At Naples they were on familiar ground; they revisited Pompeii and made delightful expeditions in every direction. George sketched happily at

Virgil's Tomb and wrote to his sons about the "perforations made by marine animals" in the columns of the Temple of Serapis, which temple "was first above the sea level, then below it, and now is some 40 feet above it". They walked and sketched and enjoyed all they saw, recalling that here "St. Paul first landed in Europe, a prisoner, on his way to Rome", and there was Capri, "the steep rock, whence Tiberius used to fling his slaves headlong into the sea, as an after-dinner amusement". As George talked, Josephine reflected: "He seemed to be completely transported into the old Greek world. . . . It was not the Latin and Roman associations which attracted him just then; for the most part they are not attractive, poisoned as they are by memories of the corrupt decadence of Imperial Rome. It was the spirits of the old Greeks which hovered about him there; all the most poetic associations being connected with the Greek colonisation of this part of Italy. . . . It was the words of Pindar rather than those of Virgil or Pliny which came into my husband's mind, and of which his memory was at all times tenacious. The whole scene was for him peopled with the shades of the classic past." As one reads the accounts of their holiday which Josephine sent to her sons and her sister, one cannot fail to realise how singularly blessed were those two travellers who could so completely enter into each other's minds and enjoy together so many literary and historical associations.

On April 10th Josephine wrote of "a delightful day at Pozzuoli, where Sir William Armstrong is establishing great ironworks for making ironclads for the Italian Government. He has sent out from England some forty or fifty picked men; they are all Northumbrians and choice men in every respect . . . tried and skilled workmen. Mr. Stephen Burrowes, my sister's helper in her work for the sailors, suggested that a Workmen's Rest or Home for our English workmen and others should be established at once at Pozzuoli." George was invited to dedicate this Home and a great party assembled and drove out there in open carriages. "Then we sang hymns, some of the old favourites of the English workmen. It was strange to hear those familiar songs, pronounced with the strong Northumbrian guttural, ascending from the ruins of the Temple of Serapis—blending of associations, past and present, heathen and Christian, ancient and modern. When the men found out that my sister and I were Northumbrians they could scarcely suppress their joy; and, after that, whenever she or I made a remark, however trivial, they cheered."

This party happened on April 9th. On the 20th they received a telegram saying that the Bill repealing the Contagious Diseases Acts had received the Royal Assent. This was a crowning mercy and Naples was bathed in a new glory. The weight of the C.D. Acts had oppressed Josephine for more than twenty years, and she had been actively engaged in efforts to remove them for the last seventeen. Now the weight was lifted and her spirits rose.

They had a delightful journey home through Florence, Bologna and Verona to Lucerne over the St. Gothard, where they "stood outside almost all the eight hours on the platform of the carriage . . . round and across the Lake of Lugano with glimpses of Como and Maggiore". George went back to Winchester from Lucerne, while Josephine went to Neuchâtel for a few days' work, and on June 1st she was at Boulogne, waiting for the Channel to calm down before she ventured on a crossing. It had been a wonderful holiday, perhaps the best she could remember since those early days when they were without anxieties. She was disappointed therefore, when she got home, to find George ill in bed; he appeared to have rheumatic fever and his heart was affected. The other Canons were most kind and gladly took over his duties. Josephine records the affectionate ministrations of Archdeacon Atkinson, who came every day to pray with her husband. Gradually his condition improved and the doctor recommended treatment in Hamburg. Thither they went therefore, but the weather was oppressively hot and they were advised to move on to Aix-la-Chapelle. But the weather was still too hot and they next moved to Grindelwald, where the mountain air seemed to do him good. At Grindelwald there was a new little English church. George had had some part in building it and had been grieved to be unable, owing to his illness, to take part in the consecration that June. He was therefore particularly happy to be well enough to celebrate the Sacrament there early in September. It was, however, only a very temporary improvement in his health and he was obliged by increasing rheumatic pains and fever to move to Berne.

The next weeks were full of anxiety. More than once he seemed to make progress only to relapse; there came a day when his son George, on the point of starting for India, was advised that he ought not to go, and went instead to join his mother in Berne. At another time Stuart and the other sons came from England. Through all this Josephine remained desperately calm. She had found the night nurse asleep at her post one night, and her husband shivering with insufficient bed covering. From that time Josephine stayed up with him all night and rested when she could find time during the day. George now had congestion of both lungs and an alarming heart condition; his doctors despaired of his life. One night, Josephine, feeling sure that there was nothing more she could do for her husband, went into the adjoining room and sat down, conscious only of exhaustion and despair. She describes the experience: "My own strength was failing and he was worse. Who would now minister to him, I asked? . . . It seemed at that moment that a voice came—or rather, I would say, a light shone—into the very heart of my darkness and despair. The promises of God in the Scriptures came to me as if I had heard them for the first time. . . . It seemed to become a very simple matter, and grace was given to me, in my pain and weakness, to say only 'Lord, I believe'. The burden was removed." She goes on to tell how, when the doctor came, he found the patient wonderfully better—well enough to be bundled off to Territet, since they feared the advent of snow at Berne. This was accomplished with the aid of Charles, who had been able to join his parents, with instructions that the patient was to be put to bed the instant he reached his destination. Josephine records, however, that the journey the doctor had regarded with so much anxiety proved beneficial rather than exhausting to the patient, and when they arrived "he had no idea of going to bed at once". Territet suited George and he steadily regained strength.

The Butlers got back to Winchester by Christmas and were able to resume their pleasant hospitable way of life. Catherine Booth stayed with them for a while and a more remarkable guest was Elisé Reclus, the great geographer, whom they had met in Switzerland. This man, Josephine says, was "not only a Communist, but a professed Anarchist; one of the most delightful men, nevertheless, that I ever conversed with". He turned up unexpectedly at Winchester immediately before the arrival of a dinner party including Arthur Shadwell and two or three clergy. There was no time to prepare these guests for the shock of meeting so revolutionary a character; the Butlers could only hope for the best and determine at least not to let Reclus fall into a *tête-à-tête* with one of the clergy, "a strong conservative and high churchman". To her horror, however, they eluded Josephine's vigilance and before dinner she found these very two in the library. "They seemed to be disputing warmly." With a sinking heart she approached, only to find their dispute was "concerning no more burning question than the comparative antiquity of Welsh and Breton poetry".

All through 1888 George seemed restored almost to his former health, interested in political matters, warmly supporting Home Rule for Ireland. He was able to visit many of his old friends, renewing intercourse with those of his undergraduate days. He stayed with Froude in Devonshire, and with Lord Coleridge, then Lord Chief Justice, in London, where he very much enjoyed a dinner party to which came Gladstone and John Morley and several others. Another time he went North and visited Tweedside friends.

In the autumn of the following year the Butlers went together to the Conference at Copenhagen. There is nothing unusual to record about this Conference; what made the visit to Denmark particularly interesting to them was the opportunity of studying the works of the sculptor, Thorwaldsen. George, who had recently resumed his writing, contributing articles to the *Edinburgh* and *Contemporary Reviews*, had been commissioned to write one on the Danish sculptor. With his characteristic thoroughness he spent many happy hours studying the works, making notes and sketches. Both found this very interesting, but the article was never published. Josephine found it—carefully written and scholarly, but still unfinished—among George's papers after his death. They had a happy day too at Elsinore as the guests of the Dean of Winchester and his wife, who were staying there with her mother. Then they went home. The sun was shining when they set sail, but the wind was rising and Josephine, knowing well her limitations as a seafarer, at once took to the cabin and remained prone, enduring as best she might the increasing violence of the wind. When, the ship being in dock, she got up and rejoined her husband, she was greatly disturbed at his appearance. He had remained on deck in the bitterly cold wind and looked chilled and pale. Josephine hurried him home and sent for the doctor, who confirmed her fears. This chill was the beginning of George's last illness. Josephine felt he never really recovered from its effects. He rallied this time and returned to the duties in the Cathedral which he so dearly loved; he had still eighteen months to live and for Josephine they were months of great happiness, though overshadowed by anxiety.

George Butler had made himself much loved during his years at Winchester. His gentleness and courtesy, his dignity, combined with a rare humility, captured all hearts and now his serene courage and unfailing patience deepened this love into reverence. He was universally known as "the dear Canon" and as he walked slowly and painfully across the Cathedral into the pulpit all eyes followed him with affectionate concern. Josephine was much touched by the kindness and sympathy extended to her. Her husband had periods of great pain and weakness, but at other times his wonderful constitution reasserted itself and he could enjoy walking and above all entertaining his friends. Many of them came to see him and as they talked his animation returned and he seemed like his old self. His first grandson was born in

1888 and this was an added joy to the household. At Christmas time that year Charles suddenly appeared, having heard in the Transvaal, where he was working, of his father's serious illness. This made the family complete and the Butlers were able to enjoy to the full three sons, a daughter-in-law and two grandchildren.

In the following autumn the doctor advised that Canon Butler should be taken south to avoid the cold weather. The Meuricoffres lent them their house at Capo di Monte, near Naples; and the journey was arranged by the kindness of many friends to be as easy as possible. Their son George took charge of them across the Channel, seeing them into their carriage *de luxe* at Calais. This, their last holiday, began delightfully. The weather was perfect and Canon Butler was sketching again and going for little walks. Watching him with loving eyes Josephine found herself almost beginning to believe that he would recover sufficiently to take his place in the Cathedral again. She knew really that this wish was father to the thought. They went from the Meuricoffres to Amalfi and were happy there, but a wave of influenza swept over the Continent. It was not to be expected that George should escape it. They did their best to keep him away from all possible contact, but in vain. He longed to get home, and as soon as he rallied sufficiently to make travelling possible, they started by slow stages for Winchester. At Cannes at the end of the year George received a letter from the Dean, asking if he was likely to be able to come into residence at the Cathedral again. George showed the letter to his doctor, who, with great gentleness and kindness, said quite certainly that he must not expect to be able to do any more. This was no more than an official confirmation of what they had really known for some time, but the spoken word seems to bring the inevitable nearer.

They got as far as London by February 1890, and when Josephine had settled George into bed in their hotel, she said to him encouragingly "We shall be home tomorrow." He was contented and smiled. But the next morning there was no greeting for her, and during the day he was only partly conscious. In the afternoon "appearing to feel he was going on a long journey, he

. . . took my hand and said rather anxiously 'You will go with me beloved, will you not? You will go with me?' The appeal went to my heart. . . . I answered without hesitation 'Yes, I will! *I will go with you*' for I knew my heart would follow him whither he was going and would dwell with him there."

GLOWING EMBERS

CHAPTER FIFTEEN

GENEVA AND ITALY 1891—1894

"The awful abundance of compassion in me is what makes me fierce".
(J. B.)

YEARS earlier, when George had had to return to his work, leaving Josephine in Switzerland, she had written to Hattie: "Except for the pain it would give to him, I always hope I may die first. For if he were to die and leave me, I do not say I could not live or work any more, but I fear I should fall into a state of chronic heartache and longing which would make me rather useless, and perhaps a weariness to others, who would never fully understand what and who I had lost." She did not, of course, react as she had feared. She faced her new life with courage, but the loss was as grievous as she had foreseen. For, with George's death, something of the perfect stability and balance which had characterised her, was lost. While George was waiting for her at home, even while she rattled over the Continent, she had known, with the lover in Donne's poem, the unity which makes two souls one—or

> "If they be two, they are two so
> As stiffe twin compasses are two
> Thy soule the fixt foot, makes no show
> To move, but doth, if the other doe.
>
> And though it in the centre sit,
> Yet when the other far doth rome,
> It leanes, and hearkens after it,
> And growes erect, as that comes home."

She had no longer his "firmness to draw her circle just", and the result was to be seen in a certain loss of steadiness in judgment. Now her husband was no longer there she was restless as she had never been before; she used her journeys to escape from her loneliness. A note of acerbity creeps into her criticisms of her colleagues; she finds the official voice of *The Shield* and the careful utterances of committees more irritating, and she speaks of someone as "the kind of man whom one is justified in asking the Lord to remove". Even the men with whom she had always had such easy and happy relations, even such old and trusted friends as Wilson and Stuart, fall short of her expectations. It is possible to exaggerate this change; she was, after all, growing old. She was to live, a widow, for sixteen years—years which were filled with great mental and physical activity. She had still domestic claims; her children and grandchildren knew they could always turn to her and count on her; her sisters, too, often needed her, but most of her time, thought and energy was devoted to the cause she had so long served. It was a constant struggle against ill health; she kept breaking down, but she had the will to live as long as she could see work to do and there was no lack of this.

The beloved house in the Close must be vacated and some plan made about her future dwelling. Her two older sons were eager to offer her a home with them; the youngest, Charles, was working in South Africa. Stanley was married and was established with his wife and two children. Josephine was devoted to her children and grandchildren and was most ready to go and stay with them —especially if there was a crisis of illness or anything else in which she could help, but no woman who has managed her own home will willingly live as a guest in another's. George, however, was unmarried and though Josephine was sure she must ultimately have some place of her own, she was glad to look after his home in Wimbledon for a time. Later, when he married, she moved to a house in Balham; and later still, when George and his wife settled in the North, she had rooms in the village of Wooler.

Wherever her headquarters, she was much away from them,

travelling, as of old, all over Europe visiting the offices of the International Federation. Besides travelling, she wrote extensively for the movement. The only book not exclusively concerned with it was her memoir of her husband George Butler. It is a moving book, a mine of valuable material rather than a well-constructed biography. Josephine wrote from a full heart; her memories tumble out, warm and living. All George had told her of his boyhood and school days, of his aspirations in early manhood, the experiences they had shared, the fun, the work, the toil and the sorrows are all here vivid and vital, and if the sequence is sometimes a little difficult to follow, because some incident has renewed in the writer's mind some memory belonging to quite a different period, there is a compensating freshness and warmth in the narrative. One of her sons remarked to her that this book, which she was then writing, could hardly fail to be an autobiography, since their lives were so closely linked—and this is true and makes the book the more valuable. It is rich in sketches of incidents, of places and of people—the Meuricoffres, James Stuart, the Humberts and many another of her foreign friends and colleagues. And it is, of course, the only authentic portrait of George that exists, for he has had less than justice done to him, outside these pages. The book shows that the work they did was emphatically *their* work rather than hers or his, and it was no doubt in part her experience of a perfect marriage that made Josephine see so clearly that all fruitful social work must be undertaken by men and women together. The other women fighting for their rights proclaimed loudly their equality with men; she alone proclaimed the mutual dependence of the sexes.

Josephine found the physical act of writing very tiring, but she thoroughly enjoyed the mental activity involved and even while she was engaged in writing the *Memoir*, she was also bringing out a quarterly paper called *The Dawn*. She had begun this before her husband's death. When the C.D. Acts were repealed in 1886 the National Association for Repeal, feeling that its work was accomplished, wound up its affairs, and while it appointed a

Committee affiliated to the International Federation, to keep in touch with developments on the Continent, it closed down its English office and ceased to exist. Though at that moment Josephine was anxiously looking after her husband, she had managed to get up to London for one day in order to exhort the Ladies' National Association not to follow this example. She was fully convinced that, though under pressure of public opinion Parliament had repealed the Acts, there remained a considerable body of the unconverted who would gladly reintroduce the system, perhaps in some slightly different form. She felt therefore that the L.N.A. must remain in being and must be ever vigilant. Soon after this, in 1888, when George appeared almost to have returned to normal health, she conceived the idea that some sort of periodical to keep all Abolitionists informed as to the progress of the work all over the world would be useful. *The Dawn* appeared for the first time in May 1888 and thereafter more or less quarterly for eight years. It was entirely Josephine's venture. She wrote a great deal of it and for the rest she collected the material from all over the world, carried on a correspondence with agents everywhere and printed the reports they sent her.

None of the European reports gave Josephine as much concern as those that dealt with India. The laws prevailing there were the responsibility of the British Government and therefore of every English citizen. It was a responsibility she took seriously. Every number of *The Dawn* carries some reference to India and her concern to abolish Regulation there overshadowed the whole of the rest of her life. For the sake of clarity, her contribution to the struggle in India is here dealt with after the history of her work in Europe.

The Dawn of April 1891 records one very remarkable adventure in which Josephine was involved within a year of her widowhood, "the most sustained and severe conflict I have ever had, in all the past 21 years, with the powers of evil". When she had got out of Winchester and established herself in her son George's house, she found herself very tired and determined to go to Switzerland and rest. While she was at Serrières, sitting over her small fire, tired and dispirited and conscious of her loneliness, according to her habit she gave herself to prayer and "again and again" she says, "the thought came to me of 'Geneva', there is something to be done in Geneva, that central city of Europe, so full of intellectual light and of moral corruption. It was almost like a voice that came down the chimney, which said 'Geneva' again and again!"

She went at once to Geneva, which seemed perfectly peaceful, but on the day after her arrival, going to see Minod, the Secretary of the Federation, she found herself the confidante of a group of outraged parents. A notorious libertine of Geneva had lured four or five little girls into his house, enticing them with sweets, and had then assaulted them. The parents had lodged a complaint, but by the Genevese Constitution every charge was examined by the Juge d'Instruction before being sent forward for trial. In this case the Juge d'Instruction—himself a man of dubious character—had confronted the children with their assailant, who in the interval had shaved off his beard, so that his appearance was altered, and who was arranged to sit with his back to the light. The children, naturally enough confused and frightened, were unable positively to identify him. The Procureur Général therefore declared the complaint *non lieu*, that is, there was no case to go for trial, and the parents in despair came for help to the Federation Office. This was too much for Josephine, and as her son Stanley said, "Mother saw the Devil triumphant and she *went for him!*" "Yes I did," says Josephine. "The whole town was roused! The iniquity itself was even less terrible, to my mind, than the cowardice and shameful injustice of the magistrates who, after a mock enquiry, pronounced this man to be innocent, white as snow! . . . One father said to me 'Could we not, at least, Madam, make a little noise?' I said 'Yes, we *will* make a noise.' "
She proceeded to make it, with the help of Mme. de Gingins, who made her house into a hall for meetings, turning out her own furniture and replacing it by hired chairs. They organised meeting after meeting, and a house to house canvass, which at least contributed to the "noise" and prevented the householders from continuing blandly ignorant.

"Never at any Congress," says Josephine, "have I ever worked so hard; and I was without the help of any of my old dear English allies. I was the only English person there, carrying on all the argument and all the battle in a foreign tongue." The demand they made was the reform of the constitution which should make it impossible that a case should be dismissed on the authority of one man, from whose decision there was no appeal. This was disheartening work, as Josephine found many of the substantial citizens of Geneva "disavowed any responsibility in regard to legislative reforms. 'We are not advocates' some of them repeated, 'we are simple citizens and know nothing of law. It is not for us to suggest to the Grand Council any change of the laws etc.' It might have been asked—how then are laws made? How are they unmade or reformed, in all countries? It is a fatal mistake, and the Genevese people will, it is to be hoped, find it out in time, to fall into the habit of leaving everything that concerns the Government, the Legislature, the Administration of Justice, and consequently the welfare of the people at large, in the hands of experts, political, legal or medical, as the case may be. This is the tendency, evidently, in some modern cities at the present time. No community can be morally or politically healthy in which the citizens take but a languid interest in public matters."

Before she left Geneva, Josephine wrote her mind to the Procureur Général. In the course of a long letter she says: "I am aware, Sir, that you, acting on the report made to you by the Juge d'Instruction, believed it to be your duty to pronounce this *non lieu*. I must believe you did it with regret. I have heard your name pronounced as that of an honourable man, and it is this which strengthens the impulse I have to write to you with absolute frankness." After affirming that it was she who encouraged the parents to resort to publicity she finishes: "I trust you see, Sir, the motives which have induced me to write to you, to convey to you the ardent desire that I have to see you come forward publicly as the advocate of justice and the defender of the weak against the violence and fraud of the strong. ... In this matter and in regard to my communication with you, I have taken no counsel whatever with anyone, and no one is aware that I now write to you." There is no evidence to show what the Procureur Général thought privately of this letter, though an appeal to a conscience which has been stifled must be disturbing. It is not surprising to learn that his public reactions were somewhat unfavourable. Josephine wrote from Neuchâtel, February 11th, 1891: "It seems the Procureur Général of Geneva is much displeased. He thinks I instigated the working men to protest. I did not, but I am glad to share the responsibility. Our legal friends are examining the probability of the Procureur prosecuting me. I think it not *possible*, though if it were not winter and I were not so suffering and tired, I would not mind going to prison, but I would not like the Federation to have to pay a heavy fine for me. How annoyed they would be! I should never be trusted by Mr. Stuart again, who has much Scotch caution! I hope this suspense will soon be over." From Geneva she went back to Neuchâtel, where she was cheered to find the work of the Federation going well and she addressed several encouraging meetings before she went home to her son George at Wimbledon. Considering the long strain of her husband's illness and all that she had done since, it was obvious that what she now needed was a real rest. She contemplated "a quiet, peaceful, decrepit visit" to Bristol, but she had reached the stage when it was impossible to stop.

She received an invitation to address a woman's suffrage meeting at the City Temple. This could not be refused. That cause had been dear to her since her early married days, for she was convinced that justice demanded that women should have the right, with men, to determine who should legislate for them. As early as 1855 she wrote a paper, which after the imposition of the Contagious Diseases Acts seemed like a prophecy: "I said (not knowing what I said) that some awful form of slavery was in store for women, and the yoke would be fastened on us because we are not represented." In 1872 she wrote to Wilson, "Do you know that the *publicans* sent out a strong whip the day before the Women's Suffrage Debate to get M.P.s in that interest to attend and vote *against us*? It is significant of the fear they have lest *temperance and chastity* should be forced upon their Honourable House by the influence of women." In June 1873 she noted that "Egerton Leigh said in his speech on C.D. Acts how needful it was to have this system extended *'before women* are represented in this House!' If I were not working for Repeal," she said, "I would throw my whole force into getting the suffrage." When, in the same year, Trevelyan was advocating the extension of the franchise to agricultural labourers, she had written: "Every argument in this applies equally to women, and yet not a word about *us*, and 'our interests being trampled upon', because *we* are unrepresented. I feel more keenly than I ever did the great importance of our having votes *as a means* of self-preservation. We cannot *always* depend on the self-sacrificing efforts of noble men ... to right our wrongs, and now that the labourers are going to be enfranchised, our case becomes *the worse*; we shall be utterly swamped and lost, if we have no representation, if we become (though more than half the nation) the one unrepresented section under a Government which will become more and more extended, more popular, more democratic and yet *wholly masculine*. Woe is me! That people cannot see it!" Through the strenuous years of her main crusade she had no time to throw herself into the Women's Suffrage Campaign, but she was always taking note of it and continually speaking of it. She was for a time hesitant about writing of it in the organs of the Federation, since she knew some members were opposed to giving the suffrage to women, but in 1892 she wrote in *The Dawn*: "I know that our Federation is not unanimous on the subject of Women's Suffrage. We should not, however, esteem each other very highly, if we sacrificed our independence of judgment, in combining for a great and definite moral aim. I am impelled to confess that every year deepens my conviction of the injustice of denying to women the right of direct representation under a Representative Government."

How valuable Josephine's contribution to the Women's Suffrage Movement might have been is well illustrated by an incident reported in a local paper from a Diocesan meeting. It was affirmed by "more than one speaker, that it was absolutely useless for the clergy to attempt to upset what Mrs. Josephine Butler had done, for she was 'perfectly invincible'." On which the Editor comments, "To confess to being hopelessly defeated by a woman in a cause in which you think she is in the wrong, does not strike one as a very manly proceeding." After this, can it be doubted that, had she not been diverted from this question to that of abolition, it would not have taken a major European war to secure votes for women?

All through 1891 Josephine was working very hard for the International Conference, which was to be held that year in Brussels. She was concerned to raise money to enable the L.N.A. to send delegates who could not afford otherwise to go, and she was touched by the generosity of many of the impecunious who were always ready to squeeze their purses to help again. She went to the Conference and came back with much material for *The Dawn*, but she had tried Brother Ass too severely. In the October issue of the paper we read: "It is with regret found necessary to give notice that Mrs. Josephine Butler took ill after her return from Brussels. In the doctor's opinion it would be a very great risk ... for her to speak at or attend any meetings during the coming winter." There followed a long period of distressing illness. Through the autumn, while she was absolutely forbidden to go about, she was not prevented from work at home, and being incapable of idleness, she was still corresponding, arranging for the publication of her *Memoir of George Butler*, bringing out *The Dawn* in December 1891. She struggled through Christmas, but then she succumbed to the prevailing influenza. It seems not to have been recognised at first for what it was, and weeks of acute anxiety followed. A consultant—a Northumbrian —called in by her son, declared: "It is just a marvel she is living ... with those lungs most people would have been swept off at once." He said to her: "You ought to be dead you know, but your state is hopeful now." Recovery was necessarily slow and she suffered that darkness of spirit which from time to time came upon her. There was no *Dawn* in March 1892, but when the warmer weather came she was over the worst and she brought out a number in July, after which she went for a recuperative holiday in Switzerland.

This holiday began with a visit to the Humberts in Neuchâtel. The Humbert household was no longer the cheerful place it once had been. Mme. Humbert had died some years previously and Humbert himself had had a stroke. Josephine was shocked to find him "an infirm, restless old man". She wrote of this visit to James Stuart "I took pains—*great* pains to arouse him, and I talked to him every day, about politics, literature, etc.—until he became quite his old self again. . . . The fact is, the complete putting off of his harness had nearly killed him." As a result of this renewed animation, M. Humbert "brought to me one day fourteen bound volumes of letters dating from 1875 to 1887, arranged by date, with an index made by himself. Many of my letters, of yours, Stansfeld's and other people's. . . . Then I found also in his study large bundles of arranged extracts from newspapers and all sorts of things." The sight of all this well-ordered material inspired in Josephine a wish to fulfil a request that had often been made to her by Stuart and others that she should write an account of her crusade. This she proceeded to do.

Personal Reminiscences of a Great Crusade occupied all her scanty leisure for the next few years and was published in 1896. It is less readable than many of her works, partly because it contains so many details robbed of interest by lapse of years and because it was written at odd moments as she could spare time. It has not the lucidity of her earlier works nor are the facts recorded always consistent with those set down contemporaneously in *The Shield*. It is, however, full of good things. The adventures at Colchester and Pontefract, in which she herself played the principal part, are written with her usual gusto and it remains the only full account of the movement for Abolition between 1869 and 1886.

In November 1893 reports from the Federation in Italy were disquieting and Josephine was asked to go there to see what could be done to forward its work. The letters to her sons, for the perusal of friends and supporters at home, and the reports in *The Dawn* describing this visit to Italy are full of interest and most revealing of her personality and of the extraordinary position she occupied in the minds of the leading actors in the Italian drama. After the Congress at Genoa in 1880 the prospects had seemed promising. On Giuseppe Nathan's death, the work had been taken up by his brother Ernest, a great deal of propaganda had been done and as a result a Commission had been appointed to enquire into the whole system of Regulation. The report of this Commission produced after most careful work, entirely condemned the system, and was at once suppressed. As Josephine writes: "The whole edition of 700 copies was purposely and deliberately *buried* in a dark cellar of the Ministry of the Interior. ... Such are the tricks of which people interested in the maintenance of old, bad systems and opposed to reformation are capable!" Owing to the researches of Nathan and the Federation, a copy of the report was unearthed and brought to the notice of Tommasi-Crudeli, who raised the subject in the Chambers, and having reprinted the report, submitted it to Crispi, Minister of the Interior. Crispi thereupon made further investigation, and being partially convinced, in 1888 initiated legislation on the subject. This legislation, though a move in the right direction, had not satisfied Abolitionists, for it had compromised with the system instead of abolishing it. However, since in fact it had been shelved and had become a dead letter, its defects were unimportant.

When Josephine reached Italy she found the country in a much disturbed state. It was facing a severe financial crisis. There had been banking scandals in which members of the Government were involved; the Treasury was depleted, the currency devalued; unemployment was serious and the general poverty, especially in Sicily and the South, deplorable. Josephine had of course come with many introductions from England. She had stopped on her way out in Florence and had taken counsel from old friends there, who had also given her introductions. She had a curious correspondence with the Archbishop of Trebizonde, to whom she had an introduction from Lord Ripon, and to whom she sent copies of various other letters. He replied: "You will do nothing in Rome. The Holy Father (the deposed Ruler) has no power to do anything, and you can expect nothing from the present Government when you look at *what they are*." Josephine adds "That is a *decided* opinion anyhow." She comments regretfully on the impotence of a man who calls himself the successor of St. Peter, who "only a poor fisherman, being filled with the Spirit of God, swayed great multitudes", and she wrote to the Archbishop that it was to her "a sad and perplexing sight to see the Church and the spiritual fathers standing aside, and refusing to touch a great moral question because others, whom they deemed unworthy (Liberal politicians) had had the courage to touch it".

Undeterred by the Archbishop's prognostications, and following the advice of her friends, when she reached Rome she set herself "to knock first at the door of the Vatican". In the Chamber, the friends of Abolition were chiefly to be found on the Left —the Liberal—side, but were not strong enough to carry any measure themselves without support from the Right. These latter Conservatives—many of them related to Cardinals and other important Churchmen, might well be influenced by a pronouncement from the Pope. Josephine carried with her letters from Cardinal Vaughan, Cardinal Manning and others, but she says, "I found it an advantage to go about the business allotted to me merely as a humble individual, not delegated by any Association or League, and having no earthly rank or dignity. In conversation, and more especially on any difficult or controversial point, my weakness was my strength, my solitariness a host to me; and I felt it an advantage to present my appeals simply as a woman, and even as a heretic! As a woman I could say all I pleased; and I must confess I was patiently heard, and in some cases with real and touching sympathy."

Though she started by knocking at the Papal door, she did not spare the doors of the State. She was invited to dine at Senator Tommasi-Crudeli's house to meet some old Garibaldians. One of the party was Count Passolini, the son of one of Garibaldi's comrades who had been greatly interested in Josephine's life of her father John Grey, which he had insisted on having translated into Italian. Josephine's heart was warmed when he said to her: "My father used to say to me, 'If I could only meet that lady, John Grey's daughter, how much I should like it. I have so much to ask her.' " "But," she adds, "I fear he might have puzzled me if he had gone very deep into land questions." After dinner, when others came in, some of them just returned from Sicily, she "learned to understand what the older patriots feel now—they who went through that period of high aspirations and hopes and who fought and laboured and suffered in order to bring in the new order of things and a new national life. They saw Southern Italy set free from the crushing rule of the Spanish Kings and they saw also the Papal Estates freed and made a part of United Italy and the capital fixed in Rome. And now, through misrule, and the want of political education of the people, through accidents, one may say, of many kinds, and through the want of religious faith, the country has gone down, down, until now fair young 'Italia Una', their ideal and idol, stands on the brink of bankruptcy, political, financial and moral."

Josephine's function was always to encourage the down-hearted, and as her host grew more and more stricken with misery at all the reports of corruption and ruin she ventured to remind him of Varro, of ancient Rome, who was publicly thanked by the citizens, after a time of trouble, because *he had not despaired* of the Republic. Tommasi only answered 'But Varro had more reason to hope than we have.' However I don't think he is *set against hope*. He comes to see me often. It is rather affecting to see him sitting in my one armchair, waiting wistfully for some words of hope."

The opinion of the Senators, as of Aicardi, the Pope's legal adviser, was that a solution might be found by attacking Regulation on economic grounds. In the extreme poverty of the country it was difficult to justify the expenditure of vast sums of money on a system of control against which "many of the Syndics (Mayors) of their districts have sent remonstrances . . .

as 'degrading to all who administer it'; and which most of the doctors throughout Italy know to be a failure and a fraud. (Some who are salaried in connection with it no doubt abstain from expressing an opinion.)" This was the difficulty. Here as elsewhere the *vested* interest in the system was very strong. An immense and ever-increasing number of administrators depended on it, for Parkinson's Law, though not yet formulated, was working in a constant multiplication of salaried officials and their assistants, and these would resist Abolition to the last.

In the hope of getting some definite pronouncement from the Vatican, Josephine was advised to see Père Rousseau who was "Visitor of the Regular Canons of the Lateran, and preacher of the Lateran Apostolic Mission—a French order which has branches all over the world, with its centre here in Rome. . . . His ideas are larger and more liberal than those of the Cardinals generally." On receiving a letter from Josephine, Père Rousseau at once waited upon her and they met many times, discussing many subjects, including St. Catharine of Siena. They were mutually impressed. Neither had any doubt of the good faith of the other; the priest said plainly to her that he would pray for her to become a Catholic—her heart "would be so comforted by the Sacrament". Josephine replied, "But I have the Sacrament in my Church." He said: "Ah! but you have not there the *real presence* of the Saviour." She replied: "Pardon me, Father, I think I have often been conscious of the real presence of my Saviour, in receiving the Sacrament." "He looked at me," said Josephine, "with a kind, wondering expression". He did not move her in this respect, but he did make the position of the Papacy clear in the matter of Regulation. If the Pope were, as he ought to be, the head of the Government, the whole system would be swept away instantly, but, since the civil authority had deposed him and he was a prisoner in the Vatican, he could take no part in a political movement. Josephine perceived the dilemma. The conclusion seemed to be that if the Pope was to speak at all, it must be not to Catholics in Italy alone, but to the whole Roman Catholic Church. To this end Josephine was advised to write herself to "known and estcemed Catholic dignitaries in several countries", in order that they might *ask* for a pronouncement from the Pope, which would then clearly have an international character and could not be interpreted as interference in Italian politics. Père Rousseau and others were very anxious that she should personally plead the cause with Leo XIII, who was known to be sincerely anxious for Abolition. To this, not without certain Protestant misgivings, she agreed and the audience was arranged.

While she was working hard and waiting for the appointed day to come, she was struck down with a malignant form of malaria. The attack was both sudden and severe, complications ensued and she became desperately ill. Her friends in Rome engaged two nurses to look after her in the hotel and summoned her son, George. Hattie came from Naples and for some time she was acutely and most painfully ill. Gradually, however, her will to live re-asserted itself and she slowly crept back to life. She was moved to Frascati and then to Naples, where health gradually returned. Meanwhile the work fell into the able hands of Agnes McLaren, a Roman Catholic friend of Josephine, a doctor and a convinced Abolitionist. The result was very happy, for in 1895 Cardinal Vaughan reported to her that Leo XIII had made up his mind to issue the Encyclical which Josephine had so much desired. She had the satisfaction of knowing that her arduous winter had not been in vain.

CHAPTER SIXTEEN

COLMAR AND GENEVA 1895—1897

"Every death of person or thing which is good is followed by resurrection". (J. B.)

JOSEPHINE reported cheerfully to the Conference of the Federation which met in London in July 1894. She was not sanguine enough to believe that Abolition on the Continent was in sight, but she felt that public condemnation of it by the Pope was an important advance and that the stirring of indignation among the masses in Switzerland was also significant. The rest of the year was, however, filled with a great personal anxiety, for her son George was desperately ill after an accident in which he was thrown from his horse and suffered a severe fracture of the skull. His wife, Mia St. Paul, who was Josephine's kinswoman and had been her ward, depended much on the support of her mother-in-law, whose unfailing courage and steadfast faith carried the young people through a most difficult period. Josephine therefore did not go abroad that winter.

It was in this autumn that Watts painted her portrait. The invitation came from him. He was painting, to give to the nation, a series of portraits of people who had made the history of the nineteenth century, and he wished to include hers. With her daughter-in-law Mia, she went to Compton for sittings. The portrait is now in the National Portrait Gallery. She wrote about it to Watts: "When I looked at the portrait I felt inclined to burst into tears. I felt so sorry for her. Your power has brought out of the past the record of a conflict . . . it is written in the eyes and face. . . . Just as an old tree bears the marks of a storm by which it was blasted long ago." Josephine enjoyed the sittings and conceived a great respect for the old man. The days she passed under his roof made a break in a very difficult time.

It happened to be a very severe winter. Her little jerry-built house in Balham had walls too thin to keep out the cold; the pipes all froze so that there could be no kitchen fire and no hot bath. The devoted Annie, who had succeeded Jane as Josephine's cook, attendant, cherisher and friend, was laid low with influenza, but a young girl whom she had imported produced surprisingly good meals cooked on an open fire. The cold was prolonged; as late as March 1895 there was still skating and in some places the Thames was frozen over—a dreary time indeed. Josephine's pity was not principally for herself but for the half-starved men who were out of work and came in succession tapping at the window, offering to do any job for the price of a meal; her heart ached for them; she never had as much money to give away as she wanted. Throughout the distresses of the winter she found relief in her work, turning her mind away from the immediate problems to write something quite unconnected with them. In this spirit she wrote *The Lady of Shunem*, which she described as a series of studies in Scripture addressed chiefly to mothers and fathers. It is not a "series", for there is no connection between one chapter and the next, nor is it in any ordinary sense a "study". It is rather a collection of reflections on unrelated episodes from the Bible. It is not an important book, but it is interesting as showing the ideas which were always at the front of Josephine's mind, and as Newman said, "She reads Scripture like a child and interprets it like an angel."

Her other activity at this time was preparing for the Congress the International Federation was to hold in Colmar in the following autumn. She was worried about certain symptoms which were appearing, especially among the Germans, dreading lest the Federation should be "nobbled" by Regulationists who gained credit by professing zeal for the abolition of the White Slave Traffic, while at the same time, by the maintenance of brothels, promoting the demand which the Traffic supplied. She was determined to get the right people to Colmar, wanting especially a large and strong group of "faithful women" from all countries so that the position of the Federation should be re-affirmed and the "Ark of the Covenant" established. It was the old trouble which had first appeared in the matter of Bruce's Bill—a tendency among the elect towards compromise, which seemed to her fatal. In the summer, when she reached Switzerland, she wrote a letter which was published as a "meagre number of *The Dawn*", which revealed her anxiety and showed no abatement of her vigour, no softening of her asperity. She saw the weakening of the Federation everywhere by the inclusion—because of the imagined prestige their name would give—of men who did not in their hearts accept the "fundamental thesis, the unalterable principle of an equal moral law, an equal moral responsibility for both sexes and the consequent necessity of equality in all human laws bearing on morality". They were willing to abolish Regulation as long as it remained perfectly clear that only the women were to blame. It was the old contention, which started in the Garden of Eden, "The woman tempted me." It was re-affirmed in the House of Lords in 1871, when it was said that "the woman sold herself for gain, while the man was merely satisfying a natural impulse". It was re-asserted by the Court Preacher at Berlin who, realising with horror that the aim of the Federation was nothing less than the legal equality of the sexes, declared "this is an aim that must be at once rejected". To which Josephine adds, "It is always good that persons should state plainly what they mean." Now in France there was a physician declaring "the vice of the man is *disinterested vice*", and claiming that "society has a right to defend itself against these women, as it defends itself against mad dogs". "But," adds Josephine, "dogs who go mad are not all of one sex, O most learned Professor."

The misgivings Josephine had had were dissipated when she reached Colmar. The place was congenial, the delegates were received by M. Camille Schlumberger, who, as Mayor, had shut all the brothels and refused to register prostitutes as early as

1883, when in England only the suspension of the Acts was being painfully achieved. The weather was good. The principles of the Federation were well and clearly stated by Mr. Pierson of Holland and a valuable paper on the legal side of the question was read by M. Bovet, who in spite of his age had surrendered to Josephine's entreaties to address the Congress. The French branch was represented by two of its sound members and from Germany no hostile delegate appeared, though the official organ, the *Korrespondenzblatt*, had said: "We have no need to be taught by others what is demanded of us, in Germany. . . . Our English friends need not come to their next conference at Colmar in order to teach us our duty. . . ." The people of Colmar, pleased, no doubt, to feel that they had been ahead of all their guests in the good cause, made delightfully cordial hosts and everything went perfectly.

Josephine had given up her house in Balham and had determined to spend the winter in Switzerland. She went to Montreux. She could write from there as well as from anywhere else and she knew that the next serious contest would be in Geneva. Meanwhile, however, there was much to occupy her. She was concerned with Guernsey, embarking on an attempt to abolish Regulation there; with British Dominions, which were causing much anxiety; she was corresponding with an Armenian woman doctor, who had been at Colmar and had contributed a paper on the medical aspects of the question in Persia. She was also maintaining all her usual correspondence with her family. Her son George had been sent to Africa to recuperate after his illness. It had been decided that he must give up his work—and the future for his family was obscure. His wife, Mia, left lonely in England, needed a very regular supply of letters.

Through the remaining months of 1895 after Colmar, Josephine's main preoccupation was with Geneva. "Geneva", she writes, "is heavy on my heart. It has been visited and stirred again and again, and yet its present condition is worse than the first. Geneva is a scandal to Europe and not only to Switzerland. It is a plague spot in the heart of the Continent. It is a very international town with a mixed population which partly accounts for its great wickedness and the difficulty of arousing public spirit there." Now she was to attack it again. A new situation had arisen. A change in the constitition had instituted a *Droit d'Initiative* which gave the right to any body of citizens, who could rally to its support a sufficient proportion of the electorate, to institute legislation on any subject. Ever since Josephine's visit to Geneva in 1891, public opinion among the working classes had been stirring on the subject of Regulation. The impulse given by that visit had been maintained by the office of the Federation, and M. Minod, the Secretary, had been busy collecting signatures to support a resolution for Abolition, an activity not always well received. One indignant husband wrote to the local paper, *Le Génévois*: "Sir, A gentleman presented himself this morning at my house when I was absent and laid before my wife a petition to which he asked her signature against the 'houses of *tolérance*' sanctioned by the authorities. Having read this interesting nonsense my wife thought it a duty to sign it without quite comprehending it. I am much obliged to the gentleman for having instructed my wife on this question, which she, I must confess, had never studied. But I hope when the signatures are analysed all those of women will be struck out which have been given without their husbands' consent."

In October 1895 there was an election for the Grand Council of Geneva, and to this Council two members of the Federation were elected, de Meuron and Bridel. Early in January the new Grand Council had its first meeting. The first subject to be considered was the question of Abolition. There were two *Projets de Loi* before the Council, one drawn up by the Government, in favour of maintaining the old system; the other, enacting Abolition, drawn up by the friends of the Federation. The President opened the proceedings by proposing the official Bill and having done so ordered the hall to be cleared and the doors closed, so that the rest of the discussion could be held in private. Josephine remarks acidly: "The defence of State-protected vice is proper to be heard by all, says the President, but the arguments against that State protection are immoral, and tend to the 'corruption of youth'!" The *Signal de Génève* protested indignantly that this was not a democratic proceeding but resembled rather the days of the Council of Ten. Bitterly the Editor wrote: "The Grand Council has always manifested an extraordinary modesty in approaching the subject of public morality. The large and important petition from Geneva citizens which was presented to them some years ago, has lain ever since in their waste-paper receptacle; because it was well not to disgust the people with the subject! The 22,000 signers of the petition did not count as a portion of the people! To the waste-paper basket then with the petition! . . . How are the people's legal rights and the modesty of the Grand Council to be reconciled? . . . By . . . the continuation of the regulation of vice; we say it plainly, the *encouragement* of vice, and the enjoyment by the Government *of the funds derived* from it!" In spite of the feelings of that paper, the result of the Grand Council's action was that the case for Regulation was reported and the opposing speeches were not reported. They were made, however, and though at the beginning there were only the two members of the Federation on the side of Abolition, when the vote was taken 32 members— one-third of the House—voted for it.

The Government then did what Governments do when they want to delay—they appointed a Commission of Enquiry and on this body only one Abolitionist sat. The enquiry was very rapidly concluded and in three days reported in favour of retaining Regulation. This, however, was not the end of the matter, for since there were two opposing "*projets*", they had to be submitted to a referendum of the males of the Canton. This then was the task that faced the Abolitionists in the early months of 1896—so to canvass that a popular vote for Abolition should be secured. They set to work gallantly. There were two months in which to prepare for this trial of strength; there was much at stake; it was the first time in the history of the movement that the opportunity had been given to the electorate to express its opinion. The Federation warmed to its task. Mme. de Gingins' house became the headquarters of the campaign. She had been a zealous adherent of the cause since 1876 when, after her husband's death, she had come to Josephine for comfort. Josephine had known how to help her—first with sympathy and then with the best tonic she knew—a cause in which she could forget herself in the service of the oppressed. Mme. de Gingins was now old, but she was still valiant and she threw herself into the campaign with vigour. Josephine had moved to Clarens in order to be accessible and friends came from Geneva to consult her there. She was constantly on the telephone, "at which the intelligent head waiter yelled for me, for I cannot yell properly myself". Early in February Mme. de Gingins asked her to stay with her for a few days in Geneva and Josephine was glad to go: "the smell of powder is always agreeable to me in a fight on a moral issue". From the moment she arrived she was busy all the time and except for a short daily walk on the terrace for the good of her health, she went nowhere. There were immense meetings of women. "I had been urged," says Josephine, "to stir up the women (nearly all quite novices in such work, and eager to learn) to see that their part in this great work for morality and justice is a very important and vital one, and I did my best to show them what women can be and do; I told them that the *woman's voice* must be heard *now*. It must sound high and clear like a tocsin, over Geneva and over all the Canton round; without it the victory would be an electoral victory, but not a vital and endurable one. I said a good deal in fact, speaking to them 'heart to heart'. . . . I begged them for the moment to forget that there were gentlemen present, and only remember God . . . I saw they were moved, by the nodding and wavering of their bonnets (mostly black). . . ."

There were, of course, other activities too, described by Josephine with immense gusto. A young Pastor in the town, "He may be about 35 to 40 . . . very broad shoulders and short neck, a square head, and altogether a bovine look . . . but you must imagine a kind looking and very *intellectual* bull", invited every other pastor of every denomination to come to a meeting in the

Consistory. Nearly all attended the meeting, and this was no small gain, for hitherto the religious leaders had strangely stood aside; they had been content to quote St. Paul's words, "But fornication and all uncleanness, let it not be once named among you", holding apparently that it was better to let a notorious evil exist than to shock the respectable by mentioning it. Old M. Lenoir too, a banker who had been a friend of the Federation since its beginning, "came quite in an agitation and fuss, to say 'You will want money for this propaganda; we must form a fund for it, and begin at once, for there is no time to be lost'." Even more encouraging than the adherence of the old was the new interest shown by the young. Students from the University were asking for meetings and when one young man had the temerity to express the view that there was something rather effeminate in this concern for prostitutes, he was so fiercely attacked by all the rest that he was obliged to seek safety in flight.

The meetings of the Grand Council throughout this period were also not without incident. Here the Regulationists had a substantial majority, but de Meuron and Bridel were indefatigable and very well supplied with facts and figures to disprove those of their opponents, and since the majority had no arguments that were effective they fell back on other methods of silencing the Abolitionists. "On Thursday de Meuron was so merciless to them, that a number of them left the Chamber in a rage, and the President beat with both hands on the table as hard as he could, to try and drown de Meuron's voice."

The principal Genevese newspaper *Le Génévois* was strongly on the side of Regulation, but the *Signal de Génève*, edited by Albert Thomas, gave the Federation clear and reasoned support, and the Catholic *Courrier de Génève*, having ascertained from Josephine the attitude of the Vatican, published "an uncompromising and strong article" on its side. Increasingly the Abolitionists believed that their cause was prospering. This view was shared by the upholders of the *status quo* and it alarmed and vexed them. The opposition hardened. The substantial citizens of Geneva resented the blaze of publicity which exposed features of their life which they preferred to keep private; they resented the intrusion of a third party into local politics. Feeling ran high. The father of Albert Thomas, the Editor of the *Signal*, a substantial business man, publicly denounced and disowned his son and forbade him to see his mother or sisters. It is not altogether easy to explain the bitterness of the respectable against the work of the Federation. There is no difficulty whatever in explaining that of the tenanciers. Like the silversmiths of Ephesus they saw that the hope of their gains was in danger. They had a powerful vested interest in the system and they were fully prepared to fight for it.

Josephine, summoned by telegram from Clarens, whither she had returned to carry on correspondence for the cause, found her friends facing a new situation. The tenanciers had formed a League to oppose Abolition; they had plenty of money at their disposal and no scruples as to the spending of it. They hired some 200 roughs to break up meetings and make Geneva too dangerous a place for the expression of any opinion opposed to theirs. The first meeting to be attacked was a large gathering in the Hall of the Reformation which was to be addressed by delegates from other towns. It went on for two hours, "Our gentlemen . . . trying to get a sentence heard now and then", but the mob became so violent they had to stop and finally the police appeared, not to quell the rioters but to escort the speakers home by a side door. From that time it was difficult for Abolitionists to hire a public hall and ten days before the vote—on March 22nd —the police ordered all public rooms to be closed to them. When they attempted to speak in the street they were stoned and pelted with dirt, when they put up posters these were pulled down and torn up. Any sort of public advocacy became impossible. The Abolitionists were undeterred. Josephine recalled that Lloyd Garrison had once said that a shower of brickbats had a re-markably good tonic effect. "Three venerable Pastors . . . were plucky enough to hold a meeting at a sort of stand, very openly in a rowdy party of the town. . . . They were stoned and pelted and dirt was thrown over them, and their clothes torn! Dear men, they had to take to their heels. . . . It was fine to see the Pastors *run*, someone told me. . . . They have preached such *much* better sermons since then, and are full of zeal." Since public meetings had become almost impracticable the Abolitionists had recourse to leaflets and posters. Visits were paid from house to house and an immense mass of literature was distributed. As posters were torn down, others were put up in their place.

Le Génévois became more scurrilous in its attacks and one favourite line was that this agitation was entirely an affair of foreigners who desired to destroy the prosperity of Geneva. All this work, in fact, was paid for by an Englishwoman sent out from England with the express intention of ruining Geneva! When Josephine was leaving for Clarens one Friday evening, it came over her "to go and call on the Editor of our mad opposing newspaper the *Génévois*. I went to the office, but he was not in, only his sub-Editor and other men. I left my card, with a courteous message. The men stared, apparently astonished that I should go there, and before they had recovered from their surprise I was gone. As I stood in the middle of that bureau whence such scandals and vileness emanate, I was filled with an *intense pity*— nothing but pity." She did, however, see the Editor on another occasion, when she was taken by Madame Ruchonnet, whose husband had been a friend of Favon, the Editor. Favon, an embittered man, obviously rather embarrassed by this echo from his past, was perfectly civil to them, but remained unmoved in his opposition, which he declared to be based upon the conviction that the only alternative to *Maisons Tolérées* was the establishment of a system of espionage: "What an *awful* thing, dear lady," he said, "what a tyranny beyond all other tyrannies it would be, should your party triumph, to have a renewal of the ancient sumptuary discipline, of the prying into the secrets of every household, and of family life. It would be the most wicked of tyrannies." "I was astonished," said Josephine "and with difficulty persuaded him that such a thought was as detestable to us as to him . . . that we had evidence of the folly and futility as well as *shame* of attempting to reach private immorality by the Law, which means necessarily by Police and the most hateful espionage. I was thankful in my heart that since the beginning of our Crusade, I had been convinced in my conscience and understanding of the folly and even wickedness of all systems of *outward repression* of private immorality for which men and women are accountable to God and their own souls; but not to the *State*." The Editor was sufficiently moved to come down to the door to see them off, thanking them for the courtesy of their visit. Josephine reflected, "I am not without hope for that man."

As the voting day grew nearer, the women too grew more and more stimulated by the general excitement and became more vocal. They were not attacked, as the men were, for the opponents thought of them contemptuously and did not care to spend their powder on such feeble adversaries. At first they were self-conscious and hesitant, but gradually indignation roused them; they spoke only to women, but they achieved considerable success in that field, and before the end of the campaign had added the suffrage to their demands. Josephine records a meeting at a *brasserie* to which they had been invited by a friendly brewer. Miss Humbert came and spoke last. "The Geneva ladies who are all young to this work have not yet learned to move people. They speak in a low voice and too meekly—careful to be very 'prudent'. Miss Humbert on the contrary went into a very natural and righteous rage. ... The crowd of women who had sat patiently listening before, all stood up, and pressed forward, and were moved like a cornfield before the wind. The friendly brewer came in to say would they please not to cheer quite so loud, as there were some of the mob around the door mocking them!"

In the Council Chamber a controversy was raging about the form of the questionnaire to be submitted to the electorate and here the Abolitionists, still decisively outnumbered, sustained a serious defeat. They desired that the question put should be "Do you desire the retention of the *Maisons Tolérées*?" This would have been perfectly clear to the least educated, for no one could fail to know what he was asked to approve or reject. The Government, however, knowing well that the opposition was

largely among the illiterate, chose rather to put two questions:
(1) Are you in favour of the *Projet de Loi d'Initiative*? Yes or No.
(2) Are you in favour of the Government *Projet de Loi*? Yes or
No. In spite of the protests of de Meuron and his followers the
second form was adopted and it was extremely confusing to
simple people unused to Government circulars. Many refrained
from voting because they did not know what the questions
meant, while some, with a general feeling that what Government
offered must be accepted, voted contrary to their intention. So
the fatal day approached. Saturday, March 21st, was observed in
all the churches in Geneva as a day of prayer, and Abolitionists
all over England and Europe were exhorted to join in this
intercession.

Josephine was staying with Mme. de Gingins and as they walked
to church together in the early hours of Sunday she enjoyed the
beauty and peace of the fresh spring morning. She was no longer
as certain of victory as she had been. There had been so much
violence and undisguised hatred let loose in Geneva and she had
been conscious of a sense of brooding evil over the place. But
she did not flinch. "If the majority is on the right side", she
wrote, "the Regulations and these horrible State-protected
houses of vice will fall, and will not be restored easily. If the
people's vote is on the wrong side, the struggle will be begun all
over again, and indefinitely prolonged."

Just outside Geneva, on rising ground, stood the home of M.
Favre. He came of an ancient family of aristocrats who, before
the days of the Reformation, had maintained themselves in this
fortress. In the days of Louis XIV it had received Huguenot
refugees, for the walls were stout enough to withstand the attacks
of any mob. Here came the leaders of the Abolitionists on the
afternoon of March 22nd. Josephine and Mme. de Gingins
arrived at about five o'clock and took what comfort they could
from the view of the town and the Lake of Geneva, which lay at
their feet like a map. It was already obvious that things were going
ill. Drink was flowing freely and there was much rowdyism. M.
Favre and his brother were kind and assiduous; he gave them

dinner and the table stood laden with refreshments of all sorts till midnight. One by one the leaders who had been presiding at polling booths all day came in "with their dusty boots and their tired faces". There was nothing cheerful to report, the vote was going against them. They realised this long before the final figures were announced—8,000 votes against Abolition and a poor 4,000 in favour. They stood silent, they looked at one another and then with one accord turned to Josephine. "Have you no word for us?" they asked. The answer came without hesitation—"Every death of person or thing which is good is followed by resurrection!" They looked at her as she stood there, beautiful, dignified, frail, utterly wearied but indomitable and hope returned and their courage revived. They stood about in groups, talking earnestly and quietly, looking forward to the next step, and Josephine as she watched them, looked at their good faces and heard their words, felt more encouraged than she had ever yet been in Geneva. "These were the men who make 'corps d'élite', who lead forlorn hopes, and who by this very defeat and disaster are welded into a more complete and convinced body of combatants than could ever have been formed by a victory, and I felt the strong brotherhood which had grown up among them in a short time. There were democrats and conservatives, protestants, catholics and free thinkers, but all 'straight men', honest and in great earnest." Presently they turned to her again and suggested they should make themselves into a committee and lay plans for the future. So they all sat round the great table—some forty or fifty men, Mme. de Gingins and Josephine and planned for the morrow and as they sat and talked they began to hear sounds from the city below and they looked out on to a scene of flashing lights and movements in the streets and they heard the sound of singing. It was the tenanciers celebrating their victory. It was not till later that the Abolitionists heard particulars of that celebration. The tenanciers had taken the *Lampes Rouges*, which were the sign of their houses, and had made a procession through the streets dancing and singing bawdy songs; they had burst into the largest Church and barring

the doors against intruders had held a blasphemous service—
a mock consecration of their *Lampes Rouges*. They had then gone
round the town breaking the windows of the Federation office
and of any other building connected with Abolitionists. They
had called on the Editor of *Le Génévois* and had insisted he should
come out and address them. M. Favon came out, somewhat
reluctantly. He was certainly in favour of *Maisons Tolérées*, but
he did not wish to identify himself with the disreputable behaviour
of the mob. He exhorted them to go home quietly, since they had
gained what they sought. It was not, however, the Editor who
sent them home, but a violent thunderstorm which burst over the
town soon after midnight, clearing the streets and enabling the
Abolitionists to leave their fortress and creep back in safety to
their own lodgings.

Through the following difficult days Josephine unmistakeably
revealed her immense power. It was to her that everyone turned;
the undergraduates, dismayed and uncertain how best to proceed,
asked for an interview with her; the women, outraged at the
result, came to her for advice and a wonderful system of education
for them was inaugurated. "Dear ladies," says Josephine, "their
hearts have been so stirred that it has sharpened their inventive
powers. Numbers of poor women have come to one another to
ask 'Will one of you ladies come to *my kitchen*, the best room I
have, and speak to my husband and sons, and a few of our
friends, men and women?" So in connection with the women's
work the proposal was adopted to have a branch called '*Le
Bureau des petites cuisines*', the office of the little kitchens, thence
teachers on this question should be sent out whenever asked
for."

There is another touching story of a rather different kind,
told by Josephine in her letters home. "One day Mme. Bridel
asked me if she might bring her little boy of thirteen to see me
alone, as he was full of grief, and she thought I might be able to
comfort him. He came, and he and I sat opposite each other on
two chairs and had a very satisfactory interview. The poor little
fellow had been frightened and brokenhearted by hearing his

father's name howled at and hissed in the streets and some older boys of indifferent character, in the school he goes to, had repeated things with mockery which little Bridel could not understand, and he had said to his mother 'What does it mean? *What has Papa done?* Why do they say such horrible things about my father?' It was quite touching to see the boy's grief and innocence. I talked to him in a very general way—but as a child could understand—of the present opposition of principles, of 'God's Order' for mankind, which is the family and family life, whence all wholesome things spring, and of the rebellion of some men against God's will and order. Then I told him how we revered and loved his father in England and elsewhere, because he was fighting the battle of justice and of the weak against the strong, and that some day he would understand better than now how good and brave his father is. And the boy's eyes began to shine, as he looked hard at me, and he turned to his mother (who was sitting wistfully behind, listening) with a look of relief and triumph."

As the days went on, solid grounds for confidence appeared. The tenanciers had over-reached themselves. Many respectable citizens of Geneva, who had hitherto accepted the *Maisons Tolérées* without question simply because they had always been there, were shocked by the excesses of the mob, they were not prepared to acquiesce in the government of the Canton by the brothel keepers and they found themselves compelled to look into the whole question again. Their complacency shaken, they called at the Federation office and many became members. Among these were a number of University professors and some doctors. Abolitionists became conscious of a very real conversion of public opinion. The National Church was shaken. "Some of the Pastors of the National Church, perceiving clearly, it seems for the first time, that the Government derives a certain revenue from the tax on every house of debauchery which it licenses . . . now hesitate to accept money from such defiled hands. . . . On the other hand, the Radical Socialists, who are always at war with the Churches, asked indignantly whether money should be given to any body which tried to deprive the State of its 'ancient rights and prerogatives' ". No one in Geneva could any longer be ignorant of the fact that the whole question of Regulation, which had hitherto seemed as natural and unquestionable as daylight, was a living issue which could never again be relegated to complete obscurity. Nor was the influence of the battle confined to Geneva.

In the Canton de Vaud, when a similar *projet* was being considered by the Grand Conseil there, a petition against Regulation organised by the Federation was signed by 6,000 women. "We arranged," writes Josephine, "that the Petition should be taken to the Castle where the Grand Conseil sits, by a deputation of working women. There was much excitement about this, and I had to put the dear bodies through a rehearsal, but it succeeded well, and attracted attention, being something quite new in Switzerland . . . I was glad to see that they looked quite 'women of the people' though with well washed shining faces and their best bonnets on. One was a remarkably handsome woman with splendid dark eyes full of wit and intelligence, and she had a little black woollen shawl pinned at the neck, *bare* muscular arms, and black woollen gloves on her hands, an interval of handsome bare arm showing between shawl and gloves. It looked so nice! They mounted up to the Castle and I waited their return. In about an hour they came back to my room. I never saw such radiant faces! They all wanted to speak together to tell me what had passed." They had been taken into the "awful and august presence of the Grand Conseil itself, sitting in full session; and they were told to sit down". The President opened the Petition and read it all through. "It was declared to be of great importance, seeing that it was signed by such a number . . . and it was proposed to appoint a Commission that very day to consider it and report to the Executive. . . . The women retired, feeling 'Well, after all, we are citizens, we had something to say to the Government, and we have said it!' " M. Bridel wrote, on hearing of this petition: "How happy we are over the events in Lausanne! . . . You could not have organised a better revenge or a more delightful encouragement for the 'Vanquished of the 22nd March'. Thanks! A thousand times thanks!"

Josephine was confident of ultimate victory, but she did not live to see it. It was not until 1927 that the system was finally swept away when the League of Nations proclaimed its belief in all the principles for which she had battled throughout her life.

During her days in Geneva, in addition to bearing the brunt of the local struggle, she had been called upon to reassure the friends of the Federation outside Geneva who were, not unnaturally, horrified at this public disavowal by popular vote of the principles for which the Federation had been contending on the popular behalf. She did not minimise the calamity. "We have had a crushing defeat," she wrote, but she added, very much in the spirit she had displayed in 1873, "A victory yesterday might have come too soon to insure deep work and a real reform", and she signs that letter, "Yours, cast down but not destroyed." Then again: "The more I think of it the more I rejoice in the awakening of the good men of Geneva. Our shaky friends in different countries very readily blame our methods; 'Why,' they say, 'did you not let the Grand Council go on *quietly* as it was doing (the minority) till it had converted *itself* and then *quietly* suppressed the "Houses", why did you act so as to arouse the mob? It only did harm'. They speak in ignorance. The Grand Council never moved a step till *pushed* on almost violently by our two good leaders . . . and the demon which the Grand Council has favoured and protected so long would not be put down by its own patrons . . . without a violent and terrible resistance. Men who have not learned what a real moral movement in politics is do not understand that it is only by the force of awakened consciences *outside* Governments as well as inside them, that real reforms can be accomplished. They do not see that this great thunder peal of the 22nd was the best thing—perhaps the only thing—to awaken dormant consciences." Defiantly she declared her conclusion: "Therefore I am *glad*, *glad*, *glad* that all this has happened!"

Josephine was on her way home. She must first put in a little work in connection with the coming Conference at Berne. She stayed at Neuchâtel and was, as ever, cheered by the Humberts: Amélie, of whom she said "I do love her; she is such a gay light-hearted being. . . . When she comes to see me we always close the door so that people shall not hear us, and think we laugh too much"; and the old man who, being told the story of all that had happened at Geneva "remained silent awhile with his head bent; then he looked up and said very distinctly and gravely 'Ce n'est pas une défaite. C'est le germe de la victoire.' "

CHAPTER SEVENTEEN

INDIA 1888—1898

"My soul is as untamed and untameable as ever in its fury against injustice". (J. B.)

WITH the repeal of the C.D. Acts in 1886 the regulation of prostitution had been abandoned in Great Britain. It might have been supposed that it had ceased to exist in any part of Her Majesty's Dominions, since these were all ultimately under the control of Parliament at Westminster. This, however, could in fact happen only if the Executive in each Dominion loyally accepted the policy of the central government.

In India this was far from being the case. The Viceroy with his Advisory Council had considerable doubt of anyone except himself being able to judge wisely about the affairs of an Empire so vast as India and so remote from Westminster. In the long controversy that followed Abolition, it is perfectly clear that the Government of India and more especially the Army authorities there were convinced that those who desired Abolition were tiresome cranks endeavouring to lay down the law on a subject of which they were totally ignorant. Lord Cross, the Secretary of State for India in the Conservative Government, wished to carry out the will of Parliament; his Under Secretary, Gorst, was uncomfortably convinced of the necessity for doing so, but his sympathy was entirely with the Viceroy, Lord Dufferin, who had no intention of conforming to the policy of the Government if there was any way of avoiding doing so. There was one, quite obvious way. The Regulations in India depended on an Order in Council (1866) authorising them, but in addition there were Cantonment Acts which gave the military power to make ordinances for cantonments wherever there were units of the British Army. It was therefore perfectly simple to repeal the law authorising Regulation and to leave the military free to make what arrangements they liked for each cantonment. This was the course pursued. Its success depended on its escaping the notice of home authorities.

Dyer, who had done valiantly in the fight in Brussels, was now in India and in 1887 wrote home disquieting reports of the state of things there. James Stuart at once raised the question in the House of Commons and from this time there was no peace for the Government. The Abolitionists repeatedly asked questions in the House as to the accuracy of the reports they were receiving from India; the Bishop of Lichfield called attention in the House of Lords to outrages reported to him; and a Conference of Bishops in Calcutta roundly asserted that the C.D. Acts were still in force. To all these questions and attacks Lord Cross could only continue to reply that he was asking the Viceroy for information; and the Viceroy, backed by his Council and by military and Anglo-Indian public opinion in India, preserved a masterly silence.

A crisis, however, arose when a document, later known as "The Infamous Memorandum", was published in the English Press. This memorandum, purporting to have been issued by the Q.M.G. in India to officers commanding troops there, said that there had been complaints about the quality and quantity of the women supplied for the troops and directed an improvement in both respects, suggesting that if the matron in charge of a brothel could not do better, she should be replaced. This Memorandum not unnaturally roused a storm of indignation and the Bishop of Carlisle asked the Secretary of State whether it was authentic. Lord Cross replied that it was so grossly at variance with the assurances he had received from the Government of India, that he could not believe it to be so, but if it proved a genuine document, it was utterly indefensible. When the reluctant admission that it was indeed authentic was made, "It was delightful to see the pale looks of some of the Government Front Bench when Sir John Gorst had to confess the ghastly story from India was true", and even Lord Cross could no longer believe in the bona fides of the Viceroy's assurances. A very peremptory telegram was sent ordering the immediate and total abolition of the Regulations. The Indian Government had no choice but to comply. The Acts were rescinded and the Government and Army Command set themselves to consider how to meet the situation. When their proposed new regulations were submitted to the Secretary of State, it was clear to Stansfeld, Stuart and the other Abolitionists that though they were superficially unobjectionable, they still made possible the re-introduction of the essentials of the old system. This being pointed out, Lord Cross replied that he could not believe that the Government of India, knowing the policy of Her Majesty's Government, intended to circumvent it. This remarkable triumph of hope over experience was not greatly reassuring to the Abolitionists. They remained vigilant. They had good reason for their misgivings.

The Press in India openly congratulated the Viceroy on his skill in circumventing the Home Government: "The religious fanatics who howled till a weak Government gave way to their clamour . . . will probably howl again now at the way the old order of things will be enforced under another name, but with very little difference in manner. . . ." The new rules are "the work of a master in the art of making a thing look as unlike itself as it well can be". The reports the Abolitionists received were so disquieting that it was determined that an independent enquiry into the whole question was necessary and it was agreed to raise funds for this purpose and to send out a special delegation. It was easy enough to pass this resolution; to find a suitable delegate was quite a different matter. It must be a woman, for only a woman was likely to be able to penetrate the secrets of the bazaars and to make contact with the women concerned; it must be someone with courage and tact, tough enough not to be intimidated by official opposition yet tactful enough to avoid being expelled by an indignant bureaucracy. It must be someone so dispassionately determined to discover the truth that her report would be accepted as worthy of credence. Neither Josephine nor her committee could think of the woman to fulfil all these conditions. Then, as they anxiously prayed and sought, the answer came in the arrival of Dr. Kate Bushnell with her friend Mrs. Andrew.

Dr. Bushnell was an American, a member of the World's Women's Christian Temperance Union. She had not met Josephine nor communicated with her, but she had read the report of her speech to the Conference which the W.W.C.T.U. had held in London in 1891, and had been greatly impressed by it. Later in the year, having finished some work she had undertaken, she was anxiously considering what her next step should be. She could come to no satisfactory conclusion and while still in this state of disturbing indecision she had a curious experience. She fell suddenly asleep and in her sleep found herself being tossed on the sea with the clear knowledge that she was on her way to meet Mrs. Butler and to do some work for her. When she woke, the conviction remained that she was called to some special work for Mrs. Butler, and this conviction was strengthened when she wrote to her friend Mrs. Andrew, who told her she had already booked a passage to England and was going almost at once. Dr. Bushnell thereupon took a passage for herself and in due course they presented themselves to Mrs. Butler. So the delegates were found and set forth on their investigations.

They spent the cold weather of 1891–1892 in Upper India and visited a great many cantonments. The task called forth all their qualities. Weeks passed while they tried fruitlessly to get information from the military side. They then engaged a native who taught them enough of the language to enable them to make some sort of contact with Indian women. With this they were able to penetrate to the brothels. The women and girls whom they found there were in a miserable state. Many were widows, still in their teens, who on the death of their husbands had been sold by those who did not want the charge of them. Conditions varied from place to place but always the prostitutes lived in premises provided by the Army and were paid a regular, infinitesimally small, wage by the "Town Magistrate". Always they were obliged to submit to regular examination and they were given tickets countersigned by the Army Surgeon to certify their state of health. They were under the authority of a sort of matron, a "Mohaldarni", whose duty it was to bring in new girls when the supply fell short. For each new girl so brought in she received three rupees.

The two Americans reported in "A Statement of Facts" in 1893, which Stuart and Stansfeld at once took up with the India Office. The result was the appointment of a small Departmental Committee to take evidence. G. W. E. Russell, the Under Secretary at the India Office, was the Chairman, Stansfeld and Wilson the representatives of the House of Commons and Sir Donald Stewart and Sir James Peile represented the Government of India. The first witnesses called were the two American ladies. Their evidence was impressive; it was not highly coloured but was direct and simple; they spoke of things they had themselves seen and repeated what the women themselves had told them. Moreover, they had with them a ticket, given them by one of the women, licensing her as a prostitute, signed by the Camp Magistrate and countersigned by the Army Surgeon. This evidence was sent to India for examination and comment. In the weeks that followed, many meetings were held at which the two ladies spoke of their experiences. Their report was published in May.

Lord Roberts, returning from being Commander-in-Chief in India at about that time, was interviewed by the Press and, as the *Westminster Gazette* reported, "declared emphatically that there was no foundation for the ladies' statement. The old system", he said, "was swept away". The *Gazette* goes on to give Lord Roberts' own words: "After the action of the House of Commons, Lord Dufferin sent for me, and we at once issued the most stringent orders. As late as July last further orders were issued in the same spirit. I made it my business recently to inquire personally into this whole matter, and I found that in every cantonment the whole system has been completely abolished. Of course, I do not deny that it is possible that here and there some of the features of the old Régime may have reappeared; I have never come across them, and if they do exist anywhere it is contrary to orders. . . . To say that any such state of things exists as this report describes is simply untrue." The *Gazette* continues: "The ladies, then, it was assumed, were mistaken and had been ill-informed. Philanthropists with the best intentions sometimes are. Lord Roberts is a disciplinarian, and the idea of his orders being quietly set at defiance by subordinate officers was scarcely anywhere regarded as a possible explanation."

By July the Committee in India had reported that the ladies' statements were substantially true. Roberts was called before the Departmental Committee in August, and could only plead ignorance to what was going on and when asked about the "Infamous Memorandum", he replied that it had been issued without his knowledge or consent. When he was followed by Lieut.-General Chapman, his Quarter-Master-General, who declared that he had shown the Memorandum to the C.-in-C. before circulating it, the Committee was somewhat embarrassed and in its report remarked that there "appeared to be a discrepancy" in the evidence on this point—a euphemism which angered Josephine, who had no doubt in her own mind as to who was lying. In a private letter quoted by A. S. G. Butler in his *Portrait of Josephine Butler*, she describes Chapman: "He is a dark, evil-looking man, lean, dried up like a piece of old tree trunk, expressionless, with a mouth of a peculiar form—thin, mechanical, which slowly opens like a steel trap to emit the lies he speaks with a face of black night and imperturbable impenitence—then shuts again, like a skeleton's mouth." Before the Report was published, Roberts took the unusual and honourable course of sending, for inclusion in it, a letter. "I frankly admit that the statements of the two American missionary ladies . . . are in the main correct. I hoped and believed that the orders issued to give effect to the resolution of the House of Commons had been everywhere obeyed. In some stations the rules have been strictly enforced, but in others it turns out that this has not been completely the case. I deeply regret this, and I feel an apology is due from me to the ladies concerned. This apology I offer unreservedly." On this letter the *Westminster Gazette* comments: "Now this is a good straightforward apology which does all credit to Lord Roberts as a man, but we must confess it is rather staggering to the civilian who reads it. For here is the greatest of disciplinarians in a land of discipline confessing that his orders were not obeyed, that his subordinates either evaded or defied them, and therefore, by implication, that he himself was entrapped into making wholly misleading denials on his arrival in England. Now what, after this, can any person of sense or humour say about Lord Roberts' further remark in the same letter that 'it would have been better if the missionary ladies had been commended to the care of the authorities in India'. What would the American ladies have discovered, we wonder, if they had put themselves in the hands of the authorities, who contrived to keep the Commander-in-Chief himself almost wholly in the dark?"

The Committee published a Majority Report signed by the Chairman and the Abolitionists; and a Minority Report signed by the representatives of the Indian Government. The Majority considered that the facts put before them proved that the old system was being re-introduced; the Minority did not question the facts, but held they were only vestiges of the old and expiring organisation. In any case the Government of India had to bow to the force of public indignation in England.

In 1895 Abolitionists got their way and the Government of India was obliged to order the abolition of all brothels within cantonments and of compulsory medical examination. But victory was not really won. Within a year the Army medical officers in India were reporting an immense increase in venereal disease. They did not point out that they had closed practically all hospitals and treatment centres, on the ground that without compulsion they were useless, since nobody would attend.

Actually, those who cared to study the facts knew that where there was a sympathetic doctor who could speak the vernacular, women were eager for treatment. Much capital was made out of the statistics and a panic set in. This, it was said, was the result of the abolition of the C.D. Acts and since Netley Hospital responded with gloomy pictures of the state of regiments returning from India, the restoration of the Acts, not only in India but also in England, was loudly demanded. Statistics can be made to prove anything, though it was perhaps going a little far to quote, as a correspondent in *The Times* did, the alarming increase in the number of cases, using the figures for London in one year and for the whole of England in the next.

By this time the Conservatives were in power with Lord George Hamilton at the India Office and the Government was by no means disposed to resist the pressure from India for the re-imposition of the Acts. Regulationists returned to the attack with energy and a petition to the Government for restoration of the Acts was sent up, signed by a Royal Duchess as well as by peeresses and other ladies of fashion. The intervention of women on this side was a dreadful blow to Josephine. It was sufficiently deplorable that any woman should support Acts so degrading to her sex, but in this case it was deeply humiliating, since the women who signed the appeal came from a class of society which could not possibly suffer under the Acts. Josephine could never forget the letter she had once had from a working man:

"These gentlemen who make such a noise about the necessity of prostitution too often forget, I think, that in order to satisfy that necessity, *the dishonour of the daughters of the people* is indispensable, for till now none of the worshippers of these medical theories have been found ready to declare their willingness that *their own daughters* should be sacrificed."

In 1897 a still more shattering thing happened. Lady Henry Somerset, speaking as President of the British Branch of the World's Women's Christian Temperance Union, a body in which Josephine herself held an important office, declared in favour of Regulation and suggested a system even more repellent than that previously in force. Josephine had become involved in this body rather unwillingly. She was not a teetotaller by conviction, though she had signed the pledge in Liverpool in her early days because some of her fellow workers were convinced it would help those among whom she was working. But she belonged to no Temperance organisation until her friendship with Dr. Bushnell and Mrs. Andrew had drawn her into the W.W.C.T.U. When the Union was on a tour of Europe she had met Miss Willard, the President, and had addressed the members on Repeal. As a result, she was invited to become "Supervisor" of the Union's "Purity" Section, and, grateful to Dr. Bushnell and Mrs. Andrew, who were working so hard for her Federation, she did not know how to refuse. She did not really wish to become so deeply involved, and one wonders if she would have accepted the position if she had still had George's wisdom to draw upon. She soon regretted the connection and in May 1895 wrote, "the fact is our cause has not gained, but is suffering sadly from the union with it of the W.W.C.T.U., and my own position is rendered painful and difficult". This difficulty was enhanced by Lady Henry Somerset's pronouncement. It was perhaps the feeling that she had put herself in a rather false position which made Josephine exaggerate the importance of this episode, for there were elements of comedy in Lady Henry's intervention. She had always declared herself entirely unwilling to study or even to hear anything about questions of morality, regarding the subject as unsavoury. This, however, had not deterred her from producing, both to Lord George and to *The Times*, on the spur of the moment a "solution" to this very complicated problem. When, however, she discovered that she had thereby embarrassed her friend Miss Willard, the President of the W.W.C.T.U., Lady Henry wrote a second letter to Lord George, withdrawing the first. Her contribution to the question was therefore negligible, but it did not seem so to the L.N.A. Of course Josephine resigned from the Temperance Union, but she dreaded lest anyone at home or abroad could suppose that there was any weakening in the L.N.A. in its central principle. A meeting of the Ladies' National Association was called to consider the situation. Josephine was in Wooler and could not attend, but the letter she wrote "almost on my knees" reveals the distress in her mind about this breach. The letter "must be read to the meeting please, if it comes in time, and it must be printed and circulated. . . . I will use no guarded or mincing words. We are on the eve of a great defeat, unless we *arise in our strength*. Please, if my letter is read at the meeting, get some *ardent* person to read it—not a Parliament man (except perhaps Mr. Wilson), for Parliament men and some women put such an official voice into any reading—and mine is not an official voice, which seems to say 'Allow me', 'Excuse me', 'I beg your pardon gentlemen' all through." She was perfectly clear that even at the cost of very undesirable publicity, Lady Henry must be disowned, that it was far better for the enemy to know that the L.N.A. was divided, even split asunder, than to believe that it was ready to compromise with any kind of regulation. "O! I sometimes wish," she wrote, "I was young and strong again, and could go about and publicly pour forth 'vials of wrath' on all false and demoniacal suggestions . . . with charity always and pity for those whom Satan has misled."

The substance of her letter was reproduced in her pamphlet *"Truth before Everything"*. There is nothing new in it to those who have read *"The Constitution Violated"* and her earlier pamphlets; it is interesting chiefly as showing that the passage of half a century had not in the least abated her passion for justice, the fury of her indignation against those who would exploit the defenceless, and her unshakeable confidence in ultimate triumph.

The L.N.A. next turned its attention to practical ways of tackling the admittedly serious question of the health of the troops. Since it held Regulation to be inadmissible, even if effective—but in fact not even effective—it was necessary to recommend quite other methods. It drew up a memorandum which it sent to Lord George Hamilton outlining the ways in which it considered action should be taken; these included the education of officers and men in a sounder attitude to sexual questions, the suggestion that the proportion of married men permitted to have their wives with them should be increased and the provision of those social amenities and opportunities for recreation which are now taken for granted in any Army establishment. These concrete proposals commended themselves to some of those in authority and a change in their attitude to the whole question of morality became apparent. Since, however, Regulation again existed under the new Cantonment Act, there was still much work to do and the need remained to keep public opinion alert.

It was for this reason that Josephine determined that the Federation, which was holding its Triennial Congress in London in 1898, should spend a whole day on India—to quote from the typed programme of meetings: "India—the whole question as much as possible, clearly set forth, statistically, historically. The truth about it generally, and what is to be done." She was busy preparing for this Congress all the spring. She took things less easily nowadays and she worried more than she had been wont to do. To get speakers was easy enough; there was Stuart to talk about the Parliamentary side, Dr. Nevins on the medical aspect, while Dr. Bushnell and Mrs. Andrew could speak with first-hand authority about the conditions in India. This was all easily arranged, but there were other things which worried Josephine. She was anxious that the foreign delegates should enjoy the Congress and that they should feel that they had been allowed to speak freely. Wilson, who took the chair at many meetings, had a bell which he rang when any speech had filled the allotted time. Josephine did not mind her own countrymen being belled to silence, but she could not bear that foreigners should be so treated; she corresponded with Wilson at some length about this. A deeper anxiety was that the foreigners, and particularly the foreign women, should be assured of the continued loyalty of the English branches to the principle of unconditional repeal. Lady Henry Somerset's incursion into this field had received wide publicity and her recantation had been greeted by some—including a celebrated Congregational Minister—with excited adulation. Josephine feared lest this should suggest to Continental friends that there was a wavering among the ranks of the Association. She hoped very much that Lady Henry's antics might not be mentioned. She did not want her, or anyone else, condemned, but she did want the suggestion of the possibility of compromise to be repudiated. It was with this in her mind that she suggested that the L.N.A. should hold its Annual Meeting immediately at the close of the Congress and that those foreign women who attended the Congress should be asked to stay on for this meeting. She writes in April about this: "Though I have been ill and weak for eight weeks now, I hope to get well when summer comes, and there has come to my mind a desire (if it is not of God it will not be permitted to ripen into action) to address my fellow women in an address which would be a sort of farewell charge, and *very* grave and earnest . . . I should like to call them most earnestly to the guarding of the great principles of Justice and Equality, which it seems to me are but loosely held by many even English women and to which some foreign women are almost strangers." She had her women's meeting, but she was not well enough to say more than a few words. Nevertheless, she was able to report that it had been a good Congress and that a cheering number of young people, both men and women, had attended; and she pointed particularly to its value as an international meeting place. "I regard every meeting of an international character as something almost sacred and solemn in these days, when all the nations seem bristling with jealousies and antipathies against each other. We seem to have the high duty laid on us of at least striking one little note of international brotherhood and peace."

CHAPTER EIGHTEEN

OLD AGE 1898—1906

"Even in old age you can stimulate the young around you". (J. B.)

IN July 1896 the last issue of *The Dawn* appeared. It carried an
announcement that Josephine felt herself no longer able to
manage it. The struggle at Geneva had taxed her severely, the
Indian affair was opening a new chapter and the immense work
involved in the single-handed production of a journal which
covered so wide a field and required such extensive correspondence was proving too much for her. It was not, however, possible
for Josephine to be long without a forum from which to address
her fellow workers and in January 1898 she issued the first
number of *The Storm-Bell*. This was a much less ambitious effort
than *The Dawn* and for the historian of the movement much less
valuable. But for the biographer it is important and revealing, for
it shows Josephine in her old age. She was almost seventy when
the first number appeared, and in those days a woman of seventy
felt and was expected to be very much older than her successor
today. The scope of *The Storm-Bell* was limited; Josephine left to
The Shield the reporting of conferences and speeches of the
Federation. She was rather reluctant to do this. "When I read
the last number I said to myself '*Shield*, you are horribly medical,
you are just an Abolitionist *Lancet*' " . . . and she said in a note to
Miss Forsaith, the Secretary of the L.N.A., "I think it is well
worth an effort to infuse a little more of the healthily human and
heart element into it." There was plenty of this "element" in *The
Storm-Bell*. It was intended for "simple" people, those who had

not the habit of serious reading, but whose hearts were right, whose support was important and who needed help to enable them to give it intelligently.

The name *Storm-Bell* was taken from a poem by Whittier:

> "The Storm-Bell rings—the Trumpet blows;
> I know the word and countersign;
> Wherever Freedom's vanguard goes,
> Where stand or fall her friends or foes,
> I know the place that should be mine."

and this sufficiently reveals its character. It was there to draw the attention of all readers to threatening dangers, to breaches in the wall, to the stratagems of the enemy. It was avowedly the organ of the L.N.A., but from the beginning it was understood that Josephine should be entirely untrammelled in her editorship. She wrote it from wherever she happened to be; from Wooler or St. Andrews or from Lausanne or any continental city. She wrote of whatever was at that moment in her mind. It need hardly be said that again and again as one turns over the pages of *The Storm-Bell*, one finds the reiteration of the fundamental principles to which the L.N.A. was committed and the triumphant reassertion of her certainty of the ultimate victory of righteousness. "We know in Whom we have trusted", she wrote, and in that knowledge she commanded, "speak to the children of Israel that they go forward". In one of her letters, when she was old and in pain, she wrote: "It would be *terrible* if we were to allow the smallest note of discouragement to be heard! How our enemies would rejoice! They would catch the faintest note of it and say 'NOW is our chance! They are less confident than they were'. ... A leader should always be *most* full of hope and courage in the darkest hour." This duty she fulfilled magnificently in every number of *The Storm-Bell*.

Sometimes Josephine dealt with current affairs, but at other times some scene or encounter recalled incidents or experiences of the past and she described these. When Stansfeld died in 1898 she wrote a loving tribute to one whom she mourned both as a close friend and a well valued colleague and adviser. On Gladstone's death she spoke, not of his contribution to the movement, which had in fact been ambiguous, but of an incident at Hawarden. "A number of Lancashire miners were given an excursion to Cheshire. They gathered round the Park at Hawarden, in the hope, before returning home, of catching a glimpse of Mr. Gladstone. The evening wore on, and they were about to retire, disappointed of their hope, when one suggested they should 'strike up' one of Mr. Gladstone's favourite hymns: 'All hail the power of Jesus' Name'. 'That will fetch him', gently remarked one of the miners; and it did 'fetch him'. Just as they were singing the last words of the last verse—'Crown Him Lord of all' —the grand old man appeared at the door of the Castle, leaning on his stick, and with Mrs. Gladstone by his side, and smilingly thanked them for their sympathetic act."

She included a whole series of "Recollections" of those with whom she had worked in the past. One was William Lloyd Garrison, the hero of the American anti-slavery fight. He was her inspiration rather than her colleague, but he had written in support of the Abolitionists as early as 1871; he had come to Liverpool to meet her, and his writings were to her "a source of strength and encouragement throughout the years of toil which we had to undergo, and in nothing more so than in that constant war which we have had to wage, and which no doubt still awaits us, against offered compromises". Then there was Mme. de Gingins, who had joined her in 1874, had stood by her side in Geneva through the dreadful night of March 22nd, 1896 and, as she turned to go to her room, had said—weeping—"I am not discouraged, but I shall never see victory in Geneva; others may live to see it, but not I." She wrote also of Dr. Nevins, whom she had called on in his old age and whom she described as like Moses who, "after he had concentrated all his labours and given his whole soul and life to the pursuit of one great aim—that of leading the people into the Promised Land . . . was forbidden to realise that aim . . . and only saw the land afar off . . . on the Mount Nebo where he died".

When Yves Guyot was received at Newcastle, "my own Northumbrian city", she made it the text for an appreciative account of his work for the cause, including his story of his introduction to it: "In his native town, when he was quite a boy, a fire broke out one night. He observed a number of women and girls running from a burning house, men and boys were chasing and insulting them, throwing mud and stones after them. The chivalrous temper of the boy was aroused. He was astonished, grieved, enraged at the brutality of these men towards a set of helpless women, fleeing from danger. He asked the meaning of this. The answer was heartless and cynical, but sufficient to make him understand that these were 'unfortunates', whom the world despised and who might be ill-treated at will. The sight and the explanation made a deep impression on the boy. Love of justice, and compassion for the weak and oppressed were born in him. That night he vowed to himself, 'When I am grown up, and go to Paris, I will take the part of these poor women'."

Josephine recommended to the attention of her readers the pamphlet by Stuart and Wilson called *Facts versus Panic*, dealing with the alleged rise of disease in India after the abolition of the C.D. Acts, the *Queen's Daughters in India*, a book by Dr. Bushnell and Mrs. Andrew about the treatment of women there and *Mothers and Sons* by Ellice Hopkins, who had long been working in much the same field, though the two women seem not to have met. Sometimes she wrote of matters which had no direct connection with the work of the Federation or the L.N.A. She was deeply perturbed by the fate of Finland, when in 1899 the Russians abrogated its constitution. This suppression of a small country by a great roused in her all the abhorrence she felt for any subjugation of the weak by the strong.

One of the subjects very much in her mind at this time was the Dreyfus case. For the sake of those too young to remember it, it is perhaps worth while to recall the facts. Dreyfus was a Jew and the victim of that anti-Semitic sentiment which even now is apt to simmer under the surface of so-called Christian society and of which we have all had bitter experience in our own day.

It broke forth in fury in 1894 when Dreyfus, an officer in the French Army, was accused of selling military secrets to Germany. He was tried in complete secrecy by a Court Martial, on a dossier later proved to have been forged and, protesting his innocence, was condemned for high treason and sentenced to life imprisonment on the Ile des Diables. The first protest against this sentence was made by a fellow officer Picardt, who demanded a reexamination of the evidence and was promptly cashiered; the next protest was made far more publicly by Emile Zola, who published his book *J'Accuse*, an indictment of the French Higher Command. This could not so easily be suppressed and though President Faure declared blandly, "There is no Dreyfus Case", the Press of Europe resounded with it, and to this chorus *The Storm-Bell* contributed its protesting tinkle. Josephine wrote at once privately to Mme. Dreyfus expressing her horror and indignation at the odious injustice and in the columns of her paper she described feelingly the barbarity with which Dreyfus was treated, the anguish of all right thinking people while the question of the revision of his trial was still in doubt and the thankfulness with which his return to France was greeted. The ardour of Josephine's indignation on behalf of Dreyfus was increased by the fact that she had many Jews among her friends and warm supporters. George Butler's Hebrew studies had endeared him to many Rabbis and other Jewish leaders and Josephine shared in the intimacy which resulted.

She was convinced that the Dreyfus affair had, throughout Europe, "sharpened the sense of justice and quickened the zeal for justice in tens of thousands of right thinking people". This, she felt, was wholly to the good, for surely those who had been so roused to wrath by injustice to one man could hardly continue to ignore injustice to all women? She thought she discerned evidence of this improved state of opinion. There were two conferences in 1899, which she had greatly dreaded. The first of these was the Medical Conference at Brussels. The conveners were avowedly Regulationists and Josephine had been most anxious lest any, not experienced in the antics of statistics, should be misled by it. She implored Dr. Nevins to attend, knowing that he was not only invincible in statistics, but also able from his long experience to give the lie to that "easy falsehood that comforts cruel men"—that chastity is impossible and injurious to a man. He maintained on the contrary that he had "never known or heard of an instance in which unchastity had really promoted either health or happiness. Young men were sometimes taught by their companions and even by medical men, that a chaste and at the same time a healthy life was an impossibility. More utterly mistaken and mischievous teaching could not possibly be put before youth . . ." Actually this Conference showed a new spirit and Josephine need not have feared. There seemed to be a misgiving on the part of some Regulationists that their methods were more fallible than they wished to believe and this made them less impervious to the truth. To Josephine's surprise, no resolutions were passed in favour of compulsory medical examination.

The other Conference which she dreaded was that of the Federation at Geneva. Here her anxiety was probably more emotional than reasonable. The memory of the 22nd March, 1896 had not faded, and she could not contemplate a conference there with any pleasure. But this one too turned out far better than she had expected. Though fewer actual members of the Federation than usual attended, a great number of friendly newcomers appeared, all eager to learn, and Josephine welcomed the presence of many young people—especially young men. After this Conference, she received and published in *The Storm-Bell* accounts of a most cheering meeting in Berlin, where, contrary to all expectations, a great company including many men attended a meeting organised by women and enthusiastically passed entirely satisfactory resolutions.

Josephine needed this encouragement at this time for on the whole life on the Continent for an English woman so devotedly patriotic as she was not easy. There was no shutting one's eyes to the fact that the English were very unpopular. The French resented the immense excitement caused in England by the Dreyfus case. They found Great Britain—not for the first time—

hypocritical and smug. The Fashoda Incident had further exacerbated French resentment. The outbreak of the South African War aroused the fury of the Netherlands and when the German Emperor sent his telegram of support to Kruger, German public opinion ranged itself against Great Britain. Josephine was sensitive to this hostility.

There was a worse trouble than this. Her own Abolitionist friends, both on the Continent and at home, were for the most part pro-Boer. She had hated the events which led up to the Boer War, for her patriotism had never been of the "my country right or wrong" type. She deplored the policy of Rhodes and distrusted Joseph Chamberlain—a Midland business magnate ("What can Brummagem Joe know about a horse?")—but she had followed events in South Africa long before the advent of Chamberlain and the Conservative Government. Her kinsman, George Grey, had been Governor in the Cape in the 1850's, and with that voracious appetite for knowledge which had been hers from her youth up, she had eagerly read all that concerned the country he administered. Her interest in missions and in the question of slavery had also led her to the writings of Livingstone and other African authorities. She did not therefore approach the subject of the Boer War with an empty mind and she was not prepared to accept the thesis that this war was simply the expression of a greedy Imperialist hunger for expansion. When members of the Society of Friends, who were her colleagues, wrote to her with confidence begging her to denounce this aggression, she felt herself bound to go into the whole question of the origin of the war in some detail. She produced a book called *Native Races and the War*. This is a most remarkable book. It is the work of an historian rather than a of passionate reformer. It displays a quite extraordinary knowledge of original documents, of Blue Books, Parliamentary papers and earlier histories. She gives her authorities—French missionaries, German and English books of travel—and one asks oneself when she found time and energy to consult them. She was no longer young, her eyesight was failing and she was not even settled in one place with library and books of reference easily accessible. There is no answer to this riddle.

Josephine believed the origin of the war to lie far back in the 17th century, when the King of Holland ceded the Cape of Good Hope to the British, to the great resentment of the Dutch settlers in that country. Since, however, the country was remote from European control, the two communities lived together in some degree of harmony until the abolition of slavery in all British Dominions in 1834 interfered with labour conditions and made it impossible for the Boers to use native labour as they had been accustomed to do. It was interference with their liberty in this particular, rather than any passion for liberty in general, that led to the trek of Boer farmers to the Transvaal. Josephine's account of the relations of the Boers to the native races has a curiously modern ring. She describes the resentment against the pass laws; the injustice of taxing coloured men for the education which their children do not enjoy; the hostility against the missionaries who recognise the equal rights of coloured people— all these are familiar subjects in our papers today. She was not so naïve as to suggest that the British Government had gone to war to protect the native races. On the contrary, it was a straight-forward clash of white races over opposing commercial interests. The British had annexed the Transvaal, then bankrupt and on the edge of dissolution, in 1877 at the request of its President. In 1881 Gladstone restored it to the Boers, including in the terms of the Convention a safeguard of the rights of the natives. The native chiefs, having no confidence in this safeguard, since they had already experienced Boer rule, hotly protested, but Gladstone, eager to be generous, failed to realise that this was generosity at the expense of those least able to meet the cost.

Josephine reflected mournfully on this transaction. "These poor natives," she said, "had appealed to the British Government, had trusted it, and were deceived by it." Admiring and revering Gladstone as she did, she would gladly have separated "the memory of that truly great man from this act of his Administration". It revealed his fatal weakness. Just as in the American

Civil War he could support the South, remaining unconscious of the rights of the negroes, so now, intent on dealing in a generous anti-imperialistic spirit with the Boers, he could overlook the rights of the native races. Josephine reflected, "His noble enthusiasm for some good and vital cause so engrossed him at times that the humble knocking at the door of some other, perhaps equally vital, question was not heard by him. The knocking necessarily became louder and louder, till at last the door was opened, but then it may have been too late for him to take the part in it which should have been his."

This action of Gladstone's, Josephine felt, was the underlying cause of the South African War. The Boers had been encouraged by his misplaced generosity to believe that the British Government was indifferent to the interests of its subjects overseas, and they were determined to get rid of British suzerainty and its restrictions. No doubt the perpetual provocation of the Uitlander was a part of the deliberate policy of the Boer Government and Kruger, watching and waiting for Rhodes to make a false move, is alleged to have greeted the news of the Jameson Raid with the grim remark that "one cannot kill a tortoise until it puts its head out". Josephine's conclusion was that the war was a bad business, that the British had, over a long period, pursued selfish ends in Africa, and were now fighting to protect their own interests. At the same time, for the native races, the only hope of freedom and civilised development lay in a British victory and the establishment of government under British sovereign rule. "Great Britain will in future be judged, condemned or justified according to her treatment of those innumerable coloured races, over whom her rule extends. Race prejudice is a poison which will have to be cast out if the world is ever to be Christianised, and if Great Britain is to maintain the high and responsible place among the nations which has been given to her."

In a letter written at the end of 1899 she sums up her feelings about war with a strange prescience: "A time of trouble like this, though sad in the extreme, does lift a nation out of all grovelling tendencies and makes people graver and nobler. . . . It will be a happy result of the war if the whole of South Africa could be united under British rule, with plenty of freedom of self-government, like Australia and Canada. . . . Though it is noble of our soldiers to be so ready to die for our country it seems a pity so much mankind should be destroyed when we shall want it for a great European War."

As the century drew to its close Josephine's abundant zest for life began to fail. *The Storm-Bell* rang for the last time in July 1900. The death of Stansfeld and of Gladstone in 1898 and of Queen Victoria in 1901 seemed to mark the end of an epoch and, like many people at her age, she began to feel that this new world around her was not hers. She had personal losses. In the spring of 1900 her brother-in-law, Tell Meuricoffre, died rather suddenly. She had always been fond of him; he had brought Hattie a bride to their house in Oxford and had always welcomed her and George most cordially, both at Naples and in Switzerland. The more she had known him the more she had come to love and admire him and she felt his loss not only for Hattie's sake but for her own. In the autumn of that year she went to La Gardonne to be with Hattie and found her "full of courage, making plans for the improvement of the place. . . . We had some delightful talks sitting in her sunny garden looking across the lake to the beautiful mountains. . . . When I left she brought me to the train . . . and we planned her long desired visit to England for the next year. . . . The last thing she said was, 'Will May be too early for me to come to England?' I replied, 'You cannot come too early, my beloved', and she smiled and waved her hand." It was a terrible shock to Josephine to receive a telegram when she landed in England telling her that this beloved sister had died. Josephine was sorely shaken. The two sisters had been so close in their intimacy that the loss was overwhelming. She set to work at once on a little book in memory of her sister. This was a collection of her letters published in 1901 under the title *In Memoriam Harriet Meuricoffre*. It is a moving little book. The letters are charming, gay and vivid. Harriet shared with Josephine the artist's eye and the enthusiasms that animated her. The book is a very intimate record of a beautiful relationship; it is of no general interest.

It was at about this time that Tolstoi's *Resurrection* was published. More than one continental paper asked Josephine to review it and she gladly consented. The English version of her review was published in *The Shield*. It was no wonder that she rejoiced at this book. Here at last was a *man*, and a genius at that, who put his finger unerringly on the essential point at issue. "The book might be called the *amende honorable* made by the masculine conscience to the womanhood of the world, for the centuries of wrong inflicted by the absence of the recognition of an equal moral standard for the sexes. The Resurrection which Tolstoi pictures is the resurrection of conscience in a man who arises to do the *whole* of his duty towards a fallen woman, a woman of the streets in fact, whose first seducer he had been. . . . The sister of the hero, a good, kind, prosperous society woman asks him, 'But do you believe it possible that a woman who has lived such a life can ever again be really elevated, morally reinstated, and restored to the nobility of womanhood?' His reply embodies a thought which rarely occurs even to the best of men: 'That is not the question which I have to answer. The question which I have to answer is: Is there hope for *me*? Can *I* be rehabilitated, morally restored and elevated to the true dignity of manhood?' "

In 1900 Josephine settled in Cheltenham, thinking that its mild climate might suit her better than the chill winds of her native North. She had been happy there as a young married woman and she had revisited it to stay with her sister Fanny. She soon found she had made a mistake. Those whom she had known in the old days had died or moved away and she found in Cheltenham society all the features she most disliked—a comfortable respectability, narrow and smug, quite satisfied that all was well with the world. Everyone knew of the existence of brothels in the place and everyone looked the other way and let things go for the sake of propriety. Only one ally could she find— a clergyman of the Lady Huntingdon persuasion. He fretted with her at the impossibility of moving public opinion and she found herself longing for a train of gun-powder with which to make a conflagration. She determined to go back to her own people and countryside and in 1902 she left Cheltenham and settled at Wooler, close to her son George and his family at Ewart Park.

Soon after her return to the North Josephine and the Federation suffered a grievous loss in the death of Mrs. Tanner, who had joined the movement at its very beginning and had been Treasurer of the L.N.A. until within a few months of her death. She, with her sisters, the Priestmans, had made a home at Bristol in which Josephine had always known she could count upon sympathy and complete understanding. "We have always worked in perfect harmony," she wrote, "although differing markedly in natural character. To speak honestly, as one conscious of faults, . . . I was too impetuous, impulsive and sometimes rash. The keen sense of injustice which possessed both her and me, was apt at times to fill me with bitterness of soul. She, on the contrary, was always calm, steady, equal, gentle—a true representative of the Society of Friends. . . . With all her gentleness, she had the utmost firmness, never wavering in the least in principle. . . . She would say she owed much to me. Few people guess how much I owed to her, to that firm, quiet individuality . . . I am full of grateful remembrance."

In 1901 Josephine had formally resigned her office as Secretary of the Ladies' National Association. This in fact made very little difference to the extent of her work, for to most members of the Federation the L.N.A. was Mrs. Butler, and it was to her they wrote when they wanted advice or help. She had always herself dealt with all the international aspects of the work and now that she was less able to get about, to go to meetings in London or on the Continent, she began to feel some anxiety about the continued close and happy co-operation between British and continental workers. She knew that here she had had a unique part to play, she had one qualification that other English Abolitionists often lacked. This was a real understanding of the mental reactions of the continental members of the Federation. The British were admirable in their clear grasp of principle, their efficiency in carrying out the task they had undertaken, but they lacked subtlety and could not realise that the differences between English and continental institutions might make a method of attacking a difficulty in England inappropriate to the same difficulty in Belgium or France. M. Minod, General Secretary of the Federation, appealed constantly to Josephine for help, certain of her understanding and sympathy when other English members were critical or impatient. She was anxious to devise a means of avoiding friction between the English and Continental Abolitionists. "The London Committee", she wrote, "should restrict its action to England, India and our Colonies (surely a large enough order) and leave intricate questions of European legislation etc. to the care of that body of really clear-headed, strong and devoted workers who form the 'Commission Administrative' on the Continent. They are persons in whom I have full confidence. I am really sorry for Mr. Wilson, he is so alone, and he does not read French, and is almost brutally English in his views. He is sometimes the only man at committee meetings with half a dozen ladies, who are all good as to English matters, but who know nothing of foreign ways and the methods of the Latin mind." And again she adjured her friends to "help as far as you may be able to keep up the *international bond* amongst workers; . . . the work on the Continent is scarcely ever mentioned at ordinary committee meetings in London because the correspondence with the Continent has always been my part and I have not been able to fulfil my part. . . . It will be a great loss to our faithful Continental friends and to ourselves if the tie should be loosened between us."

There was another peculiarity in her British colleagues which was puzzling and sometimes distressing to Continental fellow workers; this was the attitude of the Honorary Officers of the Federation to those of their assistants who were paid. "To receive a salary seems to demean a man . . . this should not be so," says Josephine. The British Committee appeared to assume that the opinions of those who were paid servants of the organisation were less to be considered than those of the voluntary workers, and that where they differed, the opinions of the volunteer must prevail. This is a strange doctrine to modern ears, when voluntary workers in any social sphere are suspect and their opinions negligible. The pendulum may have swung rather far.

Josephine spent the last years of her life chiefly at Wooler. She was old, she was tired, she was never well and often she was seriously ill; her sight became worse so that she could read and write only with difficulty. But the idea of relinquishing the struggle in which she had so long been engaged never occurred to her, and she still followed the course of events with eager attention. In spite of her physical difficulties she still corresponded with members of the Federation and others on the Continent, and with many soldiers, both officers and men, much cheered by the improved moral tone she discerned in their letters. She rejoiced that Mrs. Fawcett was appointed to the Commission of Enquiry into the alleged horrors of the concentration camps in Africa, having no doubt that the reports on them were greatly exaggerated. Some of the younger workers corresponded with her. One of these was Maurice Gregory, an American and a Friend, who had done much work for the Federation in India and now in Africa. She enjoyed his long letters, though when he took upon himself to describe features of the continental landscape, which she had known familiarly before he was born, she expressed some pardonable irritation: "He really need not tell me what Hamburg is like!" She enjoyed her contacts with the young and was keenly alive to the importance of encouraging those in whose hands she must soon leave the work she loved, for she knew that victory could never be complete and the battle must be fought in every generation. There was never anyone less inclined to lament the defects of the young. "You say that many persons do not welcome new recruits, lest they should make mistakes. They will no doubt make some mistakes, but they will learn, as we did, by our errors. This brings me to express the thought that has been uppermost in my mind for some years past—that the great hope for the future movement is in the *young manhood of our day*—in the generous heart of youth. Young women too must and will come forward. But I press the fact of the need of a great army of young men; for the great evil which we combat is the result of the egotism of men, and of the deeply rooted idea that the sin of impurity is a greater sin in a woman than in a man. This unequal standard is the devil's invention."

Josephine looked out on to a sombre world—the Russo-Japanese War, the Siege of the Legations in Pekin, the assassination of the Empress of Austria, the revolutionary uprising in Russia and the perpetual unrest in the Balkans—all these seemed to her to speak of a coming Judgment. Already submarines were in action and she foresaw a day when "overhead destruction things" would shorten the duration of wars. Threats of disaster were on every side. Her letters became increasingly apocalyptic, but she was by no means dismayed—"The waves of the sea are mighty and roar horribly and yet the Lord abideth King for ever and ever." She continued "to beat the little kettledrum of faith".

In 1905 Josephine was immensely touched to receive through Mrs. Fawcett a gift from her friends which had been subscribed from many sources, in England, on the Continent and from overseas. It was sent with an address expressing the greatest gratitude for all she had done in and for the cause through her long life. In her letter of thanks she expressed the real pleasure she took in reading the list of names recalling so many happy memories, in the beautiful script in which they were written, "itself an arduous task", even in "the appearance of the beautiful Album, lined with rich white satin" in which they were enclosed. But she said again what she had often said before—that she felt utterly unworthy to be the recipient of so generous a testimonial. This was not assumed modesty, it was the perfectly sincere expression of her consciousness of her dependence on all those who had so long and so devotedly worked with her. "How could I have answered to this call had it not been for the host of brave women who rose up with me to the battle?" She ends her letter with the hope that she may yet serve the Federation and continue to make her contribution to the cause. It was not to be.

The winter of 1906 was very severe. In Northumberland there was snow and sleet and a bitter wind from the East which Josephine, in her unscientific way, believed to be carrying influenza germs from Russia. She was not able to get up, but in the intervals of acute pain she wrote busily, letters to her family, letters to Miss Forsaith, to members of the Federation abroad. Her magnificent vitality had carried her through so many times of desperate illness that even this time it seemed that when the spring came she would rally again. She was lovingly tended. Her son George was within reach and her little grandchildren came to see her. She had always called forth devotion from her attendants, and Mary, like all who had served her before, loved to look after her. The shopkeepers and tradesfolk of Wooler took a pride in her and were eager to offer her services. So she lay in bed and wrote her letters. Her handwriting wavered but her mind was clear as ever and her expression as trenchant. She was writing on the day before her death and an answer to a letter to de Meuron arrived in Wooler after her death. But her work was done. Very quietly and easily as the year drew to its close she fell asleep and died.

SOURCES

(1) MSS *Josephine Butler's Letters*

(*a*) In Josephine Butler House, Liverpool.

(*b*) In Liverpool University Library.

(*c*) In Fawcett Library, Westminster.
    A collection belonging to the Association for Moral and Social Hygiene, including many letters from J. E. B.; from George Butler and their family; from and to Henry J. Wilson and others; some of it private correspondence, the rest relating to the work of the Ladies' National Association and the International Federation for the Repeal of the State Regulation of Vice. Also many circulars, manifestoes, etc.

(2) *Josephine Butler's Printed Works*

Woman's Work and Woman's Culture (Ed. J. E. B.),　1869
The Constitution Violated,　1871
Memoir of John Grey of Dilston,　1874
Une Voix dans le Désert,　1875
Catharine of Siena,　1879
The Hour before the Dawn,　1882
Salvation Army in Switzerland,　1883
Life of J. F. Oberlin,　1883
Rebecca Jarrett,　1885
The Dawn (Periodical),　1888–1896
Recollections of George Butler,　1892
Lady of Shunem,　1895
Personal Reminiscences of a Great Crusade,　1896
The Storm Bell (Periodical),　1898–1900
Native Races and the War,　1900
In Memoriam, Harriet Merricoffre,　1901

    There are also some twenty other articles, speeches and letters available to the student in the Fawcett Library.

(3) *Government Publications*

Report and Minutes of Evidence of the Royal Commission on the Administration and operation of the Contagious Diseases Acts.　1871.
Report and Evidence of Special Committee of the House of Commons into the working of the Contagious Diseases Acts.　1879–1882.

League of Nations. Report on the Special Body of Experts on Traffic in Women and Children: Part One and Part Two. Geneva, 1927.
United Nations: Department of Economic and Social Affairs Study on Traffic in Persons and Prostitution. New York, 1959.

(4) *Authorities*

A. *Memoirs of Josephine Butler*

Josephine Butler. A Life Sketch, by W. T. Stead. Morgan and Scott, 1887.
Josephine E. Butler. An Autobiographical Memoir, (edited, Geo. W. and Lucy A. Johnson). Arrowsmith, 1909.
Josephine Butler and her Work for Social Purity, by L. Hay-Cooper. SPCK, 1922.
Josephine Butler. Her Work and Principles and their meaning for the Twentieth Century. Written for the J. B. Centenary, 1828–1928, by Millicent Fawcett and E. M. Turner. Association for Moral and Social Hygiene, 1927.
Portrait of Josephine Butler, by A. S. G. Butler. Faber & Faber, 1954.

B. *Histories of the Crusade*

The New Abolitionists. James Stuart. Published anonymously.
A Narrative of a Year's Work. Dyer Bros., 1876.
A State Iniquity. Its Rise, Extension and Overthrow. A Concise History of the System of State Regulated and Licensed Vice, by Benjamin Scott, F.R.A.S. Kegan Paul, 1890.
A Rough Record of Events and Incidents connected with the Repeal of the Contagious Diseases Acts. Privately printed, by Henry J. Wilson, of Sheffield, 1907.

C. *Other Biographies*

Clough: Memoir of Anne Jemima Clough, First Principal of Newnham College, Cambs, by Blanche A. Clough. Arnold, 1903.
Gladstone, W. E.: A Biography, by Philip Magnus. Murray, 1954.
Hopkins: Ellice Hopkins, A Memoir, by Rosa M. Barrett. Wells Gardner, 1907.
Jowett: A Portrait with Background, by Sir Geoffrey Faber. Faber, 1957.
Nightingale: Florence Nightingale, 1820–1910, by Cecil Woodham-Smith. Constable, 1950.
Somerset: Lady Henry Somerset, by Kathleen Fitzpatrick. Cape, 1923.
Stansfeld: James Stansfeld. A Victorian Champion of Sex Equality, by J. L. and Barbara Hammond. Longman, 1932.
Stead: Life of W. T. Stead, by Frederic Whyte. 1925.
Stuart: James Stuart. Reminiscences. 1911.
Wilson: Henry Joseph Wilson. Fighter for Freedom, 1833–1914, by Mosa Anderson. James Clarke, 1953.

D. *Other Authorities*

Charitable Effort in Liverpool in the 19th Century, by M. B. Simey. Liverpool University Press, 1951.

C.D. Acts (Garrison Towns). *A Series of Leading Articles from the* Daily News, 1863, by Harriet Martineau, 1870.

Maiden Tribute of Modern Babylon, by W. T. Stead in *Pall Mall Gazette*, 1885.

Queen's Daughters in India, Dr Bushnell and Mrs Andrew, 1899.

Storming the Citadel. The Rise of the Woman Doctor, by E. Moberly Bell. Constable, 1953.

Maiden Tribute. A Study of the White Slave Traffic of the Nineteenth Century, by Charles Terrot. Muller, 1959.

The Shield. A Periodical Review of Moral and Social Hygiene. Published by the Association for Moral and Social Hygiene from 1871 to present day.

INDEX

28; his ordination, 30; makes
hall of residence for non-
collegiate students, 31; Vice-
Principal Cheltenham Col-
lege, 40; Principal Liverpool
College, 45; resigns Liverpool, 165; Canon of Win-
chester, 166–169; illness, 185;
death, 190
his educational innovations: at
Oxford, Geography, Art,
32, 33; Cheltenham, Physical
Education, 40–43; Liverpool,
Hebrew, general reforms,
48–50; for women, 60–61
his holidays: Lakes, 27; fishing,
28, 167, 168; Switzerland, 70,
133, 134, 179; France, 118–
119; Germany, 144, 145;
Neuchâtel, 169; Italy, 183
his politics: Liberalism, 28;
Italia Una, 33, 41; American
Civil War, 42, 43 *passim*
his support of J. B's work: in
Oxford, 35; in Liverpool,
54, 55, 56, 57; in private, 76;
in public, 96, 108; Berne,
134; Paris, 135, 136; Hague,
172
his writings: collation of MSS.
in Bodleian, 34; *Edinburgh
Review*, etc., 40; on sculptor
Thorwaldsen, 188
Butler, Josephine (*see also* Grey,
Josephine), her marriage, 28;
at Oxford, 29–38; Cheltenham, 39–47; d. of Eva, 43;
Liverpool, 48–65; social
work here (*see under* Education of Women, Employ-
ment of Women); joins C.D.
Crusade (*see under* C.D. Acts
and Prostitution); evidence
to Royal Commission, 86–91;
General Election, 102; first
foreign tour, 111–127; first
contact with White Slave

Traffic (*q.v.*), 134; congress at
Geneva, 138–142; suspension
of Acts, 1883, 163, 164; to
Winchester, 166–174; hus-
band's illness and death,
183–190; to Wimbledon,
then Balham, 194, 209;
Geneva, 196; Rome, 202;
Conference at Colmar, 210;
conflict at Geneva, 211–225;
Geneva again, 243; to Cheltenham, 248; last years in
Wooler, 249; her death, 253
her charm—appearance: 25, 52,
77, 152, 178, 208–209, 220;
gaiety: 24, 32, 33, 69, 151,
225; *voice:* 52, 77
her health: breakdown at Oxford, 38; illness after Eva's
death, 45; distrust of doctors,
46, 47; breakdown after
foreign tour, 128, 129; and
again after Geneva, 144;
malaria in Rome, 207; failing
health, 247, 253
her holidays: see under George
Butler
her religion: early religious experience, 23, 24; letter to
Jowett, 37; catholic nature of
her faith, 103; her mysticism,
147
her work for women: see under
Woman's Cause
her writings: see under individual
titles
Butler, Stanley, 118, 194, 197

Cambridge University, G. B. at,
27; petition for women's
education, 62, 63
Cantonment Acts, 227, 236
Cantonments in India, 229–231,
232
Carlisle, Bishop of, 227
Carter, Dr., 128, 129